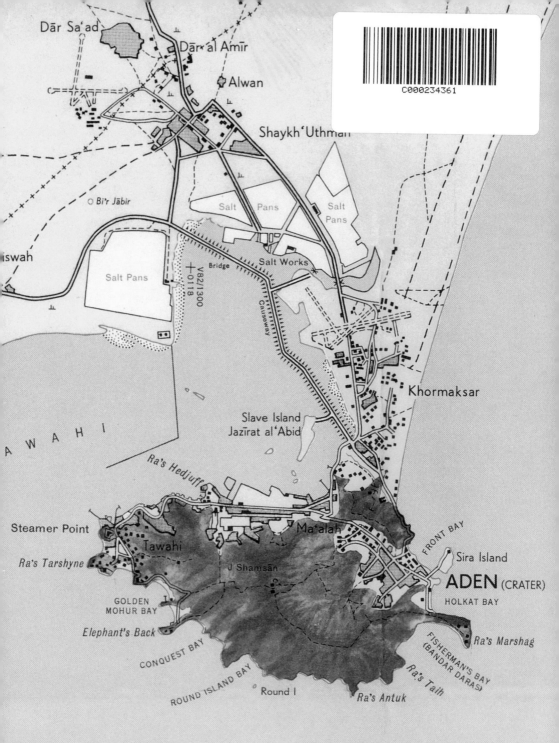

GULF OF ADEN

**ADEN COLONY 1959**

# LETTERS FROM OMAN

# LETTERS FROM OMAN

A SNAPSHOT OF FEUDAL TIMES AS OIL SIGNALS CHANGE

BY

DAVID GWYNNE-JAMES

BwB

Dust jacket painting and title page drawing by Paul Bawden,
based on a photograph of the Rostaq area taken in 1963.

Chapter heading illustrations by Fiona Gwynne-James.

Published in the United Kingdom in 2001
by Blackwater Books,
1 High Street, Kelvedon, Colchester CO5 9AG

Printed in Great Britain
by The Five Castles Press Limited, Ipswich

ISBN 0-9539206-1-5

This book is dedicated to my wife Charmian
and our two daughters Grania and Fiona

# Contents

# Maps

# Documents

# Illustrations

*Illustrations, which are numbered 1 to 100, can be found within the six plate sections. For reference purposes within the text, illustration numbers are shown in brackets.*

بسم الله الرحمن الرحيم

قبل كل شيء أعتبر نفسي محظوظاً لمشاركتي بهذه الكلمات المتواضعة في مقدمة هذا الكتاب الهام ، الذي يعود بنا عبر أسلوبه المتميز إلى عقودٍ خلت من عمر عمان ، ما زالت ذكرياتها ماثلة في الأذهان ، وبالفعل كانت بداية معرفتي (بديفد) خلال حقبة الستينات وتحديداً في كتيبة تدريب قوات السلطان المسلحة ، وحينها كنت أعمل مدرباً برتبة رقيب بينما كان هو ضابطاً ، ولست متأكداً من التاريخ بدقة . وعموماً فالجميع على إطلاع بما كانت عليه عُمان في تلك الفترة العصرية حينما كانت فقيرة من أبسط مقومات الحياة العصرية ، في مختلف قطاعاتها الحيوية كالصحة والتعليم والمواصلات والإعلام ، وليس بعيب أن يتعرض هذا الكتاب لمفارقات تلك الحقبة الصعبة من عمر عُمان ، لماذا ؟ لأن عُمان في القرن الحادي والعشرين ، وبفضل قيادة جلالة السلطان المعظم صارت كباقي دول العالم المتحضرة ، دولة لها مكانتها المرموقة بين الأمم ، ويتمتع شعبها بكافة سبل العيش الكريم .

وأنا هنا انتهز الفرصة لتقديم شكري للمؤلف لهذا الجهد الذي أتمنى أن يتكلل بالنجاح والوصول إلى الهدف المنشود ، وهو تعريف الناس وبخاصة الشباب والأجيال الجديدة بما كانت تعانيه عُمان الأمس ، كي يتأكد لهم أنهم يعيشون أياماً رائعة .


نصيب بن حمد الرواحي

# Omani Foreword

*By General Naseeb bin Hamad Salim al Ruwahi, the first local Commander, Sultan of Oman's Land Forces (CSOLF) in 1982*

First, I should like to say that I consider myself extremely fortunate to be contributing these modest words to the Foreword of this important book, which graphically recreates a picture of Oman's past that is still remembered today. I first knew David in the Sultan's Armed Forces Training Regiment in the 1960s when I was an instructor with the rank of sergeant and he was an officer. I do not remember precisely what date that was.

Everyone knows what Oman was like at that time. It was poor and lacked even the most basic elements of modern life in such vital areas as health, education, communications and information, and this book should not be faulted for touching on the paradoxes of that difficult period in Oman's history. Why? Because, thanks to His Majesty the Sultan's leadership, Oman in the 21st century has become like the other civilised states of the world and has earned itself respect among nations, and its people now have everything they need for a decent life.

I would like to take this opportunity to express my thanks to the author of this book and wish it success. It introduces the public, particularly the younger generation, to Oman's hardships and sufferings in the past and shows them clearly that they are now living in wonderful times.

Naseeb bin Hamad al Ruwahi

October 2001

# British Foreword

*By Colonel Nigel Knocker, OBE, Chairman, Sultan's Armed Forces Association*

David Gwynne-James served on secondment from the British Army to the Sultan's Armed Forces in the then virtually unknown Muscat and Oman, as the country was called, in the early 1960s at a time when oil had only just been discovered. The country was considerably underdeveloped with very little infrastructure, had very poor medical facilities and no education system. How things have changed since those days, and thanks to the far-sightedness and abilities of the ruler, His Majesty Sultan bin Said Al Said [Sultan Qaboos], the country has undergone a rapid and well-managed renaissance, survived a communist insurrection, and now plays a prominent part in affairs in the Gulf area.

The book tells the story of those early days seen through the eyes of the author by the imaginative means of extracting parts of letters to his future wife. It is well illustrated with photographs taken at the time. He paints a vivid picture of life in the Sultan's Armed Forces which was itself in the early stages of development. Coupled with the descriptions of the country and the way of life as it was then, the book is compelling reading for anyone who has an interest in and love for Arabia, and in particular the Sultanate of Oman.

Nigel Knocker

May 2001

# Acknowledgements

*My wife, Charmian*

for transcribing my original letters into an exercise book and for keeping it. Without the letters this book would not have been written; for her encouragement, patience and help in refreshing our memories.

*Our younger daughter, Fiona*

for her illustrations at the head of each chapter.

*Carol Danenbergs*

for her patience, care and consummate skill in the word processing of my longhand drafts, invariably on Sunday mornings, as well as my business typing – this in addition to a full-time job and her family responsibilities.

*Ron Horne*

a longtime business colleague who as a National Service Lieutenant in the REME during 1959–60 was responsible for building Falaise Camp in Little Aden – for editing the chapter on Aden and for generously lending his slides, photograph of Crater and his map of Aden Colony (1959).

*The Rev Father Colin McLean*

who learned Arabic with me in Aden and then joined the Sultan's Armed Forces with me. His recollections of our shared experiences and his editing of both chapters have been invaluable. He has also edited Chapter Nine (Memories without Letters) and has provided most of the information needed for me to make a draft of the second part of Chapter Ten (Oil and the Quickening Beat of Change) which he subsequently edited. Unlike me, he spent fourteen years of his life serving the Sultan and his knowledge, recall and judgement have been absolutely essential to this book. His enthusiastic encouragement to someone much less qualified than himself to write on Oman, has been exceptionally generous, and always provided with great enthusiasm despite his many pastoral duties.

*David Coppin,* GM

who was stationed at the SAF Training Centre with me in 1964. He subsequently returned to Oman in 1974–1977 and in 1984–1987, and was employed within the construction industry on various development projects resulting from oil. Initially he helped develop the infrastructure for the Capital Area in the Ruwi Valley behind Bait-al-Falaj. On the second occasion he was directly engaged in the construction of the Sultan Qaboos University. Thanks to Colin McLean, we re-established contact and despite his now being with PremierOil Plc in Islamabad, his vetting of and contribution to the last three chapters have been both significant and invaluable.

*Christopher Ballenden*

who was one of the three King's Shropshire Light Infantry 'Muscateers' and commanded 'B' Company, The Northern Frontier Regiment at Saiq during 1963. He has approved the relevant chapters and also provided some excellent colour slides of the Saiq area.

*John Darbyshire*

who had also served in the KSLI and who commanded 'A' Company, The Muscat Regiment at Rostaq during the 1963 hot season. Subsequently he became our best man in May 1965. In particular he has made significant contributions to Chapter Seven (A Baluch Company in the Jebel Foothills). He has also edited and made some typically succinct and helpful observations on the whole book. Most importantly he has kindly lent me his excellent selection of photographs, coloured slides and map of Northern Oman (1956), which have proved to be essential components of the book.

*Colonel David Betley (The Lancashire Fusiliers)*

who took over from me as Second-in-Command to John Darbyshire in 1964. During recent years he has acted as UK Resident Contact Consultant for Omanis requiring specialist medical treatment in London. On discovering this, I was keen to ask him to check out the whole book to ensure that I would not offend any of those in high office within Oman at the present time. I am most grateful to him for doing this and for his subsequent encouragement.

*Roddy and Gigi Jones*

both of whom have spent many years in Oman. Between 1989 and 1995 Roddy was Field Manager of The White Oryx Project. Those interested in Oman crafts, weaving and spinning should obtain a copy of Gigi's book *Traditional Spinning and Weaving in The Sultanate of Oman,* by Gigi Crocker Jones, published by The Historical Association of Oman, March 1989. I am most grateful to both of them for their help regarding the White Oryx Project and spinning.

### Colonel Nigel Knocker, OBE

who as Chairman of the Sultan's Armed Forces Association has been a great help in both approving my final draft and providing sources for much-needed photographs. Having commanded The Desert Regiment (1971–1973), Nigel was able to ensure that my description of the Dhofar War was technically correct and fair comment. I am very grateful to him for his foreword and for his active support and encouragement.

### Charles Butt

who between 1966 and 1978 served in Muscat Garrison, Midway, Oman Gendarmerie and Headquarters, Bait-al-Falaj. He has kindly lent me some remarkable photographs from his extensive library of slides of his service in both Aden and Oman.

### Julian Lush

who was prospecting for oil with The Petroleum Development of Oman (PDO) based at Ibri (1962–1963). His rig drilled for oil at Yibal I, Natih I and Umm al Samim. We met and climbed Jebel Misht together with Sergeant Carr of the Parachute Regiment. Having re-established contact after 37 years, he has kindly reviewed Chapter Six (Arab Company in the Desert) and has provided six excellent photographs of the Ibri area. He has edited the two sections on oil in Chapter Ten.

### Lieutenant-Colonel Christopher Hinton

who was seconded from The Royal Greenjackets to The Sultan's Armed Forces (1964–1965). He was General Staff Officer (Intelligence) under Malcolm Dennison, the Force Intelligence Officer at the time. He has edited the section headed 'Differing perceptions of loyalty' in Chapter Nine. He has also provided a photograph of Malcolm Dennison.

*Tim Callan, Information Advisor, Embassy of the Sultanate of Oman*

who, together with Rosemary Hector in the Ministry of Information in Muscat, has been enthusiastic and helpful in sourcing various items of information which I needed for the final chapter, including providing access to Ministry of Information literature, photographs, maps and statistics.

*Sir Donald Hawley, KCMG, MBE*

who was Her Majesty's First Ambassador to The Sultanate of Oman (1971–1975). As author of *Oman Jubilee Edition* and *Desert Wind and Tropic Storm* he is the pre-eminent author on the renaissance of the Sultanate between 1970 and 2000 and Vice-President of the Anglo Omani Society. His professional advice to a first-time author has been invaluable. Not only did he read through my draft manuscript but he introduced me to others who have helped me and has allowed me to source matters from his own books. Those interested in Omani silver are advised to read his wife's new book *Silver: the Traditional Art of Oman* published by Stacey International.

*General Naseeb Hamad Salim al Ruwaihi*

whom I remember in 1963 as Sergeant Naseeb Hamad, clearly destined for high rank. In 1982 he became the first local Commander, Sultan of Oman's Land Forces (CSOLF). I am very grateful to him for writing the foreword from an Omani's point of view.

*His Excellency Abdullah bin Shwain Al Hosni, Under Secretary, Ministry of Information, Sultanate of Oman*

who kindly arranged for his Ministry to review my original (unedited) manuscript. Various suggested amendments have been included and his wishing me 'every success with its publication' has been a great encouragement.

*Peter Mason*

who was in Muscat in 1953, 1958–1960 and 1968–1974 with the British Bank of the Middle East. He has kindly provided a photograph of Sultan Said bin Taimur taken in Salalah.

## Organisations

I would like to thank the following organisations, and particularly those individuals I have named, for their guidance and assistance regarding photographs, maps and other sources of such information:

*Middle East Centre, St Antony's College,* 62 Woodstock Road, Oxford 0X2 6JF – Clare Brown.

*British Empire and Commonwealth Museum,* Clock Tower Yard, Temple Meads, Bristol BS1 6QH – Peter Walton, Mary Blackley and Holly Bown.

*Royal Geographical Society,* 1 Kensington Gore, London SW7 2AR – Map Room – David McNeill.

*Ordnance Survey International,* Romsey Road, Southampton, SO16 4GU – International Library Manager, Russell Fox.

*Ordnance Survey Copyright Licensing,* Romsey Road, Southampton S016 4GU – Mrs Melanie Buckley.

*Defence Geographic Centre (Military Survey),* Government Building Block A, Hook Rise South, Tolworth, Surrey KT10 0BS – Mrs E. Manterfield.

*Soldier: The British Army Magazine,* Ordnance Road, Aldershot, Hampshire GU11 2DU – Librarian and Archivist, Stuart Robinson.

## Book preparation and production team

Finally I would like to express my sincere thanks to a talented and experienced team of professionals without whom this book would never have seen the light of day.

Editing and typesetting: *Bridget Winstanley of Blackwater Books*

Bookjacket painting: *Paul Bawden*

Book design including illustrations: *Alan Hamp of Design for Books*

Printing and production: *Michael Castle of The Five Castles Press Ltd.*

By working so well together on the various stages of preparation and production, they have been a reassuring and positive influence to a first-time author, unversed in such matters. They have made it possible to produce a good quality book at a competetive price. Our hope is that readers will agree and that it will ultimately grace many bookshelves.

# Explanatory Notes

### The Name of the Country

Oman, before 1970, was known as Muscat and Oman. However, when His Majesty Sultan Qaboos succeeded his father, Sultan Said bin Taimur on 23rd July 1970, he changed the name of his country to The Sultanate of Oman nowadays often abbreviated to Oman.

At one stroke Sultan Qaboos consigned former friction between Muscat and Oman to history. His father had been known as the Sultan of Muscat and, throughout his thirty-eight-year reign, had striven with some success to bring Oman under his rule. On succession, Sultan Qaboos paved the way for 'renaissance' by announcing the single nation state of Oman. By calling it a Sultanate he effectively extended his leadership throughout the length and breadth of Oman. Muscat became Oman's capital city and seat of government.

### The Names of the Armed Forces

During the mid 1950s there was a small armed force called the Muscat Field Force (MFF), manned by Baluchis recruited from Gwarda and the Batinah coast. They were led by a handful of British contract officers, mostly retired Indian Army, who spoke Urdu.

During 1957 and 1959 Sultan Said bin Taimur asked Britain for assistance in overthrowing two rebellions within Oman. British troops were briefly and successfully deployed and then withdrawn.

The British Government felt obliged to continue to support the Sultan by providing backbone to his forces. Not only did Britain arm, resource and pay for his forces, but fifty British Officers were seconded on a rolling programme to train and lead them.

By 1958 the force became the Sultan of Muscat's Armed Forces (SMAF), which included an air force (SAF) and a navy (SN). The majority of the force was still Baluchi.

During the early 1960's the recruitment of Omanis was given priority and Arabic succeeded Urdu as the Force language. The Force steadily increased in size and was deployed in several company outstations within Oman. The Force became known as the Sultan's Armed Forces (SAF), of which the Sultan of

Oman's Air Force (SOAF) became an increasingly significant part, while the Sultan of Oman's Navy (SON) was still in its infancy.

The Dhofar War (1964–1975) injected unprecedented urgency into recruitment and training throughout the Sultan's Armed Forces. Omanisation was proceeding apace from 1970 onwards at the same time as an increasingly bloody war.

By the late 1970s the Sultan's Armed forces (SAF) had become too large and unwieldy to remain a single entity and consequently it was divided into three arms:

Sultan of Oman's Land Forces (SOLF)
Sultan of Oman's Air Force (SOAF)
Sultan of Oman's Navy (SON).
Somewhat later The Royal Guard (RG) was created.

## Arabic Transliteration

The spelling of Arabic names and words in English usually causes writers and readers despair. The variations appear endless as there is no right way. However, inevitably some give the reader a better idea of pronunciation than others. It is for this reason that the author has included a glossary of terms which afford the reader some consistency throughout the book. In classical Arabic there are only three vowels. If transliterated to proximity to the Arabic sound, they should be pronounced:

| Vowel | English sound | Arabic sound | Meaning |
|---|---|---|---|
| a | father | barusti | shelter |
| i | feet | bin | son of |
| u | food | suq | market |

| Consonants | English sound | Arabic sound | Meaning |
|---|---|---|---|
| dh | the | fudhl | gathering for food |
| kh | kind | sheikh | headman |
| gh | good | shamagh | headscarf |

## Arabic usages

Said bin Taimur means 'Said, the son of Taimur'.
Women's names replace 'bin' with 'bint'.

The Arabic title 'Sultan' (accent on final syllable) has the same meaning as 'King' in English. Indeed occasionally the ruler of Oman is called 'King'. Like King in English, Sultan in Arabic is also a personal name.

# Glossary

| | |
|---|---|
| aghal | double headcord used to keep the cloth headdress in place |
| Ar rub al Khali | name given by bedouin to the great desert in the south-east corner of Arabia. In English this is referred to as the Empty Quarter. |
| askari | soldier |
| bait | house, often used to mean family and a component of the names of villages, e.g. Bait-al-Falaj |
| barusti | palm frond screen or shelter |
| bedu | desert dwellers who do not permanently settle |
| bin | son (of) |
| bint | girl, daughter (of) |
| birqa | a rigid black or indigo face mask worn by women |
| bisht | outer cloak, worn over a dish-dasha |
| dish-dasha | an ankle-length white garment |
| Eid el fitr | the feast celebrating the end of the fast of Ramadhan |
| finjan | coffee cup |
| fudhl | party or gathering for a meal |
| ibn | son (of), often abbreviated to 'bin' |
| insh'allah | as God wills |
| jebel | mountain, mountain range |
| khanjar | an ornate curved dagger worn at the waist |
| kohl | eye shadow worn to reduce the glare of the sun |
| Koran | the Muslim Holy Book |
| kummar | flat-topped, brimless, embroidered cap |
| majlis | room where men receive their visitors |
| massar | An ornately-patterned headshawl |
| Ramadhan | Lent, forty days of daylight fasting in which Muslims celebrate God's gift to man of the Koran |
| Ra's | head; headland |
| Rial | currency, the large Maria Theresa thaler (from the Spanish 'real') |
| shamagh | headscarf |
| Shar'iah | Islamic law, based on the Koran and the tradition of the Prophet Muhammed |

| | |
|---|---|
| sheikh | headman or elder, an acknowledgement of respect |
| suq | market place |
| surwel | women's baggy trousers gathered at the ankle |
| wadi | rocky watercourse, dry except in the rainy season |
| wali | a holy man |
| wiqaiah | a patterned shawl worn by women |

# Chapter One

# My Reasons Why

Why I went there in 1962 – Why I wrote this book 36 years later –
Who might enjoy it?

## *Why I went there in 1962*

How did fifty or so British Army officers come to be seconded to the Sultan of Muscat's Armed Forces in the 1960s? At the time Muscat and Oman was a poor and feudal country gradually awakening to the prospect of oil development. At the time Sultan Said bin Taimur refused to grant entry visas to the press – yet he welcomed British officers to his Armed Forces.

Nowadays such extremes of attitude appear difficult to reconcile. However, as my story unravels the background to this era of profound change, the reader will begin to understand why Sultan Said bin Taimur invited British Officers to lead and train his army.

Britain's involvement in the Arabian peninsular, derived historically from her need to protect her trading routes to India, had spawned a 'Treaty of Friendship' with Muscat which had been operational since 1800. Britain's withdrawal from Egypt in 1956 signalled her waning influence on Middle Eastern affairs in the face of burgeoning Arab nationalism masterminded by Egypt's President, Colonel Nasser. This was a period of frenzied oil exploration and discovery within the Gulf, intense diplomatic manoeuvre and conflicting international interests. Indeed the Cold War rendered Arabia's flanks an ideal breeding ground for Marxist subversion, extending earlier successes within the Yemen.

Against this external backdrop of insecurity, intrigue and propaganda, Muscat and Oman appeared as an isolated feudal country with oil potential and ripe for picking. Internally the age-old tensions experienced by the rulers of Muscat and Oman were fanned by external threat and internally by rumours of oil discovery. It was small wonder that the Sultan, during this time of great uncertainty, turned to Britain, an old and respected friend. Invoking earlier treaties of protection, he requested that some British officers should be seconded to his armed forces to help repel outside aggressors and calm internal unrest.

But from my personal point of view the need for a fresh challenge was the crux of the matter. Since I had joined my regiment five years earlier I had enjoyed a purple patch of variety in Kenya and the Radfan on the border between Aden Protectorate and the Yemen. How could I perpetuate this exciting life? I had spent an uneventful six months in Germany and the prospect of two years in that country did not appeal. Secondment to the Sultan of Muscat's Armed Forces seemed to promise action and interest in an exotic part of the world.

During the 1950s and early 1960s life in the services offered a bewildering choice of opportunities. These were the days of National Service, before the withdrawal of garrisons from Singapore, Malaysia, Hong Kong, Kenya, Aden and Cyprus. During this period there were a variety of overseas conflicts and emergencies to which Britain felt obliged to respond. Since the Korean War (1950–1954) there had been an unbroken series of internal security campaigns in Malaya (1948–1957), Kenya (1952–1958), Cyprus (1954–1959), Suez (1956) and Aden (1958–1967). Britain's three services had responded well to each emergency and were experienced and highly regarded. This led to an increase in demand for secondments or attachments to other armies all over the world. The King's African Rifles (KAR) and Gurkhas were just two much sought-after examples. However, following the Anglo-French withdrawal from Suez in 1956 there gradually emerged an overdue and reluctant acceptance by Britain that she could no longer afford to exert her influence on the world stage. Arguably her military professionalism during the 1950s had perpetuated a cycle of overseas defence expenditure which her declining economy could no longer sustain. In any event the main threat to her security was much closer to home: the defence of Europe from the military power of Soviet Russia.

In January 1957 Harold Macmillan succeeded Anthony Eden as Prime Minister and was determined to reduce the size and expense of the Armed Forces and to abolish National Service. Later that year the Defence White Paper announced that National Service would cease from 1960. From 690,000 in the three services, of whom 300,000 were National Servicemen, the services' strength was projected to reduce to an all-regular total of 350,000 by 1962. The Army's share was expected to be 165,000[1]. At the time the 'regulars' were torn between sadness at the loss of such a heady infusion of personalities with a variety of skills, and the promise of a smaller more mobile highly professional regular army.

Within Europe the overriding concern was to deter the threat of Warsaw Pact forces with NATO (North Atlantic Treaty Organisation) forces in a nuclear warfare setting. Emphasis was on the fast deployment of armoured battle groups, supported by varying levels of nuclear weaponry, to withstand, contain and annihilate Russian nuclear-supported attack. BAOR's (British Army of the Rhine's) contribution to NATO was about 55,000 servicemen and women. Because of the nature of nuclear warfare, the composition of teeth arms favoured armoured, artillery and engineer regiments at the expense of infantry battalions using armoured personnel carriers. Consequently, it became the norm for armoured and artillery regiments to alternate between BAOR and UK postings. In contrast, the infantry spent more time further afield on conventional internal security postings. Arguably this made for a more varied and exciting existence.

Since joining my father's regiment, the King's Shropshire Light Infantry (KSLI), from the Royal Military Academy Sandhurst in 1957 – some five years earlier – I had spent only six months in Germany. After completing School of Infantry Courses at Hythe and Warminster I joined the 1st Battalion in Kenya, becoming Rifle Platoon Commander of 7 Platoon in C Company. Although the battalion was based in tented accommodation at Muthaiga Camp, Nairobi, the majority of our time was spent on patrol in the forest from company camps in Naivasha and Thompsons Falls. By then the Mau Mau Emergency was in its last throes, but there was still an urgency about everything we did in a beautiful country.

Some six months later Battalion Headquarters, together with B and C Rifle Companies, were flown at short notice to Aden to take part in internal security operations in the Radfan. For some of us this was our first experience of active service. Being shot at by Yemeni tribesmen and mistakenly bombed by the RAF were memorable moments. Soldiering in the oppressive heat and barren openness of the Radfan was in complete contrast to the intense humidity of Kenya where we used pangas to cut our way through the dense undergrowth of the forests. Within six months, having forced the Yemeni tribesmen to take refuge within Yemen, we were on board the troopship HMS *Dunera* en route for Southampton and a two-year posting in Colchester where we joined the Spearhead Brigade, on standby for immediate redeployment wherever we might be needed.

There followed a busy and happy two years where, in between brigade and battalion exercises, live firing and standby duties, we all took full advantage of sporting and recreational opportunities. Being Mortar Platoon Commander provided marvellous opportunities for detachment for live firing on Stanford and Okehampton Ranges. Not only was I fortunate enough to play cricket for the Army and rugby for the Harlequins but I also met Charmian, who was to become my wife five years later.

The battalion was then posted to Münster in Germany where it was absorbed into the BAOR scheme of things. Like many others, I did not much enjoy the round of nuclear warfare exercises. However, travel by autobahn brought skiing and so much else of interest within easy reach. Nevertheless, I remember being pleased when after only six months I was posted to Shrewsbury to become adjutant of the KSLI Depot and also captain of the Army Cricket XI.

In early 1962 the KSLI Depot became the Light Infantry Brigade Depot and being asked to captain the Army Cricket XI for a second year, I remained in Shrewsbury as assistant adjutant to the 4th Battalion KSLI (Territorial Army) throughout that summer.

Come the autumn, the prospect of returning to BAOR as a company second-in-command seemed rather dull. By then I had decided that I did not wish to be labelled as just a sport-playing soldier and that it was the right time to seek some experience outside my regiment, preferably on active service. I promptly made enquiries about a two-year tour in the Army Air Corps, the Special Air Service and the Sultan of Muscat's Armed Forces.

To my disappointment I failed the eye test at Biggin Hill, so learning to fly helicopters with the Army Air Corps was not possible. As I harboured some reservations about the SAS, I did not proceed with my application. This left the Sultan of Muscat's Armed Forces. Not only had I thoroughly enjoyed my time in the Radfan three years earlier but Muscat and Oman was the only active service theatre at the time. The discovery that as a seconded officer I would receive double pay and six weeks mid-tour leave clinched matters.

However, life was not that simple. Despite the prospect of two years in Muscat and Oman, where no women were allowed, I unreasonably asked Charmian to become engaged to be married to me. I was very disappointed when she quite sensibly turned me down. However, most importantly, we had agreed to write to each other.

## Why I wrote this book 36 years later

During the next two years, first in Aden learning Arabic, and then in Muscat and Oman, it never entered my head to write a book. At 25 years of age it would have seemed pretentious to have done so. While most of us took photographs and wrote letters home, life was much too busy anyway. For my part, I was just happy to write to Charmian describing my experiences and was overjoyed to receive her wonderfully newsy letters in reply. Not until after we married in 1965 did I discover that she had transposed my letters – suitably edited – into a hardback exercise book.

Equally, I was much too busy during my remaining eight years of military service even to consider writing a book. After I left the Army in 1970 at 33 years of age, the need to make a success of my new career in London remained uppermost in my mind. In 1990 after 20 years with Ernst & Young and aged 53, I, in common with millions elsewhere, found myself redundant during the recession. This prompted me, somewhat late in life, to establish my own

6

independent management consultancy practice, which has kept me profitable and busy ever since.

Over the years we had occasionally shown our two daughters, when quite young, slide shows of our various travels, including those taken by me in Muscat and Oman. These scenes seemed to catch their imagination and, on more than one occasion, they suggested that I should write a book.

As our daughters grew up our attic gradually became an overflowing depository for things that 'might come in useful someday'. After 28 years of such squirrel-like behaviour, none of us could find anything we were looking for. Finally we removed everything, threw out as much as possible, and became better organised. It was during this process that we came across an overnight bag containing Charmian's hard-backed exercise book of extracts from my 'Letters from Oman'. Fortunately these were intact and had escaped the attention of mice.

And so it seemed that the time had finally come to write about an earlier chapter in my life. Finding that exercise book acted as a prompt. The combination of becoming less busy and discovering some aptitude for writing had stripped away all reasonable excuses.

If this was not sufficient to persuade me to start writing, Fiona, our younger daughter, during her BA (Hons) Illustration degree course at Falmouth College of Art offered to illustrate my book. After negotiating a success-related fee, she typically added 'Go for it, Dad!'

## Who might enjoy it?

If the reader is hoping for a story of derring-do, then to avoid disappointment he or she should set aside *Letters from Oman*.

On the other hand I hope that many readers will enjoy discovering that the vividness of my early letters, when stirred with mature reflection, produces an intriguing blend of insight and impressions of Aden and Muscat and Oman in the early 1960s.

In particular this book provides glimpses of a remarkably beautiful Muscat and Oman – little known at the time – before feudalism was swept aside by the exploitation of its new-found oil resources. It gives some indication of the stresses and achievements of its resilient people during an intense period of cultural change.

For those readers who do not know either Aden or Muscat and Oman, it will help them understand how, on opposite flanks of the Arabian Peninsula, they differ utterly from each other in terms of geography, history and culture. Their respective attributes and contrasting historical relationships with Great Britain account for so much that followed. Indeed when Great Britain's declining influence in the Middle East during the late 1950s seemed to herald fundamental change within both countries, it explains Aden's antagonism and Oman's continuing debt of gratitude. We would do well to preserve the latter, if we are to continue to exercise any influence on events in a strife-torn Middle East.

MIDDLE EAST 1962

For all those who have been there before – whether in the services, as oil company staff, or as advisors or officials – my hope is that they will wish to read and enjoy this book. Each will cherish different recollections from mine, while many, unlike me, will have held high office and have profound experience of one or both countries. My hope is that where my impressions differ from theirs, they will understand my point of view.

Whether or not the reader knows either country is not important. The combination of instant communication, global travel and relentless search for knowledge renders the Middle East's continuing insecurity a matter of real concern to us all. It is particularly so for British people who are aware of our historical links. Now increasing numbers work or take their holidays in the Sultanate of Oman, which only recently has become the subject of travel articles and tourist guides.

My hope is that my earlier impressions and recent thoughts, combined with some historical background, will help put today's issues in context. If this persuades people to wish to see this remarkable country for themselves, so much the better.

# Chapter Two

# Aden: A Brief History to 1962

Eden or Aden? – Aden as a trading centre  –  Aden's links with
Great Britain – Twentieth-century history – Qat and the Radfan –
The Colony of Aden – The Aden Protectorate

## Eden or Aden?

The first authentic recorded mention of Aden can be found in the Bible (Ezekiel, Chapter 7, Verses 23 and 24):

> Verse 23 'Haran, and Canneh, and Eden, the merchants of Sheba, Assur and Chilmad, were thy merchants'

> Verse 24 'These were thy merchants in all sorts of things, in blue clothes'

While Arabic versions of the Scriptures confirm that 'Eden'[2] was spelt in the same way as it is in Arabic today, the indigo impregnated garments (or blue clothes) were still worn in the Protectorate in the early sixties. Word has it that Cain worshipped fire here, while a tower on Jebel Hadid is billed as the site of Abel's grave.

## Aden as a trading centre

Since early Christian days the heady combination of Aden's strategic position and natural harbour has attracted envy. Her harbour acted as a trading beacon to shipping from India, the Persian Gulf, the Red Sea and Africa. It is small wonder that the early rulers of Yemen – Abyssinians, Persians and Ottomans – were attracted by her thriving port. Indeed a number of dynasties ruled Aden during medieval times. It was the Tahirids, succeeding the Mongols, who are credited with recognising Aden's great potential and reviving the port by introducing preferential duties.

By the twelfth and thirteenth centuries the best trade route between India and Europe lay up the Red Sea, overland to the Nile and then downstream to Alexandria. Thereafter the door to the Mediterranean was open for sailing to all of Europe's trading ports. Aden's prominent position at the entrance to the Red Sea and her harbour offered a timely and safe anchorage to sailing ships, who needed fresh supplies before embarking on the oppressively hot sail up the Red Sea. The same logic applied in reverse when sailing for home. In this way Aden became the entrepôt for the spice and silk routes from the Indies.

However, when Vasco da Gama discovered the Cape route to India in 1498 the old and prosperous Aden lost its powerful position. The continuous sea passage between East and West soon became the preferred trade route. For the next three centuries, Aden, devoid of international trade or local commerce, sank into abject decline. By the early 1800s it was no more than a pirate village, preying on the lesser traders of the Indian Ocean.

## TRADITIONAL TRADING ROUTES

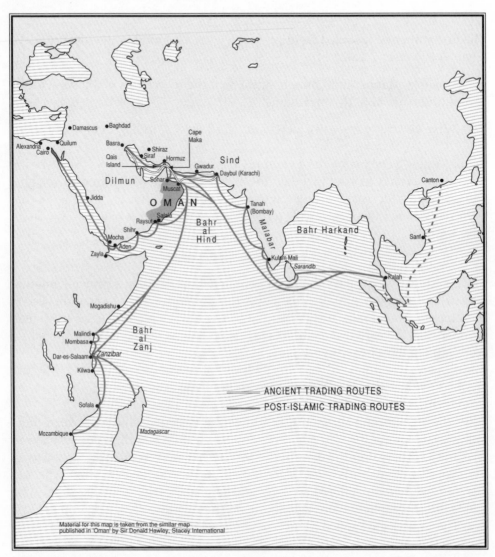

Material for this map is taken from the similar map
published in 'Oman' by Sir Donald Hawley; Stacey International

Aden's decline in the early 1500s invited predators. The Portuguese tried
unsuccessfully in 1513 to seize it. However, in 1538 the Turks were successful
and still retained control when British ships first arrived in 1551. Ultimately
frustrated in their efforts to subdue the mountain Yemenis, the Turks also
withdrew in the early 1600s, leaving Aden, which they used as a punishment

centre, in a state of decay. Thereafter the settlement, which now had little to offer, remained free from further invasion for two hundred years.

## Aden's links with Great Britain

In 1799 the British garrisoned the little island of Perim, in the Bab al Mandeb Strait, to prevent the French from sailing to India. Forced to withdraw because of lack of water, the British subsequently returned to establish a coaling station to service the Suez – Bombay run.

In 1839 Britain annexed the Port of Aden. According to records of the time, the reason for this action was to avenge the maltreatment of the crew of an English ship wrecked on the coast near the port. In riposte an armed expedition was mounted from India, under the command of Captain Haines of the Indian Navy. However in all probability this was a convenient cover for Britain's wish to control the only good harbour between India and Egypt.

Captain Haines has left on record his first impressions of Aden:

'The little village (formerly a great city) of Aden is now reduced to the most exigent condition of poverty and neglect. In the reign of Constantine this town possessed unrivalled celebrity for its impenetrable fortifications, its flourishing commerce, and the glorious haven it afforded to vessels from all quarters of the globe. How lamentable is the present contrast'[3].

Having secured this community of five hundred people in a scene of 'barrenness beyond belief' in 1839, Captain Haines became the first resident of Aden, which formed part of the Bombay Presidency. Inevitably, hinterland tribes launched numerous attacks on Aden to test the British regime: response was a mixture of brute force, courtship of selected rulers and encouragement of trade. Haines ran Aden for sixteen years, caught inextricably between the East India Company's Secret Committee in London and the Governor of Bombay. Gradually a mixture of investment and commercial flair helped to stem the decay and begin to revive Aden. The opening of the Suez Canal in 1869 helped restore Aden's status as an entrepôt and trading centre. During this period Haines and his successors realised that the port, whose only natural resource was salt, had to be supplied from the interior. Consequently protection money was paid to rulers progressively further inland from the port. Aden's sphere of influence and costs multiplied. By the 1870s Bombay complained that it was costing £150,000 a year, but even so it was not until the early 1900s that Ottoman expansion to the North forced Britain to limit its sphere of influence. By then Aden had been safe from foreign aggressors for sixty years from the time of Captain Haines's arrival.

## 20th-century history

By 1913 after much flexing of muscles between the Ottoman and British Empires, a border treaty was ratified between the Sublime Porte and Whitehall. This delineated a boundary running north-eastward from Bab al Mandeb, effectively partitioning Yemen from the Aden Protectorate. However in the following year the two powers went to war rendering their agreement useless. The Ottoman forces advanced on Aden and met British Forces at Lahej in 1915. Outnumbered, the British withdrew, whereupon the Turks advanced to Sheikh Othman, sending forward raiding parties to Ma'alla. The British big guns were pointing out to sea.

However, the clash of empires was a chivalrous affair and the Turkish commander, who refrained from interfering with Aden's water supply, did not press home their initial advantage. Instead in the words of Sir George Younghusband 'their army sat down and incidentally began to die of heat . . . Some said advance, but most said retire and did so'. Thus ended a somewhat comical First World War sideshow. The Treaty of Versailles effectively forestalled further Turkish intrusions towards Aden.

By the early 1930s fresh water from wells in Sheikh Othman made possible Aden's recovery into a flourishing town. However in 1932 political developments in India had reached a stage which made a break with Bombay inevitable. In 1937 Aden became a Crown Colony under the direct control of the Colonial office in London, who stipulated that it should remain a free port.

While Aden is blessed with an ideal strategic position and natural harbour – both priceless assets – her security and status as a duty-free port were at risk. While a firm British military presence could safeguard the security of the Colony, the decision in 1937 regarding duty-free status was infinitely more problematic. As it turned out the Arab leaders and their advisors were agreed that the imposition of export and import duties, an obvious source of revenue, would have a disastrous effect on the trade of the Colony. Accordingly the guarantee that Aden should remain a free port was a precondition of transfer. The Aden Port Trust was established to keep pace with Suez Canal development and Aden's rival, Djibouti, across the Gulf of Aden.

Two entries in the Trust's records[4] some years later give some indication of the considerable expansion of business and changes in cargo:

1948: 220 ocean-going ships of over two hundred tons per month. Six pilots. Oil replacing coal as ships' bunkers.

1956: 5000 ships per annum. Four million tons of oil, much of which supplied by Aden Refinery, completed in 1953.

In retrospect it is clear that the first signs of cultural change within the Arabian Peninsula stem from the collapse of the Ottoman Empire during the First World War and the subsequent emergence of the independent status of Yemen and Saudi Arabia. This introduced a measure of challenge to British authority around the fringes of the peninsula.

However after the Second World War three developments began to convert this cultural change into a revolution. Britain's withdrawal from India in 1947 coincided with a rise in Arab nationalism and accelerated political change. The oil industry swept much of the peninsula into unprecedented economic boom. Finally, the communication revolution – motor cars, aeroplanes and radio – began to transform attitudes towards government and frontiers.

By the mid-1950s the cultural and economic revolution was in full swing and the peninsula was being opened up to an inquisitive and materialistic world. By the late 1950s Aden had become the second greatest maritime trading port in the world after New York. While her continuing duty free status and oil refinery had been catalysts for sharp business growth, this boom invited a huge influx of all sorts of nationalities hell-bent on getting their share of Aden's good fortune. Britain's withdrawal from Suez in late 1956 exacerbated the situation still further. The combination of American encouragement and Cold War paranoia persuaded Britain to reinforce its Aden base and this introduced large numbers of servicemen and their camp followers from Egypt into an already over-crowded Colony.

Over the centuries Aden had been used to the ebb and flow of a mixed transient population according to varying cycles of trading prosperity but this influx of chattering masses was unprecedented. The Aden Government creaked in its efforts to administer the Colony, let alone co-ordinate the Protectorate.

Britain's decision to enlarge its Aden base appeared to offer some compensation for the loss of Suez, but it was inconsistent with her surrender of imperial responsibilities elsewhere. Meanwhile Britain's loss of face in Suez, consistently trumpeted by Radio Cairo, gave the chattering masses much to talk about and had a serious destabilising effect on the security of the Colony. Nasser's finger of derision was pointed not only at the British but also the Indians who had come to dominate commercial and political life.

In November 1956 Nasser closed the Suez Canal to the world's shipping causing Aden's bustling prosperity to falter and generally putting her port in limbo. During the following months many port workers returned to the Yemen

15

until Suez reopened and the ships returned. However, this period of upheaval signalled the birth of Arab nationalism, which exploited the earlier introduction of the Trade Union movement to full effect. Strike action and general agitation were the instruments used to begin to subvert the old order and disrupt labour relations and productivity. Photographs of President Nasser and the Imam of the Yemen appeared everywhere, accompanied by radio pronouncements from Cairo and Sanaa providing focal points for Arab nationalism. While the President and Imam differed on many matters, they agreed that the British had to go.

In 1959 in order to impose some order over some fractious Protectorate rulers, Britain formed the Federation of South Arabia. The idea was that each ruler's goodwill and compliance would be won by financial incentive, a ministerial portfolio and a share in oil revenues. While a dozen signed up, those in the larger Eastern Protectorate refused, partly due to their unwillingness to share their potential oil wealth with their neighbours.

## Qat and the Radfan

If this was not more than enough to challenge the resolve of the Aden Government, the growing addiction to qat was undermining the fabric of a mixed society and putting the security of the Aden Protectorate at risk. Qat is a shrub cultivated in the Yemen and Ethiopia and at Dhala in the Protectorate. The leaves of what looks like a tea bush are chewed, while fresh and green, and the practice is habit forming. While medical opinion was divided on the precise effect of the drug, by 1956 addicts in the Colony were paying £2.5 million a year for it. A growing drug culture was emerging which damaged the health of addicts, who could not afford the cost and neglected their family responsibilities.

In 1957 the Aden Government prohibited the entry of qat into the Colony but had no jurisdiction over the Protectorate. The Sultan of Lahej, through whose territory qat from the Yemen and Dhala had to pass to reach Aden Colony, was unwilling to co-operate with the Aden authorities. He even allowed further imports from Ethiopia to be landed on the Lahej coast. Consequently Dar Saad, on the Colony boundary, became one vast qat-chewing den. In addition to feeling that there was unjustified infringement of his State's liberty, the Sultan probably contravened the prohibition order because of an unwillingness to annoy the Yemen Government for fear of retaliation along his border and fear that the Imam might close the frontier with consequent loss of revenue.

His refusal to cooperate made nonsense of the Aden Government's prohibition order, which was in due course rescinded. This perceived weakness coupled with the flourishing trade route between the Yemen, Dhala and Aden Colony encouraged Yemen's tribesmen to infiltrate the Protectorate, commanding the Dhala road and generally preying on the Colony. By 1958 the internal security situation within the Protectorate was so parlous that the British Government was forced to deploy military forces to secure the Dhala road and push the Yemen's tribesmen back within their frontier.

These wiry riflemen from the Yemen hill tribes were natural marksmen having carried rifles since boyhood. Armed and trained by the Russians, they represented the People's Republic of South Yemen. By a combination of laying Egyptian plastic mines and very effective sniper ambush from mountainous country dominating the winding track of the Dhala road, they had rendered the main supply route to Aden from Yemen practically impassable.

My good fortune was to be a Rifle Platoon Commander during these operations which were known by the name of the region, the Radfan. My regiment, the 1st Battalion The King's Shropshire Light Infantry stationed in Kenya dispatched two rifle companies to reinforce The Buffs (The Royal East Kent Regiment). Our combined force included the Aden Protectorate Levies and was supported by The Life Guards in 'Ferret' scout cars, light artillery and RAF fighter ground attack and bomber aircraft.

This operation involved the painstaking re-securing of high ground by 'picquetting' tactics, last used in the North-West Frontier of India. Having 'reopened' the Dhala road the final assault from Dhala towards the Yemen border involved a daylight assault up the 8,000 ft Jebel Jihaf supported by RAF and artillery. This was followed by the well-publicised release of Fitzroy Somerset, the British Political Agent, who was being held hostage in Fort Assaria.

This had been an exciting six months for everyone. However, having seen Russian T34 tanks deployed beyond the Yemen Border at Sanah, we did wonder as we left whether we could hold the line next time.

Undoubtedly the deployment of British forces in the Radfan had helped restore respect for the Protectorate rulers and the government of the Colony. However this was against a backcloth of British withdrawals from Suez and Palestine, which showed the British Empire to be in decline. The sheer cost of maintaining the Colony and its garrison seemed to be spiralling out of proportion. Meanwhile Marxist agents, already prevalent in Yemen, were exploiting ideal circumstances for destabilising Britain's tenuous hold on Aden still further. Moreover, despite their recent defeat in the Radfan, the Yemen people whose country had been separated by Turkish and British empire building for 120 years, sensed the end of an era. The time appeared to be

17

approaching when they might achieve their destiny by reclaiming Aden, the Eye of Yemen.

Yet in the face of all this threatening uncertainty, much of which was only apparent if you thought to scratch the surface, life went on as normal. Clearly that was all that mattered. To scotch any doubts the 1962 Defence White Paper pronounced that the British base would be maintained for at least ten years.

## The Colony of Aden

In 1960 the Colony of Aden was 75 square miles in extent with the huge harbour nestled within a lobster claw. Aden including Tawahi, Ma'alla and Crater on the eastern claw and Little Aden, renamed Bureikha, on the western claw. Both promontories are hilly and are connected by a narrow strip of plain enclosing the northern side of the harbour (front endpapers).

The boundary of the Colony had been demarcated and in 1960 had not been in dispute for many years. The small island of Perim, at the mouth of the Red Sea, taken by the British in 1799, subsequently becoming a coaling station, was later largely deserted but remained part of the colony.

On the eastern claw there are three distinct entities. The main commercial centre is in the middle of an extinct volcano and is called 'Crater' (1). The trading and maritime suburb of Tawahi was often referred to as Steamer Point by passengers from ships, while Ma'alla, a mile-long strip of identical blocks of flats, is built on the slopes of Jebel Shamsan (1,700 ft).

Aden is connected to the mainland by a narrow isthmus, called Khormaksar, a flat place on which were built a Royal Air Force station and military and civil airports. The original port of Aden, so key to its early prosperity, was on the east side of the peninsula in Front Bay and Holkat Bay. Never a safe anchorage this old port gradually silted up and was abandoned. Not until the 1850s was the present harbour on the west side of the peninsula at Tawahi brought into use.

In the 1960s the housing and hotel accommodation varied in the extreme from the basic dwellings in the Crater to the garish Rock and Crescent Hotels at Tawahi. And in between was an architect's nightmare. Harold Ingrams, the pioneer British Administrator of the Hadramaut gave a vitriolic description:

'For soulless, military officialdom did its best to see that nothing picturesque or beautiful was ever allowed to raise its head among the depressing, severely practical and utterly uncomfortable barrack-like structures it erected itself.'

18

However it is always easy to criticise the British who built against the odds of urgency and restrictive budgets.

In response to the Daily Mirror's report on the appalling accommodation provided to RAF families during 1959, much improved family quarters were built as a matter of urgency. A strategic decision to pre-position an Armoured Squadron ready for redeployment within the Middle and Far East, led to the speedy construction of Falaise Camp, Bir Fukum in Little Aden during 1960 (3).

To meet the accommodation needs of the Oil Refinery in Little Aden there were four grades of housing: detached, semi-detached, terraced houses and flats with 'yards for the purdah ladies to take the air'.

While the Crater was a mixture of warehouses and dwellings within the rim of the volcano, Tawahi enjoyed greater space and elegance, overlooking the harbour.

Ma'alla's mile-long ribbon of identical apartment blocks contrasted with Khormaksar's bungalow jungle, built to house the influx of servicemen following the British withdrawal from Suez in 1956.

## The Aden Protectorate

The Aden Protectorate was originally perceived by the Colonial office as

'a *cordon sanitaire* for the Port of Aden, protecting British Commercial and Strategic interests from the depredations of wild tribesmen, invading Turks, interfering French or Egyptians'[5].

Originally Britain had no wish to be entangled in the barren wasteland of Arabia but during the 1930s the new state of Saudi Arabia, clearly intent on extending its frontiers, posed a threat to the Colony's back door. This prompted Britain to appoint Political Agents to approach the rulers of the various tribes throughout the Eastern and Western Protectorates as ambassadors and advisors. Their task was to offer protection from external aggressors in return for accepting the advice of the Governor of Aden in all matters concerning the welfare and development of their territory, except as it affected Islam and its customs. By the 1950s these advisory treaties were accepted as normal working instruments throughout the Protectorate. Somewhat incongruously, following the independence of India and all major Arab states within the Middle East, Britain then established a legal right and practical power to exercise indirect rule as well as providing protection. It was no fluke that this coincided with the birth of Arab nationalism within the Colony.

19

In 1960 the Aden Protectorate was 25 per cent larger than the United Kingdom, including Northern Ireland, and was inhabited by nearly three-quarters of a million people. Although by the early 1950s the birth of Arab nationalism was changing attitudes towards territory, the majority of Protectorate inhabitants still lived within the thirty or so ill-defined tribal states spread out between the Red Sea and Dhofar.

Here the sheer remoteness of their villages and ruggedness of the country provided a protective blanket from the chattering agitation of Aden Colony. Although radio propaganda from Cairo and Sanaa was getting through loud and clear from 1956 onwards, many rulers who had signed treaties with Britain questioned the need to overthrow the old order. The dissidents or those that had refused to sign up found themselves marginalised and at considerable financial disadvantage. Indeed since the early 1950s Yemen had offered money, ammunition, rifles and food to tribesmen everywhere in the Aden Protectorate to encourage them to rebel against their leaders, who in the main wished to remain friendly to the British, who had deployed Political Agents to bond their numerous treaties.

Consequently, unlike in Aden Colony, the wind of change took several years to have real effect in the hills and deserts of the Protectorate. Meanwhile, government of each tribe remained as it always had been, an individual matter with its inherent instability. Fixed frontiers, although now on the Arab nationalist agenda, were of no immediate concern. Nomadism remained essential to survival.

By reference to the map (8), the frontiers of the Protectorate can best be summarised by points of the compass:

South – Bounded by the sea, the Gulf of Aden and the Indian Ocean. From Sheikh Said, a rocky outcrop of hills in the SW corner opposite the island of Perim – 740 miles E to Ras Darbat Ali to the frontier with Muscat and Oman. The coast is mainly rugged and mountainous, except near Aden.

East – Frontier with Muscat and Oman. A straight line drawn inland from Ras Darbat Ali at right angles towards Ar Rub al Khali (Empty Quarter), which was by then full of oil prospectors. At latitude $19^{o}$ the most northerly point of this frontier, three frontiers converge – Muscat and Oman to the East, Saudi Arabia to the North and Aden Protectorate to the South. The Eastern Frontier between the Aden protectorate and Muscat and Oman has never been demarcated, nor has it been in dispute. That between the Protectorate and Saudi Arabia was more problematic.

West – Frontier with Yemen, a Turkish province between 1872 and 1918. In 1902 the British Government and the Sublime Porte agreed that this frontier should be demarcated. Mountainous terrain, innumerable tribal disputes, lack of security and remoteness forced the Boundary Commission to withdraw in 1904, having progressed from Sheikh Said in the South West to Qataba. Thereafter the Turkish and British Governments agreed to draw a line on the map – the violet line – between respective spheres of influence of both Empires. This was drawn at $45°$ up into the reaches of the Empty Quarter. It was ratified by both Governments in 1914 as the Anglo-Turkish convention. When Turkish forces marched on Aden during the First World War the convention became meaningless, but, following their withdrawal, was ratified once again at Versailles in 1918.

North – After years of consultation and conferences this is a reasonably straight line just north of latitude $19°$ and generally follows the southern limits of the great sand dunes of the Empty Quarter.

These frontiers had been established gradually and with considerable difficulty between 1902 and 1955 (see key to each on the map). By then those in the west were still openly flouted by dissident tribesmen, while the straight-line solutions to the north delineating the southerly limits of the Empty Quarter and the easterly frontier with Muscat and Oman were generally respected.

For those unfamiliar with the Aden Protectorate of the late 1950s and early 1960s, there is a need to elucidate a little on this region and its people. The sheer inaccessibility and remoteness of this rugged and inhospitable land had to be seen to be believed. It helps to put in perspective the culture of these hardy, resilient and resourceful people who took great pride in their simple and mainly nomadic lifestyle, so essential to their survival. Those of us visiting the Protectorate for the first time were invariably struck by the wall of suffocating dry heat which was nevertheless preferable to the humidity of Aden Port. A daunting panorama of serried jebel and foothills stretched away into the heat haze. Occasional clusters of palm trees pinpointed where water and people might be found. Good sunglasses were essential to counter the glare and also offered some protection against dust and hot wind when in an open Land Rover. Binoculars were fundamental to route selection and navigation in a country still largely unmapped.

My experience in the Radfan in 1958 helped me to understand why the Boundary Commission of 1902 had been forced to give up demarking the Western Boundary after two years. The combination of marauding tribesmen, rugged terrain and lack of water had made it an impossible task. Fifty years later very little had changed. Small wonder that Britain's efforts to instil a semblance of administrative co-ordination over these remote and troublesome Protectorate villages continued to prove so difficult. Those acting against the law became known as dissidents. Some dissident villages were so remote that it required a fortnight's march to reach them.

In this context it is easy to understand why, since the late 1930s, aerial bombing of remote dissident villages emerged as an acceptable tactic to enforce the law. After all a precedent had already been set in both India and Iraq. In 1958 I remember being alarmed to discover this fact. However, after observing such an incident first hand, I realised that it was hardly the brutal act of colonial oppression trumpeted by Cairo Radio. First the dissident village was warned in advance that if it did not comply it would be rocketed on a certain day so that the inhabitants could evacuate their homes taking their livestock with them. After everyone had retreated out of harm's way to a suitable position where they could view proceedings, then an RAF Venom or Hunter would rocket the empty village, while dissident tribesmen practised their marksmanship on the striking aircraft. Invariably there were no casualties, while the damage to dwellings constructed mainly of bamboo and brushwood were repairable within a matter of days. Such tactics were considered a prompt, affordable and firm means of concluding a village's reluctance to conform. Many sheikhs felt that until their village's honour had been satisfied in this way it was inappropriate to acquiesce.

However, while this became an accepted law enforcement procedure between the late 1930s and mid 1950s, events elsewhere in the Middle East during 1956 brought Britain's very presence in Aden Colony and the Protectorate into question. The Anglo-French withdrawal from Suez triggered the birth of Arab nationalism under the leadership of President Nasser. By then shipments of Soviet arms and ammunition were arriving in the Yemen for deployment on the frontier of the Western Protectorate. Those Russian T34 tanks we had seen near Sanaa in 1958, seemed to give notice of wholesale change. On my return to Aden four years later in 1962 it appeared on the surface that little had changed. However it was not long before my new colleagues and I became aware of a tension for change, simmering relentlessly beneath the surface.

Here we were, four 25-year-old subalterns, delegates on a course to learn colloquial Arabic within three months. Since my previous visit in 1958, the Aden Protectorate Levies (APL), a platoon of which I had under command during the assault up the Jebel Jihaf, had been re-titled the Federal Regular Army (FRA). They were to provide the tutors for our course.

# Chapter Three

# Learning Arabic in Aden

# November 1962 to January 1963

The language course – Arriving in Aden – Impressions of Aden –
A description of Aden – A visit to the Federal Regular Army at Mukeiras –
Swearing-in ceremony for recruits – End-of-course celebrations

## The language course

The language course was designed to give us a sound introduction to colloquial Arabic so that when we arrived with our respective forces we would be able to converse with our soldiers sufficiently well to do our job. In all probability each of us would serve with a rifle company of about 120 soldiers who would speak little or no English. It was likely that our company would be on detachment at a base camp either in the desert or on the jebel, where we would simply have to become proficient in Arabic. Each of us would probably become second-in-command to an experienced company commander, who could be either an officer seconded from the British Army, like ourselves, or alternatively a contract officer. In either case the prospect of their superior experience and fluent Arabic seemed rather daunting.

Consequently there was a real incentive to acquire a good grounding in an entirely new language. We needed not only to pass our Preliminary Interpretership Examination at the end of January but, more importantly, to build our confidence in Arabic so that we could become effective commanders of Arab soldiers.

There were four of us on this course administered by the Command Arabic Language School, Aden Protectorate, abbreviated to CALSAP. Two of us (Tony Parsons, Royal Northumberland Fusiliers and Ian Hurley, King's Own Border Regiment) were destined for the Trucial Oman Scouts (TOS); Colin McLean, Argyll and Sutherland Highlanders, and I were destined for the Sultan of Muscat's Armed Forces (SAF).

After attending a preliminary general briefing on Muscat and Oman at the Ministry of Defence the four of us got better acquainted during our flight to Aden. By the time we touched down at RAF Khormaksar we had discovered not only a shared excitement at the prospect of our secondment to Arab forces, but a determination to savour every moment. If a sense of humour was to have anything to do with it, all of us appeared to be well endowed. We wondered, somewhat naively, whether there would be anybody to meet us.

## Arriving in Aden

At the RAF Movements Desk, not only was there nobody to meet us but no messages either. At this point Ian Hurley took command and commandeered a Bedford three-tonner to convey us to the officers' mess. We piled ourselves and our suitcases into the back.

On arrival we came upon a strange scene of disarray. Every stick of furniture was in the process of being removed from the mess building and there was nobody around who spoke English. After much gesticulation and general ferreting about, a rather worse-for-wear British NCO emerged to tell us that we had been booked into rooms at the Rock Hotel. Nothing daunted we climbed back into the three-tonner. By then Ian had decided to stand on the passenger seat and in Rommel-like fashion, hand raised, directed a grinning driver 'Rock Hotel!'

From hereon our fortunes improved. We booked ourselves into this landmark hotel in Tawahi where we lived in some comfort while commuting daily to Arabic language tuition at CALSAP in Singapore Lines.

Here are some selected extracts from my letters to Charmian during the first three-month period.

*November 2nd 1962*

*A quick note to let you know a) my address – don't forget KSLI after my name – MOST IMPORTANT! b) that I am well c) that it's very hot and humid.*

*Sunday November 4th 1962*

*. . . Postal arrangements have been quite infuriating here. There used to be a CALSAP Officers' Mess until four days ago. It was then decided to renovate this Mess. In the meantime all Officers on the Arabic Course have been banished to the Rock Hotel. This is extremely pleasant – the second best hotel in Aden, but miles from the BFPO (British Forces Post Office). Yesterday I spent two hours trying to discover some method of getting our mail posted to the UK, avoiding a two-mile walk! In the end I made friends at a Naval Shore Station, a quarter of a mile away.*

*. . . Tomorrow the course starts. We leave the hotel at 7.15 am after breakfast and work through until 1.00 pm. We then break off and are given 28 Arabic words to learn each day.*

Those who have served or worked abroad for any length of time will understand my original concern about postal services. In my case I had left behind a girl I loved and had seconded myself out of the British Army for two years to Muscat and Oman, a then little-known and apparently remote part of the world. Letters to and from home become a life-line in such circumstances.

*November 6th 1962*

*. . . We reach CALSAP at about 7.45 am each morning and are instructed quite excellently by mixed Arab and English instructors until 12.45. They all write the most horrifying*

28

*hieroglyphics on the blackboard and we have to read back the answers. It certainly has its amusing moments.*

*. . . The afternoons are spent either lying on the beach muttering the 28 words prep (probably writing in the sand) or sitting at one's desk with pencil and pad. I seem to favour the latter followed by an evening swim.*

*Sunday November 11th 1962*

*Aden tummy struck a couple of us down this week – makes you feel unreasonably depressed.*

*. . . Aden is to my mind acceptable for a short while – but to be stationed here on a three year tour would be a nightmare.*

*. . . The winter is really quite a reasonable climate but is not conducive to hard work. Air conditioning is essential for any European who has to work hard for long hours – humidity being the enervator. Most work stops midday and restarts (if at all) at 4 o'clock. Shops are open in some cases to 11 o'clock at night. The summer is quite unbearably hot – how any worthwhile work gets done during the summer months I shall never know.*

*It certainly is a multiracial port – Arabs, Somalis, Chinese, Pakistanis, Yemenis, Europeans all live here. Large ships arrive daily spilling many more nations, colours and creeds into the already crowded streets in quest of duty free luxuries. It is a thoroughly dirty port – this being a little surprising as it is a British Colony. Some of the Adenis have ghastly deformities – one Arab walks around the litter strewn streets on all fours with sandals on his hands. The amount of begging that goes on is surprisingly small. The British Government has certainly sunk a tremendous amount of money into this place and of course the Adenis are very reliant on British Forces for their livelihood. BP has the largest share in the oil, especially obvious in Little Aden. The unrest here is not obvious at first sight, but the Yemenis are the cause of this. There does seem to be considerable feeling about the Yemen Republic, the United Arab Emirates and Saudi Arabia. I feel the King of Saudi Arabia's days are numbered. What will happen here in the next decade can only be conjecture.*

*Thursday November 15th 1962*

*This course has now got to the stage when we imagine that if Arabic remains as difficult to learn for a period of three months we will end up in a lunatic asylum! It boils down to four hours learning an afternoon. Many of us find it impossible to learn our words lying on the beach with thousands of small children screaming their heads off! Any real change from Arabic is bliss – letters and newspapers being top priority. However we had a word of encouragement from our Chief Instructor this morning saying that we were well above average. I cannot believe it!*

29

The Arabic language is not very familiar to Westerners nor is it an easy language for English people to learn. It follows from the Koran and is for the greater part uniform throughout the Arab world.

To an Arab the spoken language is used to establish the mood and rhythm for conversation. For example Westerners' brief greeting of 'Hello', is in complete contrast to the lengthy exchanges of friendly enquiries and assurances favoured by Arabs. Their often rather repetitive greetings are an essential and flamboyant prelude to what they really want to say.

Arabic is in some ways simpler than English. For example verbs are only conjugated in two tenses – perfect for the past tense and imperfect for present and future tenses. All this is achieved by attaching suffixes to root words. The main difficulties arise in pronunciation, either where counterpart sounds do not exist in English or where some distinctive guttural sounds are difficult to master.

Written Arabic is a beautiful art form that we find difficult to learn because the alphabet is so foreign. The twenty-eight letters appear in four different forms, depending whether the letter is at the beginning, middle or end of a word or standing alone. To make matters worse it is written and read from right to left except for numbers which are written and read from left to right.

*Saturday and Sunday, November 17th and 18th 1962*

*. . . You have certainly started something with my present of* The Nutcracker! *This evening I bought Puccini's* La Boheme *and am now listening to Vittoria de Los Angeles's fabulous voice. Lovely music gives me exquisite pleasure. I hope to increase my knowledge of classical music during my stay here. It seems an ideal opportunity.*

*On the way back from the music shop it was apparent that there was a Sikh troopship in the harbour. Everywhere there were these tall fine looking men with their light blue turbans – very handsome and inspiring soldiers to look at. With very few exceptions the NCOs had all seen service in the Second World War and boasted several rows of campaign medals. It made one wish that one had the opportunity of soldiering with them. As you may know, their army is if anything more truly British in its methods than the British Army itself. However for all their fine appearance they have a slightly questionable recent record. During the War many were found to be collaborating with the Japanese Police – and at the partition in 1947 they caused a tremendous amount of trouble, notably massacring Pakistanis on the border railway between India and Pakistan. Many say however, that they are the finest soldiers imaginable – others that they are utterly untrustworthy. It would be good to form one's own opinion. Anyway they are returning from the Gaza Strip and are bound for their homeland.*

*. . . Out of touch with the news. Newspapers arrive three days late . . . not possessing a wireless that will get a proper news bulletin one just wonders what is going on.*

*November 21st 1962*

*. . . Another go of Aden tum – infuriating and extremely enervating. I have however obtained some extremely potent pills (made at 85 Worli Junction, Bombay 18, India), which really seem to work wonders!*

## Impressions of Aden

*November 25th 1962*

*. . . This afternoon Colin McLean (fellow Muscateer) and I went to the Crater, the old part of Aden. It consists of very narrow streets and ramshackle little stores and shops carved out of crumbling low buildings. It is rather like a warren – packed to bursting point with dark skinned people buying and selling their goods. It is filthy by British standards but quite fascinating. In the wider streets cows and goats wander about completely ignored. Stalls overflow into the narrow pathways which divide them. Leather goods, shoes, draperies, clocks, gold and silversmiths abound. Fruit stalls overflow, wireless shops bristle with transistors – there is no end to it all. We ventured right into the heart of it and the noise was quite something. Car horns blare away in the background while cars scatter all before them as they force their way down the 'main streets'. I think you would be fascinated with it all (2).*

*. . . The senior course have just heard the result of their examination – 33.3% failure. My goodness I rather think I will go mad if I fail at the end of this slog!*

*. . . There have been three general strikes since we have been here – only the most recent one being effective. This meant that I, amongst others, had to cook our breakfasts and lunches in the hotel. Our 'school bus' did not arrive so we had to run a shuttle service in one small car. The Yemenis are behind all this and the Hotel Yemeni staff have all been given the sack (40 of them); the Somalis remain.*

*November 27th 1962*

*Short note I am afraid. Arabic calls. It was a wretched word group to learn today. I would love a copy of "A Shropshire Lad".*

*December 1st 1962*

*Saturday mornings we work in civilian clothes. Each of us has bought very gaudy shirts –
palm trees, sea etc. You will seldom see a more colourful array anywhere. The
Commandant held his head in agony and took out a pair of sunglasses as protection.*

*I have sent you a copy of my article on Switzerland. Actually I am heartily fed up with
it and now see so many shortcomings that I am sending it to you to avoid destruction! It is
too long, humourless and cheaply dramatic.*

During September 1962 Ian Robertson (Duke of Cornwall's Light Infantry) and
I had climbed the Matterhorn together. As our Alpine expedition had been
funded by the Light Infantry and equipment loaned from the Army
Mountaineering Association, we were asked to write an article describing our
fortnight of Alpine climbing. We hoped it would be published in the British
Army Review.

*Saturday December 8th 1962*

*. . . It is really quite enjoyable learning word groups sitting on a rock in the warm sun
practising pronunciation as loudly as one likes to the crashing of waves. A vast
improvement on our previous method of learning.*

We used Dunhill red cigarette tins to hold each daily batch of word group
cards. Each day we wrote out twenty-eight cards, Arabic script on one side and
English on the reverse. They fitted perfectly into these tins, which were water
and sweat proof and could be slipped into a breast pocket. They were constantly
pulled out, referred to and slipped back again until each of us felt that we were
word perfect.

*. . . The ragging which goes on during this course is out of this world. Nobody gets away
with anything! Meals are hilarious. I have been christened 'hoovermatic' for my
unbeatable eating speed. The Somalis find it impossible to stop grinning when they
see us.*

While early in the course I won the name 'Hoovermatic', it was not long before
each of us acquired an Arabic nickname. Mine became 'Dub' which is Arabic for
bear – something to do with my hairy chest!

*Monday December 10th 1962*

*There was a boat on fire in the harbour yesterday – quite a frightening sight. I was very surprised it didn't blow up. I still don't know the cause of the fire. Two British merchant seamen were burnt to death. The fire tug was under repair at the time. You would have thought they might have had a stand-in. This makes the second accident in a fortnight.*

*December 12th 1962*

*. . . No news – this school existence palls terribly. How I long to get up to Muscat and start soldiering again. However tomorrow we are exactly halfway through the course – and I think we are through the worst.*

*December 15th 1962*

*I have had a very nice letter from the Light Infantry Brigade Colonel (Colonel Freddie de Butts OBE). He had received my article ('Bugle on the Matterhorn') and thinks it is worth while sending it on to the British Army Review. I feel almost embarrassed about this as I know it not to be good enough. He also tells me that our mountaineering expedition to La Paz in the Andes in 1965 is passing through its embryo stages.*

[While 'Bugle on the Matterhorn' was published in due course, our planned expedition to the Andes in 1965 did not materialise due to lack of funds.]

*The dissident insurrection in Brunei sounds to be quite exciting. I know several officers in the Queen's Own Highlanders and 1st/2nd Gurkhas. I must say I envy them their active service. Muscat is supposedly an active service station, but little seems to happen there these days.*

*Have you read the papers about the Yemen? The reports one hears in Aden are quite ridiculously paradoxical and I long to know what really is going on, and whether the Royalists are going to survive. Some of the atrocities which are taking place on the Egyptians are certainly feudal. The Americans are in a fair predicament I feel.*

*Friday December 21st 1962*

*. . . Ever ambitious I am still hoping that this might get to you for Christmas!*

*December 29th 1962*

*Christmas here was pretty quiet – completely unlike any other Christmas I have ever spent! Nevertheless it was a good break. Try as I did – and we all did – we could not quite get the spirit. The hotel had a Christmas lunch party where everybody (some 80 people) mixed – and generally put on a show of heartiness!*

*However the afternoon consisted of a very pleasant time on an uncrowded beach reading 'The Other Wise Man' by Van Dyke.*

*Next weekend we go 'up country' (frightful expression) to Mukeiras where we are guests of the Federal Army. The object is to get us talking to the Arab soldiers and NCOs as much as possible. It should be great fun. I really do feel that the end of this course is in sight at last – and that the Arabic is slowly coming on.*

*January 2nd 1963*

*As I came out of my oral exam I entered the anteroom and faked a collapse for the benefit of waiting candidates – passing out on the floor! I was lifted on to the sofa and your letter was thrust in front of my nose – result instant recovery! I am pleased to say that the exam went quite well – 143/200, which is well over the pass mark. We had the written today . . .*

## A description of Aden

*January 3rd 1963*

*Several weeks ago I promised to describe Aden to you. Forgive me for having postponed such a description for so long. Aden is divided into three parts. There is the Old Aden or Crater, Ma'alla, and Tawahi. I have already given you a rather poor description of the Crater. A sunbleached warren teeming with market stalls, Arabs and duty free goods – a nightmare to the hygienic.*

*Ma'alla is an example of ribbon development of blocks of flats (RAF), which stretch virtually from the Crater to Tawahi (several miles). Behind these flats there are Arab hovels and shacks in danger of being razed to the ground at the first breath of wind. Most of these are Arab 'houses' made of piled wooden boxes each of which seems to serve its purpose containing something of vital importance. Sometimes when an Arab has found a suitable stall for selling his goods he makes a more permanent shack and may even paint his boxes the most bilious of colours!*

*The RAF flats are large, essentially practical buildings – usually 6 to 8 storeys in height. Each flat varies in size a little, but on the whole they seem too small for the number of children that abound. Most windows have balconies, which are littered with drying clothes, bathing suits etc! They are badly designed as far as the safety of children is concerned – three children were killed last week from climbing over these easily surmountable barriers. At ground level there is either a port for cars or there are shops and stores pandering to the requirements of forces' families. Ma'alla as you can see is typically a Service community – a complete reversal of the Crater warren.*

*Tawahi (where the Rock Hotel is situated) is again different. This is the smart quarter of Aden! Large hotels, banks, shops, stores, official buildings (shipping lines) etc, rule the roost. However despite this, if you turn down a back street you will soon come across*

*Arab markets etc. The vast majority of the larger shops are Indian run – while the smaller pokier shops bustling with transistor this and that, are proudly possessed by Adeni or Yemeni Arabs.*

*The roads are an interesting sight. Generally the main road from Ma'alla to Tawahi is a good surface, but should there be any road repairs necessary, nobody seems to bother themselves about filling in and levelling off afterwards. The result is that cars have to periodically reduce speed to 5 mph in order to cross a trench which would break every spring in the car if taken at speed!*

*The service drivers are good. The taxi drivers and Arab lorry drivers are MAD! They never look in their mirrors and assume they can stick out a chocolate-brown arm and turn right simultaneously – as if the signal was a charm. That there is other faster traffic bearing down on an outside lane matters little! The taxi drivers usually have one arm dangling out of the window – if not dangling it is gesticulating at a friend or another madman. This leaves only one hand for steering and changing gear – the latter being clearly quite unnecessary! They tear up to traffic lights – never change down – and stamp on their brakes. How there are not more accidents never ceases to amaze me! The horn is like a musical instrument to them – and must be used at the slightest provocation. Any European who is walking is fair game. It is their way of inquiring whether you want a taxi.*

*The pavements are a pretty sordid sight – litter strewn everywhere. Small boys and girls seem to be continually caught short so that the stench in the heat of the day makes you keep your mouth firmly shut. Beggars sit cross legged on these pavements. Many are old men – apparently blind – or withered old women. Others walk up to you – show a withered hand or arm and pester you. It is extremely difficult to know what to do on such occasions – as some are genuine, but others certainly not. In time one certainly becomes hardhearted – and some of these beggars are so cheekily brazen that I get intolerant – and then feel repentant later.*

*Some of the small children are perfectly charming with their big brown inquisitive eyes. The small girls are invariably quite lovely, but rascals. The Indian children look spotless and are very colourfully dressed. The Arab women also in their long flowing highly coloured dresses are heavily veiled. They walk gracefully. The Adeni Arab is a pretty uninspiring chap – small in stature and seemingly unfit. Many chew 'qat', a kind of drug, which is supposed to quicken the brain and produce a happy frame of mind. It also, in the long term, does untold harm physically making the addicts emaciated in appearance. It is also meant to reduce sexual desires – so my qat-eating taxi driver informed me!* [Did I understand him correctly, I wonder?]

*The Somalis are, I think, delightful people – tall, graceful and good looking with a ready sense of humour. Not businessmen perhaps, but nevertheless a thoroughly attractive people.*

## A visit to the Federal Regular Army at Mukeiras

*January 7th 1963*

*This morning we flew down from Mukeiras and this afternoon we have learnt our last word group (9,10).*

*January 12th 1963*

*I have been wanting to tell you of our visit to Mukeiras. We arrived at the airport at 3 o'clock expecting to fly at 3.15 pm, but we were soon told that the plane would not take off until 4 o'clock. It is only some 85 miles in a North Easterly direction to Mukeiras, but looking out of the window of the aircraft it was easy to understand that it is the best part of 150 miles by rasda (colloquial Arabic for road implying track as opposed to M1). It is a practically impenetrable mountainous area – the occasional wadi winding its way up through the foothills soon to peter out into the red brown of the jebel. As we flew north it became noticeably more cloudy and cooler. Half an hour after take-off we banked rather sharply to starboard to land on the Mukeiras Airstrip. After having a quick word with the RAF pilot I discovered from him that he had been given a "dud bearing" from Aden and as a result we had flown over the Yemen for 10 minutes. Only when we came out of the cloud did he realise his error. Good job we weren't used as target practice. Not altogether unlikely at the moment as everything seems to have reached a stalemate in the Yemen. Anything seems fair game there just now.*

*Getting out of the aircraft at Mukeiras was like turning back my life 5 years. Our operations in Dhalla in '58 were in very similar country though more mountainous. We were taken by Land Rover to the 1st Battalion Federal Regular Army's camp some 10 minutes away. Over the inevitable but nevertheless welcome cup of tea we met 6 British Officers who serve with the Battalion – 3 of whom we had already known at CALSAP.*

*We were shown to our tents and met our Arab bearers whom we practised our Arabic on mercilessly! We then went for a walk down a nearby wadi – amazingly green for this part of the world. The FIO (Force Intelligence Officer) who is an RAF Officer has been at Mukeiras 6 years now. He has got some Arabs to build him a house down in the wadi – and he had the necessary mod cons flown up from Aden. Four years ago his wife moved up from Aden and his two children come out and stay during their holidays. This is all strictly illegal now, but he got his wife out a week before the matter became law – and since then this exception has been allowed. He is clearly doing an excellent job on the*

36

intelligence side. He speaks fluent Arabic and seems to have his finger really on the pulse – most important of all he doesn't seem to mind what he says to anyone.

After the walk we each had a bath in a tin tub – our bearers producing steaming hot water. My tub wasn't big enough! Refreshed we had a good dinner in the one building in the camp – converted into a mess. After dinner we went to bed (in our tents).

Up early leaving the camp at 7.15 am. The Commanding Officer, Lieutenant-Colonel David Pontifex, had previously decided on a flag march to Merta some 25 miles north-east. Every now and then such shows of force are vital out here so that the dissident tribesmen over the border don't start fancying their chances too much. Rifles are a sign of manhood – ammunition is wealth out here. A well-disciplined Army speaks volumes to them.

As Arabic scholars (!) this was an ideal opportunity to speak to the soldiers. Each of us was therefore bundled into the back of a 3-ton truck bulging with 30 Arabs. The rasda was very bumpy and precipitous at times so that conversation dropped off occasionally. However I can truthfully say that I personally talked Arabic for 3 hours until we reached Merta.

The convoy speed was an average of between 6 and 8 mph – so that the journey was not the most comfortable one of my life – but the Arabic was invaluable. They fired questions at me until I nearly screamed – trying to decipher them being almost more than I could cope with.

We arrived at the Frontier Post – adopted a tactical position and then the CO and bodyguard plus 2 'muscateers' advanced towards the main fort. A Federal Regular Army Guard of Honour (looking like nothing on earth) produced themselves from somewhere for the benefit of the CO. We were then invited into the fort for an hour's talk and the customary tea. The crockery had seen better days. This was another heaven sent opportunity to practise Arabic which by now was beginning to be rather fun.

Later we left the fort and started on our return journey to Mukeiras. By now my brain was beginning to boggle with Arabic. We arrived at the camp mentally pretty exhausted – but generally pretty pleased with ourselves. Bed was good.

The climate up country is most invigorating. We were all up an hour before breakfast and walked into Mukeiras – had a close look at some wells and returned by a circular route back through the wadi. We had a 2 hour intelligence briefing from the CO after breakfast on the Federation etc. Most interesting. An Arab Corporal then gave us a lecture in Arabic, some of which we understood! At lunch the Arab officers came over to our Mess for a squash and curry lunch. One of them had got an MC in the Dhalla operation in '58 so I was well away. They were a very nice friendly crowd – and delighted to meet you half way as far as Arabic was concerned. After lunch a brief respite then back over to the Arab officers' mess for tea at 3 o'clock. Then a conducted tour of the *camp with an Arab corporal each. I visited one occupied tent and started speaking to a couple of soldiers – they offered stim (E African lemonade). There were 4 photos of Nasser around the tent. I was asked my views on Egypt – Brigadier Silaal etc – an awkward situation. I was not forthcoming.*

*The rest of the day was pleasantly idle and we left Mukeiras Monday morning. We all thoroughly enjoyed the trip – the climate and countryside is such a welcome change from Aden Colony.*

## Swearing-in ceremony for recruits

*January 12th 1963 (continued)*

*However I am relieved that I am not going to the Federal Regular Army (FRA) as:*

*a) Muscat is reputedly a far more beautiful country.*

*b) Out of the 6 British Officers, 4 are purely administrative. All Companies are commanded by Arab Officers, therefore no prospect for the likes of myself commanding a Company.*

*c) The FRA is run exactly as a British Battalion, ie mounds and mounds of paper. I came here to get away from the stuff!*

*d) No separate Company Camps in Aden.*

*There are many other material as opposed to functional preferences for the Sultan's Armed Forces, ie pay, leave etc. However basically with the recent Arabisation of the FRA there is far less scope for the British Officer than previously.* [It was not until 1970 – some seven years later – that Omanisation of the Sultan's Armed Forces was to begin.]

*January 19th 1963*

*I must concentrate on revision these two days. All of us are very weary, slightly on tenterhooks over this exam, and simply longing to relax. This time next week we shall be able to do so.*

*This morning we had another visit – this time to a place called 'Lake Lines' which is the training centre for the whole of the Federal Regular Army. As I told you a great deal of Arabisation is under way. This means that the British Officers are working like mad to get the Army into a state of efficiency when it will run with the minimum of supervision by British Officers. I understand that in 2 years time every Battalion will be commanded by an Arab Lieutenant-Colonel and under him he will have no British Officers on establishment, except perhaps advisors. Judging from what I saw this morning I believe they have a well nigh impossible task. I think that this is a great shame that the whole thing has to be hurried through as it is going to have to be – for standards will drop. However I can see that now that Aden Colony is in the Federation the quicker the British slide out of the Federal Regular Army the better – politically. Undoubtedly the chief problem is education.*

*There is no doubt in my mind that the British Government has financially done wonders for this Arab Army – and the British officer has again done a marvellous job in educating these men and making soldiers of them.* [Some three years later, in 1966, the Labour Government under Harold Wilson discovered that the Colony and Federation was costing about £60 million a year[6]. A decision was soon made to drop Aden itself, Federation, Sultans and all. The British finally left on November 30th 1967.]

*I did watch the swearing-in ceremony this morning of 30 new recruits. They were all drawn up on the square in their Arab dress in between two escort guards. Then an Arab priest said or I should say sang a long passage from the Koran (some of which I could vaguely catch but not much!). He then followed this with the 'swearing-in passage' used for the Federal Army – all of the recruits repeating each phrase after him. Then all the recruits filed up to the Colour Party – the Regimental Colour was lowered and they touched the Colour and then passed on to the desk. Here they put their thumbs on an ink pad and then on to a sheet registering their enlistment.*

*The recruits seemed quite a fine bunch of men. Evidently 500 had answered the call for recruits which is always done strictly by tribes. They go through a very stiff medical and that is about it. TB is rife so many are turned away on account of it. 95 per cent are illiterate – hence the thumb prints – which also serve as foolproof identification should they desert to the Yemen. It was grand to see so many fit-looking Arabs – some contrast to the typical Adeni Arab who is so often a poor specimen.*

### End of course celebrations

*January 23rd 1963*

*We have finished our written exam – cheers! The day after tomorrow is the final and all-important oral. Then it will all be over – wonderful! (6,7)*

*January 26th 1963*

*Forgive a scrawl – am decidedly worse for wear this morning. I passed the oral – by ONE MARK! Had a decidedly off day + examination nerves. One of us – Tony Parsons I'm afraid – failed. It was certainly a more difficult exam than the previous one. A staff sergeant after a year in Oman also failed.*

It was at this stage we all decided to enact a Word Group Burial Ceremony at sea. Despite any reservations that each of us might have had that we might still need to refer to some of these cards in our respective forces, we agreed that it had to be all or nothing. The ceremony took place high on the rocks of Tarshyne Beach, where of an afternoon for the past three months we had resonated Arabic to the crashing waves far below. Under Colin's eagle eye, who conducted a Burial Service at sea, we committed four packs of word group cards to the deep. The gulls were totally confused! Unbeknown to us at the time, this was to be the last course on which students would be taught Arabic script.

*We threw a party in the hotel last night – inviting all the instructors from the School – Lebanese included. We gave them and their wives, girlfriends an excellent dinner, wine and so on in a private room. After dinner we went up to the Roof Bar (highest building in Aden) and had more drinks. There is an ENSA (Entertainments National Service Association) group staying in the hotel at the moment, having done a tour of the Middle East. We persuaded them to do a cabaret for us. It really was surprisingly good! Perhaps it was the Kummel but the girls looked surprisingly attractive! I set up my record player and loudspeaker and we had some good music – Los Valdamosa and Ray Conniff, so dancing started. Quite a party for Aden. The Lebanese instructors thoroughly enjoyed themselves. They left at midnight for Ramadhan starts today! It was a good evening – our second party in 3 months.*

*I can't quite get used to the fact that this course is really over!*

*January 29th 1963*

*So you are skiing in St Moritz – how I wish I could join you.*

*Yesterday I had a giant spending spree. I have bought 12 paperbacks, a wrist watch, Parker 21 (any improvement?), camera, gramophone record and some items of clothing, which I need in Muscat. I am going to be hopelessly overweight in the plane. I believe we fly to Bahrein tomorrow.*

*. . . The Director of Infantry was out here a week ago. He did a tour of the Middle East. He went up to the Trucial States and then sent a message to the Sultan asking permission to visit his forces. The Sultan signalled his assent. Then a further message was sent as it was suddenly realised that a Staff Officer would accompany the General – "Could Colonel accompany D of I on his visit?" The Sultan signalled back "What is one more slave among so many!"*

40

**1** General view of Crater from the South-East rim, showing how the town lies on a small level plain in the bed of an extinct volcano, 1943. *By kind permission of R. Horne.*

**2** Street scene in Crater, 1960. *By kind permission of R. Horne.*

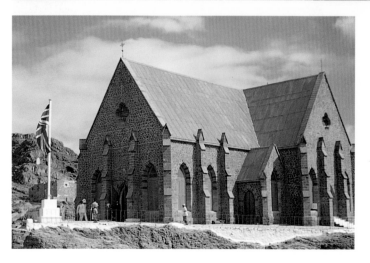

**3** Foundations being installed at Falaise Camp, 1959.

**4** View of the oil refinery, Little Aden, 1960.

**5** HM Governor opens the Legislative Assembly, 1960.

*3, 4 & 5 by kind permission of R. Horne.*

**6** Tuition on the roof of the Rock Hotel, 1962. Left to right; Ian Hurley, our Lebanese tutor Daud Dallal, the author, Colin McLean and Tony Parsons.

**7** Our CALSAP Course (11/62–1/63).
Left to right; back row – author, Ian Hurley, Sergeant Smith: front row – Colin McClean, Daud Dallal, Major Williams, Captain Bradley, Tony Parsons.

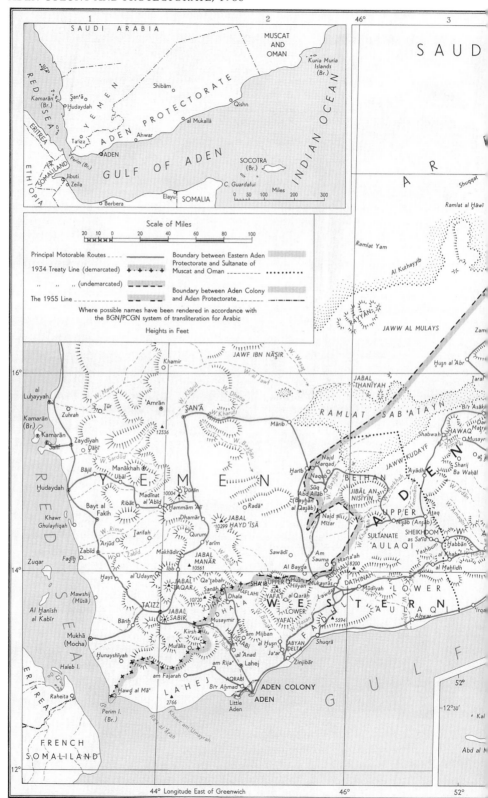

Reproduced by permission of Ordnance Survey on behalf of The Controller of Her Majesty's Stationery Office.
© Crown Copyright MC 10033918

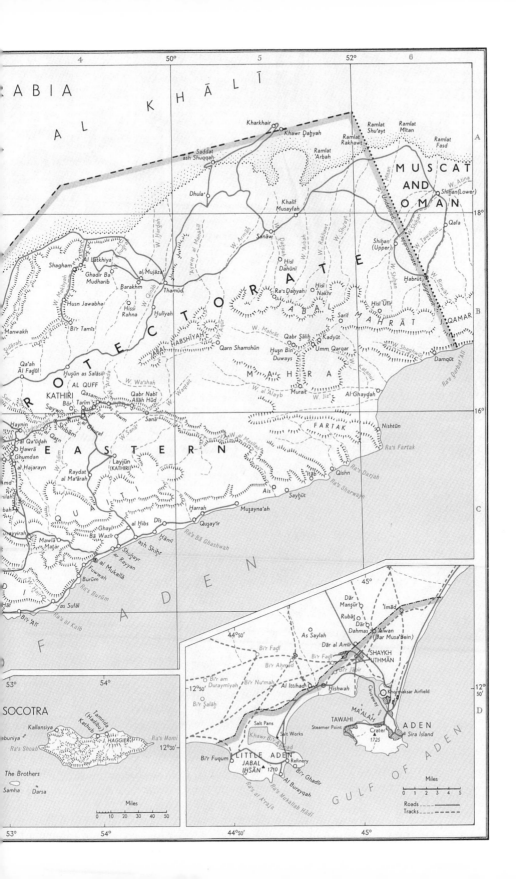

**9** Arrival at Mukeiras for our visit to the Federal Regular Army. Left to right; the author, Tony Parsons and Colin McLean.

**10** An Argyll and a Light Infantryman. Colin McClean points the way to the author.

**11** Practising our Arabic with askaris at Salalah. Left to right; Tony Parsons, Ian Hurley, two askaris, the author.

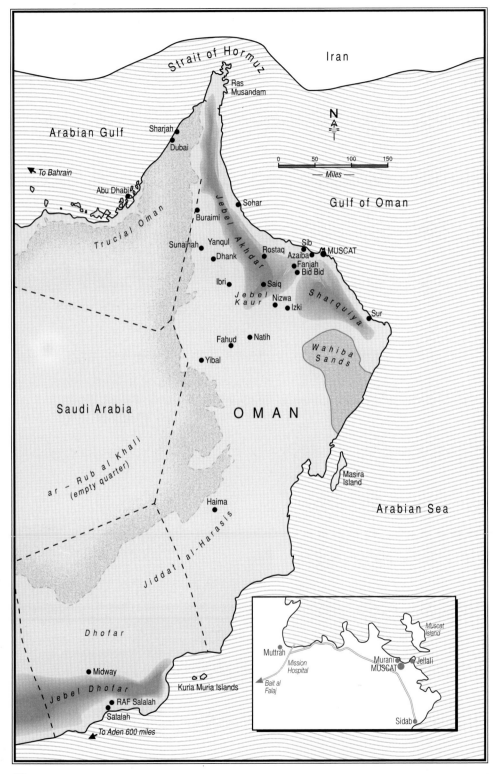

**13** Headquarters, The Sultan's Armed Forces, Bait-al-Falaj. *Photograph courtesy of* Soldier, *The British Army Magazine.*

**14** His Majesty Sultan Said bin Taimur, Sultan of Muscat and Oman, 1932–1970 on the steps leading from the courtyard into the Old Palace in Salalah. *By kind permission of P. Mason.*

**15** At the Saluting Battery, Murani Fort. The author (left) with Major Richard Anderson, known as 'The Drum'.

# Chapter Four

# Muscat and Oman:
# A Brief History to 1962

Rise and fall: historical background – Muscat hibernates, 1870 to 1960 –
Awakening to the prospect of oil, 1950 to 1962 – Buraimi Oasis as the
focus of an international dispute – British troops in three small campaigns,
1955, 1957 and 1959 – Natural divisions within Muscat and Oman

## Rise and fall: historical background

In the early 1960s Muscat and Oman was still living in feudal times. All of her Arabian cousins had fallen prey to some form of revolution, mostly since the end of the Second World War. Yet Muscat and Oman had remained a sleepy observer of Middle Eastern events for over one hundred years. Sultan Said bin Taimur, who came to power in 1932, remained determined that his country should not become spoilt by the burgeoning demands of the twentieth century.

While prospectors from the Petroleum Development of Oman (PDO) seemed to pose a threat to such feudalism, Muscat and Oman had not always been a reluctant debutante. Indeed some four hundred years earlier the Portuguese, who dominated the trade routes, built a factory in Muscat and formed a trading settlement in Hormuz. When they finally withdrew in about 1700, the Sultans prospered and became overlords of Zanzibar, Mombasa and Mogadishu in East Africa (Page 12). Their agents gathered slaves and trade from Lake Victoria to China and the Sultan's navy boasted 75 ships of the line.

Between 1700 and 1840 Muscat and Oman was the greatest independent power in the Arabian Peninsula (16, 17). In 1798, due to Muscat's pre-eminence, the Sultan was the first Arabian ruler to be invited to sign a Treaty with Britain. Through the agency of the East India Company, which hoped to enlist the Sultan's navy against the pirates of the Persian Gulf, the Sultan was persuaded to side with Britain against France in the Napoleonic Wars. In 1800 the Sultan admitted the first resident British Political Agent[7] in Arabia. In 1833 Muscat was wooed by the USA who sent a mission to persuade the Sultan to sign a treaty of friendship and commerce – the first formal agreement between America and any Middle Eastern power.

It was only after one hundred and fifty years of carrying the torch of Middle Eastern power that the Sultanate entered a long period of decline which lasted from 1870 to 1960. The trigger for this decline was Britain's Treaty with the Sultans in 1873 abolishing the slave trade throughout the Sultanate and declaring the import of slaves illegal.

While this severed the sinews of Muscat's trade, the use of new steamers on the Bombay-Suez route, which could now refuel at Perim island, reduced the number of ships using Muscat's ports. Further trading decline followed when dynastic rivalries and naval weakness cut Zanzibar adrift. These three commercial blows were then compounded by insecurity at home when the growing power of the Wahhabis from Central Arabia threatened the authority of the Sultans among the tribes.

Rather than fight for survival or seek alternative trading opportunities, the Sultanate's people, feeling impoverished and attacked, went into a prolonged period of hibernation. Lacking the stimulation of a colonial power, Arab nationalism, oil riches or a visionary ruler, it remained feudal and largely undisturbed until 1960.

While it may have been supposed that the arrival in residence of Britain's first political agent in 1800 would herald Britain's increased direct involvement in Muscat's internal affairs, this was definitely not the case. While railways and Colonial officers were imposing significant changes in Africa and Asia, British foreign policy in Arabia was to keep other powers from interfering with her maritime trade routes to India. This policy required no territorial sovereignty over a hot, inhospitable and remote interior. On the contrary, by entering into friendly trading agreements with selected states at strategic points along these maritime trading routes, secure access to suitable ports and coaling stations could be guaranteed in return for financial reward and trading opportunities.

To prevent escalating piracy on her Indian trade, Britain imposed a maritime truce on the Sheikhdoms of the Persian Gulf. This effectively excluded other great powers from her back door to India. These truces were later extended to a series of agreements that gave Britain the right to conduct the foreign affairs of many of the local rulers in return for an undertaking to defend them from their enemies.

However, all of these special treaty relationships with Britain confirmed that the rulers retained a varying measure of independence by deliberately restricting Britain's right to interfere with their internal affairs. If such treaties could help Britain keep other powers at arm's length along her trade route to India, then surely mainland Arabia could be left to look after itself? While other Arabian states reluctantly emerged to face the demands of the twentieth century after the First World War, Muscat and Oman preferred to remain remote and unseen for another forty years. It was the oil prospectors and their cartographers in the 1950s who threatened to disturb this feudal country.

### Muscat hibernates (1870–1960)

In defiance of progress Muscat remained the only capital in the Arabian Peninsula whose people were still locked within their town walls. Each evening three hours after sunset, ancient cannons roared from the battlements of Murani, one of a pair of Portuguese forts that dominate the harbour. As the echoes faded, the guards slowly shut the iron-bound doors in the mud wall. This continuing tradition secured the Sultan's Palace, his Police quarters and the

44

British Consul-General – epitomising the old order. No one could enter or leave the capital until dawn, when the gates were reopened. Anyone failing to carry a lantern with a lighted flame at night was arrested and fined.

Daytime was not a bustling contrast either. Few vehicles passed through the gates, sandy alleys muffled footfalls and voices were hushed. The crucible of the surrounding hills seemed to capture the simmering afternoon air and induce coma. Occasionally the arrival of a ship stirred the harbour with siren hoots and the rumble of anchor chains. Such intrusive activity soon subsided. Islam's puritanical ban on music, alcohol and smoking suppressed any spirit for change.

Closing of the gates against twentieth-century progress was symbolic of Sultan bin Taimur's rule over his people from 1932 onwards. Despite an excellent education, Sultan Said bin Taimur al bu Said was profoundly conservative, isolationist and distrustful of the modern world. By Western standards his punishments, allied to his innate reluctance to improve the health and education of his people, seemed oppressive. But, unlike many of his contemporaries, his justice was consistent and temperate and his habits modest. He was an intelligent, charming man, who, while admitting the necessity for change, said to David Holden[8] 'Of course it must come. But slowly, for in Muscat there is very much to do, and as you say in English – more haste less speed'.

His fundamental yet understandable conviction that change must come slowly, pervaded everything. Instead of presiding over 'those many things to be done', he seldom visited the capital, never stayed except in emergency, preferring to live in Salalah, a cooler, tiny and dilapidated settlement five hundred miles away in Dhofar (14). Here, separated by the desert of the Empty Quarter and sheltered from interruption, he turned his back on the world and viewed the rollers of the Indian Ocean.

Consistent with his wish to keep Muscat out of world affairs, he refused to join the United Nations, was contemptuous of the Arab League and preferred that British spokesmen represent his country, regardless of the damage to his standing.

His schooling at the Indian College of Princes made him the best educated of all Arabia's traditional rulers, but he decided to save money by denying education to his family and people. After intense pressure from his advisors, he allowed his son, Qaboos, to leave the country at 19 for the first time, to attend a much-needed crammer in London and then go successfully to the Royal Military Academy, at Sandhurst. His own brother Tarik[9], a man of ability, vision and a linguist, fled the country with his two sons to ensure that they enjoyed the same American education in Istanbul as himself.

To understand the Sultan's attitude to money we need to turn the clock back to 1932, when his father abdicated leaving the young Sultan Said bin Taimur, thirteenth in the dynasty, with a pile of debts and limited income from customs dues. To recoup his family fortune, he determined to keep his purse strings tight and divulge nothing. Requests from the British Government to reveal the extent and nature of his finances were studiously ignored. In his view they could make up their own minds how much Muscat was worth to them; his money was his own affair! Meanwhile hospitals, schools, hotels and roads were luxuries which must wait. This frugality personified his aloofness. Not for him the generosity and common touch of other Arab chieftains.

Consequently, his country's infrastructure remained feudal and wholly inadequate for a large, diffuse and sparsely populated country well into the 1960s. This fact, coupled with his wish to keep the world at bay, made visitors from abroad unwelcome and publicity for his country stubbornly resisted. Entry visas were nearly impossible to obtain and did not permit travel beyond the coastal towns. As neither transport nor accommodation existed for the traveller, anyone wanting to see the interior had to become a guest either of his army or the oil companies busy prospecting for oil. A special concern of his was that neither should connive at the raping of his country any faster than absolutely necessary. Consequently the activities of both remained unobserved and unreported, conducted behind a screen of secrecy greater than any in Arabia.

Yet despite all the efforts of the Sultan and his government to delay change, some signs of the inevitable were beginning to emerge in Muttrah, the twin port to Muscat barely three miles away. Rather more accessible than her comatose twin, Muttrah was beginning to throb with activity. It had emerged as a focal point for fishermen, date growers and camel trains bringing charcoal from the burned scrub of the Oman mountains. With them came reports – often embellished – of military incidents and oil company operations. The gradual increase in oil drilling operations made rumour rife. It seemed to herald an uncertain mix of vast oil wealth and profound cultural change.

## Awakening to the prospect of oil (1950–1962)

In 1949 the discovery of oil in Qatar heralded a change in attitudes towards territory and brought a reluctant Buraimi Oasis under the spotlight. This remote oasis of palm trees, dusty gardens and a few wells, dominated by a whitewashed 'beau geste' fort, was destined to become focal to an international dispute for the next fourteen years.

Buraimi resembled a tiny island – a small settlement visited only by travelling tribesmen – surrounded by desert that belonged to nobody. It stood sentinel to three cultures and was variously considered as the principal oasis in northern Oman and gateway to both the southern desert of Saudi country and the harbours of the Trucial Coast. It 'belonged to' whichever power was predominant at the time. In the nineteenth century, the Wahhabis from Saudi country had been dominant but in the twentieth century either the Sheikhs of Abu Dhabi or the Sultans of Muscat prevailed. The only military presence was a company of the Trucial Oman Scouts within Buraimi fort and a small detachment of the Sultan of Muscat's Field Force in a mud-walled compound a few miles away.

While initially this appeared to be no more than an obscure frontier struggle in the remotest region imaginable, it soon became apparent that this protracted dispute symbolised the emergence of the new Arabia. Not only did it draw in both Britain and America on opposing sides, but more importantly it heralded some fundamental changes in Arab thinking. As the dispute moved through its various stages, the Arab protagonists discovered that if they wished to compete for oil wealth, modern nation status must prevail over tribalism and fixed frontiers over nomadism. Meanwhile the older Bedouin felt utterly discredited.

## Buraimi Oasis as the focus of an international dispute

Peripheral events brought this dispute into even sharper focus. The oil discovery in Qatar was swiftly followed by intensified exploration in the Trucial States. This prompted the Saudis to make substantial territorial claims which included several miles of Qatar, four-fifths of Abu Dhabi and a substantial piece of Muscat and Oman. Britain's evacuation from Palestine seemed to signal decline and so provided an ideal opportunity for Saudi Arabia to challenge Britain's fading dominance in Middle Eastern affairs. America's oil company ARAMCO (Arabian American Oil Company) which had been prospecting within Saudi country, now concentrated its survey teams in the disputed south east. While some interpreted the Buraimi dispute as an Anglo-American oil war – a considerable oversimplification – both pragmatism and prejudice tended to drive the British and American governments into opposing camps, while the Saudis were encouraged to pursue their claims by the knowledge of Washington's tacit approval. Meanwhile the British, with some justification, considered ARAMCO to be a Saudi instrument for furthering Saudi ambitions. American Secretary of State John Foster Dulles spoke openly of British 'aggression' in Buraimi and referred to 'public opinion' in Saudi Arabia.[10]

This was the prelude to four distinct stages in this dispute. The British acting on behalf of both the Sheikh of Abu Dhabi and Sultan of Muscat dismissed the Saudi claims, proclaiming that they lacked historical or recent precedent. While this was generally fair comment, it oversimplified the situation because there had been a Wahhabi influence in Buraimi during the previous century and a few Saudi merchants still lived there. Also because of the Sultan's reluctance to pay his local agents, some unrest existed in two nearby villages which tended to undermine the British stance against the Saudis.

By 1952 the talks stage had clearly failed whereupon the Saudis, grasping the opportunity to exploit local unrest, occupied Hamasa, immediately next to Buraimi, with forty Saudi soldiers under the command of Amir Turki ibn Utaishan. In response to Saudi provocation British advisors recommended that a combined Trucial and Muscat force should eject the Saudis from Hamasa. The Political Agent in Dubai offered a detachment of the recently recruited Trucial Oman Scouts to assist. With Whitehall's approval, the Sultan assembled an army of 8,000 tribesmen at Sohar on the Muscat coast. He then ordered his regular Field Force, commanded by British contract officers, to provide professional backbone to the proceedings. Within a matter of weeks both forces, presenting admirable if distant solidarity, were ready to converge on Buraimi and throw out the Saudis.

This prompted the Americans to exert great pressure on Sir Anthony Eden at the Foreign Office to avoid a bloody confrontation. He in turn sought reassurance from British officials on the spot that the recapture of Buraimi was achievable without bloodshed. Although they felt this unlikely they could hardly give the guarantee that was being asked. Consequently Sir Anthony Eden immediately gave orders that, as bloodshed was unthinkable, the combined operation must be called off immediately.

By this time and in the absence of instant reliable communications, cancelling the advance of both forces posed practical and emotional difficulties. While it proved possible to stop the Trucial Oman Scouts in their tracks, contacting the Sultan's force in remote Sohar, out of cable communication and 150 miles from Muscat, posed serious practical difficulties. By then the Force was fired up and about to begin its long march towards Buraimi.

A cable message was sent to the British Consul General in Muscat, Major Leslie Chauncey, with instructions to deliver it immediately to the Sultan. What depressing news to convey after the exciting preparations of recent weeks! He knew the Sultan would be furious. While Major Chauncey may have been tempted with a 'diplomatic breakdown' as he hurtled his car along the dusty track to Sohar, he did not waver in his resolve. His former training as an Indian Army Officer had instilled honesty and duty above all else – regardless of the frustrating disappointment this personal message to the Sultan would cause.

Not to be made personally responsible for such cowardly betrayal before his patriotic force, the Sultan insisted that this message be handed to him by Major Chauncey, his Consul-General, in full view of his assembled army. Then insisting that Major Chauncey remain at his side, he read out the message and, by so doing, made it clear that the British Government was responsible for cancelling the operation. His bewildered soldiers then returned to their homes and the Saudis remained in Buraimi.

This public humiliation undoubtedly had some far-reaching consequences. The first was that the British would ultimately bow to pressure from the American State Department. Indeed, this experience encouraged Sir Anthony Eden to try to achieve a *fait accompli* in Suez four years later rather than consult and succumb to pressure. The deception and misunderstandings that this caused made for ignominious withdrawal. Secondly the Sohar incident must have reassured the Saudis that Britain was on the run. Thirdly, the Sultan from hereon used this *débâcle* to brandish it as an example of Britain's bad advice on his country's affairs. Fourthly, the Saudis, by remaining in Buraimi, continued their subversive activities, suggesting that they now exercised sovereignty. Having abandoned the threat of force, Britain could only go to arbitration.

In July 1954 an arbitration agreement was signed in Jeddah requiring both sides to withdraw their forces from the Oasis to undisputed country and replacing them with police groups of no more than fifteen men each. In effect the Saudis had established their right to share in the control of the Oasis.

However, arbitration could not achieve an agreed settlement to the dispute. The Saudis, who felt that they had gained some ascendancy, used the period of arbitration to strengthen their grip on Buraimi by subterfuge and bribery. When eventually the arbitration broke down, the Saudis were in an even stronger position than before. Ultimately, in sheer desperation, the British decided that the situation was intolerable. On October 26th 1955 the Trucial Oman Scouts and Sultan of Muscat's forces moved into the village of Hamasa whereupon the Saudi Police surrendered their fifteen men. Sir Anthony Eden proclaimed the Riyadh line as the Saudi frontier.

If this had happened in 1952, it is just possible that this would have been the end of the dispute. However, much had happened during the intervening years to put this positive step in jeopardy. During their three-year stay in Buraimi, the Saudis had infiltrated the tribes of the neighbouring mountains of Oman and had generally unsettled and excited them with their greater wealth and talk of oil prospects in their territory. Many of these Omani tribesmen who had loyally joined the Sultan's force at Sohar in 1952 had felt let down ever since. Indeed, Saudi ascendancy was such that barely two months after the Saudi Police surrender in Hamasa the flag of rebellion against the Sultan was raised in Oman. This prompted the Sultan to dispatch his Field Force led by British contract officers to put down the rebellion. To an intrigued outside world here within the space of two months British-controlled forces and British-protected rulers had taken military action – first against an independent Arab State and second against Arabs, who claimed their independence. Not surprisingly, Britain was accused of attempting to crush the Arab nationalist revolution. The cry of 'imperialist aggression' – suggested by Mr Dulles – united everyone. It was of little consequence that the feudal leaders of the Omani rebels had little in common with nationalist revolutionaries in Cairo nor that the Saudi regime was probably more reactionary and subversive than any other in Arabia at the time. Indeed over the preceding years, the Saudis had been financing opposition movements to bring pressure on Britain in Jordan, Iraq and Kuwait, whose governments were regarded as British puppets. By now Saudi money had become the mainstay of the Arab nationalist movement. Meanwhile Nasser's political dexterity, supported by unrelenting Egyptian propaganda, rendered Arab nationalism pre-eminent on the world stage.

In this way the reoccupation of Buraimi Oasis in 1955 – a minuscule event – propelled this long standing dispute into international significance. Gradually the merits of the case on either side became submerged in the generalities of a power struggle throughout the Middle East. Britain's ignominious withdrawal from Egypt in 1956 prompted Saudi Arabia to break off diplomatic relations with Britain and stand four square with Egypt as an anti-imperialist Arab power. By now Oman was a topic discussed in the same breath as the Cold War because the Soviet Union had begun to exert such a strong influence. Britain's historical position as protector of Abu Dhabi and ally of the Sultan of Muscat had drawn her, albeit reluctantly, into an impossible position which seemed to promise only further costly embarrassment.

This stage in the Buraimi dispute seemed destined to escalate into a major Arab nationalist and British imperialist clash of arms with both America and the Soviet Union jockeying to pick up the best pieces. However, somewhat surprisingly, and no doubt to Britain's intense relief, it gradually petered out. There were several reasons for this. First the Saudis, who in recent years had spent huge sums domestically and as paymaster to foment Arab nationalism elsewhere, ran short of money. Consequently, soon after the successful suppression of the second rebellion in Oman, the pressure on the Sultan of Muscat eased noticeably. Secondly, soon after President Nasser's apparent triumphs in 1958, the much-vaunted Arab Front ignominiously collapsed. Not only did this weaken the pressure on Britain but during the fallout the Saudis discovered that Nasser was only marginally less hostile to them than the British! Third, once the wretched aftermath of Britain's withdrawal from Suez had crystallised, the American and British policies in the Middle East began to converge. While the Americans had become disillusioned with the Saudis, whom they had championed against Nasser, their main reason for realigning with their old ally was Britain's weakening influence on Middle East affairs in the face of Russia's growing strength. Indeed by 1960 after some intense diplomatic activity, many of Washington's old reservations about British colonial attitudes in the Middle East seemed to have been dispelled or at least become better understood in their historical context. As Cold War paranoia gathered pace, America came to accept that Britain's special position in the Persian Gulf was essential to Western strategy.

### British troops in three small campaigns: 1955, 1957 and 1959

During the 1950s, while the Buraimi dispute diverted attention to the northern borders of Oman, there were some stirrings of unrest within the interior, which together with prospecting for oil, seemed to herald the end of Muscat and Oman's long hibernation. However, Sultan Said bin Taimur's refusal to grant entry visas to the press meant that three small campaigns during 1955, 1957 and 1959 remained unobserved and unreported[11]. But suffocating proper reporting channels caused rumour and exaggeration that was exploited to the full by Cairo's 'Voice of the Arabs'. The 'Oman Question' became a weekly programme for a decade reporting on 'the free and independent state of Oman', where 'freedom fighters' have 'won heroic victories' in the face of 'colonialism's aggressive war against Oman'. Other Arab capitals followed suit and the 'Committee for Rights of Oman' established itself in a little office near King's Cross Station to arouse the conscience of the British people.

Fortunately most of this nonsense became discredited by its own absurdity. For example the notorious claims that thousands of British soldiers had been killed or injured by freedom fighters could not be substantiated. However, rumours were rife. The Sultan's embargo on press reporting had the opposite effect to that intended. Indeed, for several years other Arab delegates to the General Assembly of the United Nations complained of 'the savage and overwhelming use of British armed force'. The Sultan's refusal to attend UN meetings, sending a British spokesman to represent his country, made matters even worse.

Consequently, many absurd accusations remained largely unanswered allowing unchallenged propaganda to widen the yawning gap between fiction and fact. Contrary to hearsay, there was not a war in Oman, but only three small campaigns. At no time did the Omani rebels number more than six hundred although more may have sympathised from a distance. No British regular troops were deployed throughout this period except during the brief campaigns of 1955, 1957 and 1959.

The first of these, in December 1955, resulted in the Sultan entering Nizwa, a small town in central Oman, unopposed. This was to reassert his authority after a small-scale tribal uprising. The only soldiers of the British Army deployed were a small Royal Signals detachment seconded to the Sultan to provide wireless communications. A few British contract officers commanded the Field Force.

'The only shot in a bloodless campaign was fired at, or more probably in the general direction of, a Land Rover which had me on board.'[12]

The second and biggest campaign in 1957 was witnessed by David Holden:

'In less than a month of occasional shooting, daily air attacks and minimal bloodshed, some 500 British soldiers subdued the rebel villages and then promptly were withdrawn.'[13]

In the third campaign in January 1959, two hundred men of the Special Air Service were deployed to winkle out the last of the rebels from isolated strongholds on the summit of the Jebel Akhdar. From then and until 1963 the peace of Oman remained largely undisturbed except for occasional mine incidents and ambushes.

However, while in retrospect we can now see that these three brief campaigns did not mean that Oman was at war, nor that they amounted to 'savage and overwhelming use of British armed force', this does not mean there was no trouble. On the contrary, unrest between Muscat and Oman was once again evident. The natural divisions of geography, tribes, race and religion were fanned with propaganda from Cairo.

## Natural divisions within Muscat and Oman

Muscat, the country's capital and seat of the Sultan, also comprises most of the coastal strip stretching from the Straits of Hormuz to the tip of Arabia at Ras al-Hadd (12). North of Muscat stretches the Batinah Coast, a long green strip of date palm groves. Interspersed between these groves were palm-thatch villages and mud-walled forts. Dry wadi beds with outwash from the mountains disgorge into the broad sandy beach, highways for occasional camel trains.

In sharp contrast to the fertile Batinah plain, the coast stretching south towards Sur is a rugged inhospitable series of red cliffs and dark caves that dominate a particularly treacherous and squally seascape. Occasional mixed settlements are tucked in under the lee of cliffs. The port of Sur, once thriving, but by the early 1960s semi-abandoned, whose unexpected lagoon offered a safe anchorage, was well positioned to benefit from earlier Indian and Persian trade routes. Here could be found a seafaring mix of Baluch, Persian, Arab, Indian and African descendants from more prosperous times.

Unlike the coastal region of Muscat, Oman is mountainous and landlocked. Wherever a spring sprouts from the rocks, water is nursed into terraced strips of land hewn from the flanks of the jebel. Wherever water fails a barren emptiness prevails.

In contrast to the mixed races which inhabit the Muscat coast, the people of Oman are Arab to the bone. From the moral and physical high ground of the mountainous interior they look down on the corruptions of the coast with undisguised contempt. This conflict between the two regions – highlanders and seafarers, Arabs and Mongols, puritans and worldly-wise – has been perpetuated from one generation to the next.

These natural divisions of geography, tribes, race and religion have made overall leadership of this country highly competitive and variable. For example during the eighteenth and early nineteenth centuries the Sultans of Muscat were the acknowledged leaders of both Muscat and Oman. At other times Sultans of Muscat and Imams of Oman have coexisted. Occasionally there has been no Imam at all. However Omanis take pride in the knowledge that it was they who, by their dominance of the coast from the mountainous interior, finally forced the Portuguese to withdraw in 1650. Moreover it was they who founded the present ruling house of Muscat, endowing it with their Ibadhi faith.

Oman's comparative weakness has been further compounded by disputes between the two predominant tribes, the Ghafiri and the Hinawi. Normally divided, they accepted the Sultan's authority by default rather than choice. During rare periods of unison they asserted some Omani autonomy. During the

First World War they combined to secure from a weakened Sultan an acknowledgement of their power under the Treaty of Sib, signed in 1920. While this has since been championed by the 'Free Omanis' as their formal title to independence, it only granted the Omanis a form of home rule. In effect, this allowed them the right to administer their own local affairs and to elect their own Imam in place of the Sultan of Muscat who had held both titles for the previous one hundred years. Consequently Oman's autonomy was tribal and religious while the Sultan of Muscat never relinquished his sovereignty over Oman.

As the Ghafiri and Hinawi were mostly at loggerheads during the next thirty years, the Treaty of Sib was of little consequence. However, by the early 1950s, traditional discontent with the Sultan's rule was augmented by Omani fear that unless they exerted their combined strength they would fail to reap the rewards of imminent oil discoveries on their land. Suliman bin Himyar, the strongest figure in the Ghafiri federation and paramount Sheikh of the Beni Ryam, tried to obtain the status of independent ruler of the Jebel Akhdar. In 1954 the old Imam died and was somewhat dubiously succeeded by his former secretary, Ghalib. He then teamed up with his ambitious brother Talib – both Hinawi – to unite with the Ghafiri in preparing for Omani rebellion against the Sultan.

On this occasion the Omani rebels were able to get some help from outside. The Saudis, who by then had been rebuffed in their attempt to occupy Buraimi Oasis, seized the opportunity to outflank the Sultan's position by supporting a rebellion in Oman with arms and money. This rebellion was suppressed by the Sultan's prompt response in December 1955, whereupon Suliman bin Himyar came down from the Jebel Akhdar to make his peace with the Sultan. Sultan Said bin Taimur was conciliatory and promised the Omani leaders in Nizwa that he would not interfere with their traditional way of life. As a gesture designed both to uphold the Ibadhi faith and also to impose Koranic discipline elsewhere, he banned public smoking in Muscat. While Ghalib was allowed to stay in his native village in return for his promise of good behaviour, Talib fled to Saudi Arabia to enlist more support for another Omani rebellion.

Some two years later Talib returned from Saudi Arabia with four hundred men, trained in Dammam and paid for by the Saudis. During the interim, the culmination of Russian arms agreements with Syria, Egypt and the Yemen and Britain's humiliating withdrawal from Suez had transformed the balance of power in the Middle East. So the timing of Talib's return with reinforcements to support the cause of the Oman freedom fighters was ideal. The resurgent rebellion, buoyed with propaganda from Cairo Radio, became symbolic of the need to challenge Western Power – particularly Britain – throughout the Arab world.

In effect this linked Egypt, Saudi Arabia and Oman in a challenge to Britain's influence over an increasingly isolated Sultanate. The Arab League championed the Omanis as valiant freedom fighters for progressive Arabism against British colonialism and her puppet, the feudal Sultan. On closer examination the new alliance between the revolutionary regime in Cairo, the despotic Saudis and the tribal Omanis was not a convincing example of progressive Arabism. However, it served its purpose to portray the British as enemies of all progressive Arabs and the Sultan as an isolated despot. In this way the Egyptians could continue to harass Britain, the Saudis could seek revenge for their defeat in Buraimi, while Omani tribalism and oil-inspired greed swelled the ranks of the freedom fighters.

While the Sultan had achieved some short-term success by subduing the Omani rebels in 1955, the pan-Arab support for the Omanis in 1957 now posed a significant threat to the Sultanate. It was extremely doubtful if the Sultan's Army had the resources to subdue the rebels for a second time. Britain was committed by treaty to support the Sultan. To its credit the British Government did not hesitate to respond to a temporary call for help. It knew full well that to renege would have wrecked Britain's standing, not only in Muscat, but throughout the British-protected States of the Gulf on whose oil supplies Britain's industry and finances depended.

In effect the British Government realised that for the first time since 1800 when its Political Agents had first resided in Muscat, they had no alternative but to extend 'Pax Britannica' beyond the coasts of Muscat deep into the interior of Oman. In contrast to the Egyptians and Saudis, who supported the Omani Freedom fighters from a distance by a combination of radio propaganda, training, weapons and cash, the British deployed five hundred Cameronians, supported by RAF Venom air strikes, to help the Sultan subdue the Omani rebels.

This was achieved within a month with minimal bloodshed, whereupon the British troops were immediately withdrawn. Having broken new ground by deploying some British troops within the interior the British Government had no alternative but to continue to support the Sultan by ensuring that his armed forces could become the backbone of his country and provide a real deterrent to future internal rebellion or invasion. It did this by seconding some fifty British officers to train and lead the Sultan's Armed Forces, while it also armed, resourced and paid for the Sultan's army, navy and air force.

From hereon the composition, size and duties of the Sultan's Armed Forces underwent wholesale change. Hitherto the Muscat Field Force had been manned by Baluchis recruited from Gwarda and the Batinah Coast. They were led by a handful of British contract officers, mostly retired Indian Army, who spoke Urdu. Now Arab tribesmen were recruited within Oman in equal numbers. The Army's strength increased to well over two thousand men and Arabic succeeded Urdu as the Army's principal language.

To effect this development the Sultan gave his qualified agreement to certain aspects of his country's infrastructure being improved at last. On British advice he agreed to the establishment of permanent company stations throughout Muscat and Oman to foster good relations and to preserve peace. Consequently, the British Government had to pay for new camps, airstrips, wireless communications and some new roads. To win the hearts and minds of the locals, a programme of repairs to crumbling village forts was put in hand. By 1960, this latter-day extension of Britain's support for the Sultan within Oman was costing nearly £1 million a year in direct subsidies.

Hardly surprisingly, in the wake of Britain's prompt suppression of the 1957 Omani rebellion, Cairo Radio described these initiatives as a reactionary programme of military aggression under British occupation. But such propaganda from a distance bore little relationship to what was happening on the ground. The Army's new recruitment policy meant that many Omanis and Dhofaris were learning to read and write, improve their standards of health and fitness, maintain vehicles and generally gain pride and stature in their new found military discipline. Their soldiers' pay in Indian rupees helped to advance their families' well-being.

Originally the Jebel Akhdar had indeed been a green mountain of trees and fruits – 'pomegranates, citrons, almonds, nutmegs, walnuts with coffee bushes and vines'[14]. But following the suppression of the slave trade in 1873, which heralded ninety years of decline, many Omanis migrated to the coast and Zanzibar. The irrigation channels, known as falajs, which formerly brought water and fertility to much of the Jebel Akhdar began to collapse through neglect. Those still operating effectively were destroyed by air raids in support of the Special Air Service in 1959, causing the remaining villagers to start abandoning their homes for good. However, once again Britain responded appropriately by sending a Royal Engineers' officer and her Chief Agricultural Advisor to the Middle East to see whether the falaj network could be restored. Happily this was possible and they remained to supervise the restoration of the original system augmented with diesel pumps to improve the water flow. To put icing on the cake they opened an agricultural research station at Nizwa.

By 1962 the earlier decline had been arrested and reversed with former inhabitants who had sought refuge on the Batinah Coast returning to the Jebel villages. Many Omani exiles in far away Zanzibar, hearing of Jebel Akhdar's restoration, returned to cultivate their ancient family plots again. In celebration the Nizwa research station held its first recorded vegetable show.

Indeed, the restoration of peace stirred a new will for improvement. The combination of money spent on restoring old forts, the payment of Omani soldiers, the building of company camps, clearing of airstrips and the levelling of roads were the first hesitant steps towards self-improvement.

Yet the Sultanate in 1962 was still a land where tribalism and feudalism were overwhelmingly important. Horizons were limited, administration minimal and the laws of the Koran supreme. Isolation and secrecy prevailed. Lack of schools persuaded Omanis to seek their education elsewhere – in Bahrein, Kuwait, Dhahran or Qatar. Lack of hospitals and a general disregard for health and hygiene – with little effort to rectify the situation – meant that in many Omani villages not a single healthy inhabitant could be seen. Commonest diseases were trachoma, tuberculosis, malaria, rheumatism and decaying teeth. To this cocktail needs to be added self-imposed inbreeding and involuntary underfeeding. There was only one hospital in the country – the American Missionary Hospital in Muscat.

Meanwhile the Petroleum Development of Oman (PDO) was intensifying its prospecting activities in the interior. More roads were being levelled. Yet the country's infrastructure was non-existent. The permanent deployment of the Sultan's armed forces throughout Oman was beginning to open Omanis' eyes to new opportunities and to impose some modern order upon an old tribal society. But without huge investment in the basics of health, hygiene, schools and roads the country still clung to its feudal origins. Oil seemed a betting certainty. But when? Would the resources compare with Qatar? How soon would the revenues be deployed to bring Muscat and Oman into the twentieth century? How would her people respond?

This was the scene in 1963, when Colin McLean and I joined the Sultan's armed forces. And these were the ideas in our minds. How lucky we were to be there! What would happen in the next two years?

# Chapter Five

# Joining the Sultan's Armed Forces

# Headquarters, Bait-al-Falaj, February 1963

Extracts from an information sheet about Muscat – Stopover with the
Trucial Oman Scouts at Sharjah – Arriving in Muscat at last – Induction at
Headquarters, Bait-al-Falaj – A dinghy-racing mishap –
The intelligence situation – Joining The Muscat Regiment at Nizwa

## Extracts from an information sheet about Muscat

During January Colin McLean and I received an Information Sheet, giving some basic information on Muscat and Oman. In my letter to Charmian dated January 19th 1963, I extracted the more salient points, as it was before the days of ubiquitous photocopiers!

*January 19th 1963*

*I have been wanting to tell you a little about Muscat. Forgive me if I now lapse into a tabulated letter.*

### General

> *Sultan's Armed Forces Headquarters (Muscat (Bait-al-Falaj))*
> *Training Centre (Ghalla)*
> *Northern Frontier Regiment (Bid Bid)*
> *Muscat Regiment (Nizwa)*
> *Sultan of Oman's Air Force (SOAF) (Muscat) – consists of 11 seconded RAF Pilots who fly 5 Provosts and 4 Beavers.*
> *Sultan's Navy (Muscat) – consists of 13 Arab Sailors who crew 2 Motor Dhows which are used for coastal patrolling against arms smuggling. Commanded by an RAF Squadron Leader! [Jasper Coates.]*

### Army

> *Each regiment has 3 rifle companies (A, B and C Companies), normally on detachment at Company stations such as Ibri or Rostaq.*

### Languages

> *Each Rifle Company is comprised of 100 to 120 soldiers. Companies are either all Arab or all Baluch, the latter speaking Urdu. (PLEASE may I be posted to an Arab Company!)*

### Topography

> *Large range of mountains run from Northern Frontier with the Trucial States in a SE direction to meet the sea. Jebel Akhdar (Green Mountain) is the highest mountain – over 8,000 ft. Between mountains and the sea – Batinah Coast.*

### Products

> *Mainly dates and dried fish. Also corn, millet, bananas, limes, cotton.*

## Climate

> Winter Temperatures (November – February)
> Muscat: Day 70°–85° F, Night 65°–75° F
> Inland: cooler
> Summer Temperatures (April – September)
> Muscat: Day 110°–120° F very humid, Night 85°–95° humid
> Inland: Day 125° F much less humid, Night 85°–90° F

## Social

> Nil except for small English business community in Muscat.

## Sport

> Muscat only – bathing, water-skiing, sea fishing, underwater swimming, sailing and tennis.
> Batinah Coast – shooting duck, partridge, pigeon and sand grouse.

## Other

> Photography, falconry, climbing.

## Shops

> Muscat – very limited.

## Post

> Deliveries and collections – twice weekly.
> Hope you get the gist!

All four of us finally left Aden at the end of January, two for the Trucial Oman Scouts based in Sharjah and two of us for the Sultan's Armed Forces based in Muscat. After a brief stop at Salalah where we tried out our Arabic on some askaris (11), we flew on to Sharjah where Tony Parsons and Ian Hurley joined the Trucial Oman Scouts. Colin McLean and I waited for the next flight to Muscat.

## Stopover with the Trucial Oman Scouts at Sharjah

*HQ Trucial Oman Scouts, Sharjah BFPO 64 February 1st 1963*

*I am just about as bored as you were lying in bed with flu! We left Aden on the 30th, first hop to Salalah – then here. We stayed the night and were hoping to continue to Muscat yesterday. However light aircraft are in short supply and we unfortunately seem to be low priority. It is not outside the bounds of possibility that we will still be here come Wednesday.*

*There are few things more boring in the Army than staying with a unit of which one is not part – for any length of time. Nothing to do all day, and come the evening when people get together – people are charming, but have that look which says "You STILL here?"*

*Needless to say rather than remain here waiting for the next RAF Transport Command Aircraft, I have concocted a signal saying "McLean and James stranded Sharjah. Earliest flight Wednesday. This uncertain. Any chance of an aircraft?" The SAF (Sultan's Armed Forces) have an airforce. I don't see why they should not rescue us, do you?*

*The TOS HQ does not appeal greatly to Colin or myself. Rather like any Staff HQ anywhere in the world – life seems to revolve around the whisky bottle too much for my liking. I have no doubt the outstations in the desert are different – but here they even have dinner nights and mess kit!*

*Sharjah is quite a large port – 25,000 Arabs live here. Not as warm as Aden but very humid. The soldiers in the TOS seem a good type, and clearly love their life. There are no roads at all and the local Arab is refreshingly unspoilt by Western influence compared with the Adeni Arab. Hygiene is non-existent here, but this doesn't seem to matter much. This is a great fishing port and some of the dhows make a classic picture.*

*I have bought an Arabic record called 'Promenade' by Fairuz – a Lebanese girl with a lovely voice.*

## Arriving in Muscat at last

*HQ Sultan's Armed Forces, Muscat BFPO 63(A) February 4th 1963*

*Here at last – and what a marvellous place. Mountains, forts, dhows, date palms, oasis communities – and much else besides. And perhaps above all else the people. They are wonderfully friendly. It is most refreshing to be serving in a country, which is 'pro' the Army. I had forgotten that this situation could exist. It goes without saying that this country is hundreds of years behind the times!*

*I think I am going to enjoy life here enormously – restrictions and red tape seem minimal. We are only here at Headquarters being briefed before being flown to our respective companies. It will be good to be part of something again. Being in transit seems very impersonal after a full battalion life.*

*If we had not taken the law into our own hands we would still be at Sharjah. RAF Transport planes were not forthcoming – the Sultan's Air Force (SOAF) were short of flying hours, so we rang up the 'Gulf' – the local civilian airline and got on the once-a-week Heron flight down to Muscat. We paid our way, hoping for a refund, which the Commander here has agreed to do.* [Colin McLean, a true Scot, has reminded me that the Paymaster did not refund us after all.]

*Just arrived back from the beach. A friend of mine in SOAF en route for a company outstation in the hills flew barely 15 feet above us in his Provost, whilst we were lazing on the sand. No restrictions over low-flying here!*

## Induction at Headquarters, Bait-al-Falaj

Soon after arrival Colin McLean and I discovered which regiment each of us would join. Colin would join the Northern Frontier Regiment (NFR) based in Bid Bid under the command of Lieutenant-Colonel Dougie Dalglish, MC, whereas I would join The Muscat Regiment (MR) based in Nizwa under the command of Lieutenant-Colonel Clive Chettle, MC. Our recollection is of a carefully devised induction programme at Headquarters in Bait-al-Falaj where we were kitted out with our respective uniforms, briefed thoroughly on Muscat and Oman, the Sultan's Armed Forces and issued with a *Guide to Officers and Junior Leaders Serving in Oman* compiled by Lieutenant-Colonel Colin Maxwell, Commander the Sultan's Armed Forces (see Appendix 1). We were also given a conducted tour of Muscat by Major Richard Anderson ('the drum').

*February 5th 1963*

*I have heard from Nizwa (HQ Muscat Regiment) that I am to be posted to 'B' Company at Ibri, which is one of the most cut off companies in The Muscat Regiment. Mail only once a week by Beaver! Fortunately this Company at Ibri is Arab speaking so my 3 months in Aden will be of value, thank goodness! We are now in regimental uniform – in my case bright red stable belt, lanyard and of all things a red balmoral! This brings a sharp colour impact to khaki aertex shirt with silver star badges of rank, desert coloured whipcord trousers and Bata chukka boots.*

*Evidently the Sultan admired the balmorals worn by the Cameronians when they took part in the Jebel Akhdar Campaign in 1957. Not content with just their red bobble, he decided that his Muscat Regiment should sport an all red balmoral. The seconded British*

*Officers to The Muscat Regiment have no alternative but to wear the thing, but fortunately they do bleach after a time! When out of camp and on patrol you can wear either the much more practical red shamagh or even a 'forcemeister' style peak cap.*

During our induction programme at Bait-al-Falaj (SAF HQ) I recall being impressed by the care taken to ensure that we understood some fundamental differences between ourselves and the soldiers we would soon be commanding. In particular we would need to exercise a greater degree of flexibility in our dealings with soldiers. Colin Maxwell was at pains to point out their temperamental and educational differences from British soldiers. Moreover, unlike their British counterparts who are innately aware of the demands of military discipline born of centuries of standing armies, routine habits and military discipline were new to them. Such essentials needed to be taught and explained to them. As newly seconded officers we were fortunate to have the thoughtful, caring and enthusiastic guidance of experienced contract officers such as Colin Maxwell and Malcolm Dennison. To my mind, Colin Maxwell's guide (Appendix 1) was an exceptionally fine and intuitive document. I recall obtaining a second copy to send home to Charmian, who taped it into her hard-backed exercise book of extracts from my letters.

In retrospect it seems odd that none of my letters at this time described our conducted tour of Muscat by Richard Anderson. It was enthralling seeing such apparently timeless scenes. The tour included a visit to Muttrah suq and to Ramniklal B Kothary[15] to purchase a Tilly lamp and a primus stove each – essential items for the next eighteen months. Some of my letters did go astray but it is more likely that running short of time to write, I felt my photographs would tell the story (13, 15, 18–21).

## A dinghy-racing mishap

*February 8th 1963*

*John Darbyshire [who was to be our best man] and I were dinghy racing this afternoon (haven't been up country YET!) and we turned the boat completely upside down when standing a good chance of winning. It took ages to right her. I had to swim underneath – fix a sheet as far 'up' the mast as my lungs would allow – then John sat on the keel and I tugged on the sheet as hard as I could. Not until we got the Colonel (Hugh Oldman DLI) to add a little weight at the keel end did we right her. Don't ask whose fault it all was!*

*Most of the force is down here at Muscat for an Operation Conference (2 mine incidents last week).*

## The intelligence situation

Part of our briefing was an intelligence briefing by the Force Intelligence Officer, Malcolm Dennison, giving the latest situation regarding Talib and Ghalib. As explained in Chapter Four these two revolutionaries were funded and reinforced from Saudi Arabia and enjoyed propaganda support from Radio Cairo. They were self-styled leaders of the Freedom fighters who were intent on overthrowing the Sultan. They infiltrated various tribes so as to increase their following. They used mine and ambush tactics in the mountainous interior to destabilise the country. As newly seconded officers, it was made abundantly clear to us how we should do everything we could to acquire vital information from locals within our areas of operation.

Because of the distances between battalion HQs and company outstations and the relatively poor wireless communications at the time, much of the communication of troop movement and air supply was conveyed by morse code, invariably using Baluch operators for this purpose. As there were risks of ambush and mine incidents, every vehicle departure was 'signalled' out ETD (Estimated Time of Departure) and an ETA (Estimated Time of Arrival) so that search parties could be dispatched for any overdue convoy or patrol.

## Joining The Muscat Regiment at Nizwa

In the course of our introduction to the Sultan's Armed Forces we paid a brief visit to the Training Centre several miles north up the Batinah Coast at Ghalla. It was here that all recruits underwent their basic training before being posted to their respective regiments. While I do not mention this visit in my letters to Charmian, this was a half-day visit when we were shown various intakes of recruits at varying stages in their programme of basic training. Perhaps a combination of lack of time, laziness or a relatively typical training camp scene dissuaded me from describing what we saw. Had I known then that in fourteen months time I would be appointed Training Officer, I would probably have taken greater note of what I saw.

*February 10th 1963*

*Have been on a long convoy – 6 hours – and am now at Nizwa. At last I am away from HQ – tomorrow I fly to Ibri (22, 27).*

My recollection is of a one- or two-night stopover at the battalion headquarters of The Muscat Regiment which was based in Nizwa. Here I was welcomed by the Commanding Officer, Lieutenant-Colonel Clive Chettle, MC, and other key battalion officers such as the Adjutant, Quartermaster, Intelligence Officer and Signals Officer. I was thoroughly briefed on The Muscat Regiment and the current operational situation with particular reference to B Company based in Ibri. I was told that I would fly to Ibri the following morning as passenger in a Beaver.

These robust and reliable light aircraft were flown by RAF pilots seconded to the Sultan of Oman's Airforce (SOAF). Essential supplies were listed and signalled by morse code to the quartermaster by set "closing" times each week. The assorted manifests were loaded and then flown per schedule to airstrips close to company base camps twice a week. Among the most eagerly awaited regular items were sacks of coins and the mailbag. The soldiers were paid in over-stamped Indian rupees at pay parade every Thursday; local providers of goats and lucerne were paid in Maria Theresa dollars. Those meeting flights in Land Rovers were expected to clear the strips of potentially dangerous stones. In the absence of windsocks, which invariably disappeared, smoke grenades were used to show the approaching pilot the direction of the prevailing wind.

During my final afternoon in Nizwa there was time for a leisurely tour of Nizwa town and a visit to its fort. Although I failed to write to Charmian about this visit, I recall being deeply impressed by the biblical beauty of the scenery, the feudal existence of the inhabitants and persistent flies in the suq (market place). Photographs give some indication of these scenes (23–26).

# Chapter Six

# An Arab Company in the Desert

# B Company, The Muscat Regiment, Ibri, February to June 1963

First impressions – An escape from Jellali prison – Ramadhan – A bargain with the Wali of Dhank – Feasting at Eid – Climbing Jebel Misht – A sandstorm shortens a patrol to Yanqul – Ibri – Searching for rebels in the Balad Sait region – Impressions of Omani people – Sickness in the Company – Combined operations – Leave transport and monsoon rains – A visitor from the United Nations – Rising temperatures and a visit to the Sheikh of Yanqul – Teaching Arab soldiers to play hockey

*First impressions*

*February 13th 1963*

*Bernard Mills, my Company Commander, has had no other officer to help him for 3 months. The result to my mind – unholy chaos. Now is the first time I have had a moment to myself for 3 days. I have just unpacked and now at last have a bed. I have slept on the floor for the last two nights.*

Although I naturally did not criticise Bernard Mills in my letters to Charmian, possibly through fear of their being read by others, Bernard and I, on reflection, were complete opposites! He had enjoyed several years of experience in the SAS and, as I recall, had little time for typical regimental soldiers which fairly described me! However, despite my previous fairly varied experience with an elite Light Infantry regiment, I was seeking a complete break from routine soldiering by joining the Sultan's Armed Forces. To make matters worse I still harboured some reservations regarding the SAS whose apparent ill discipline on joint exercises in Germany coloured my view, probably unfairly. One thing was clear. Bernard badly needed help at Ibri. No doubt he would have preferred an SAS colleague who spoke fluent Arabic. Instead he had to make do with me – something of a perfectionist who had much to learn about the realities of life with an Arab company in the desert. The early stages of relationship posed quite a challenge and required me to learn the ropes and improve my Arabic as quickly as possible.

*An escape from Jellali prison*

*February 15th 1963*

*We have spent the last 2 days in a succession of false alarms. 40 rebel prisoners – complete with leg irons – have escaped from Jellali prison down in Muscat. One company has been sent down from Nizwa to round them up – we have to stand by. Coupled with this we should now be 40 miles away on a cordon and search for rebels. Tomorrow evening we leave – so the latest signal reads – but destination still unknown! At the moment we have a number of visitors staying in our mess. As the Arab cook is ill I did the honours tonight. You would have laughed had you seen me. There are only 3 gas rings. Perhaps I was over ambitious but I did manage to cook for 5 people the following menu:*

*Asparagus Soup (excellent)*
*Boiled Spaghetti (overcooked) and Mince (cordon bleu)*
*Spinach (too much water) and Poached Eggs (OK)*
*Hot Gooseberries (cold)*

*I never realised that one packet of spaghetti went so far. Half way through I got cold feet and put in two packets (gauging my friends' wolf-like appetites), but then forgot to put more water in. Result MOUNDS of spaghetti which hopelessly overflowed the colander – and owing to the lack of water it looked like macaroni. Despite all it wasn't too bad!*

*February 18th 1963*

*I am at Ibri for a few hours and then out to Yanqul again. Only two of the rebels are now at large – one of my 3 tonners was blown up by a mine yesterday – the donkey truck of all things. None were hurt – don't worry!*

## Ramadhan

*February 19th 1963 (Yanqul)*

*Bernard Mills is away for 2 days to Buraimi on a recce, while I hold the fort with the company here. I am now sitting under a tree which gives a little shade. From where I am I can see the whole company – all of whom are resting today. The vast majority of the Arabs are fast asleep (Ramadhan), a few lorries bake in the sun, the camel section separate again keep an eye on the camels (one is sick). Someone has just killed a goat and they are preparing it for their fast-breaking at 6.15 this evening. Everything is quiet – though a slight breeze is welcome.*

*One of the reasons that I have been weary – as has the company commander – is Ramadhan. As you know Muslims will not eat or drink anything during daylight hours during Ramadhan. Bernard has it in his head that it is not a good thing for them to see us eating. This means we fast too! For the last 3 days I have had no food or drink during the day. I now consider the thing is a load of nonsense – and my fasting has definitely stopped and am feeling the better for it. The Arabs eat a great deal during the night instead and make an awful noise doing so. During the day they are too weak to be of great value – their tiredness peak is mid-afternoon. (Mine was all day!) So what with no food by day – and excited cooking noises at night – life could have been better!*

*Three days ago – before fasting – I climbed a mountain which is only quarter of a mile away from where I am now sitting. It looks a bit like the Matterhorn so could not resist it. Bernard wouldn't come so I went alone, breaking all my principles. Actually it wasn't difficult. I will show you some photographs I took of it, if they come out.* [No record that they did!]

**16** Muscat from the Harbour, 1813.

**17** A view of Muttrah from the East, 1813.

**18** Muscat dockside.

**19** Murani Fort.

**20** Jellali prison. *By kind permission of J. R. Darbyshire.*

**21** Moving sacks of grain at Muttrah. *By kind permission of J. R. Darbyshire.*

**22** Early stage of our first journey to Nizwa, approaching Fanjah.

**23** Nizwa street.

**24** Nizwa arch with a shaft of sunlight. *By kind permission of J. R. Darbyshire*

**25** Tinsmiths in Nizwa suq.

**26** Through the 'hole in the wall' at Nizwa fort. *By kind permission of J. R. Darbyshire*

**27** A Beaver takes off from Nizwa airstrip. *By kind permission of J. R. Darbyshire*

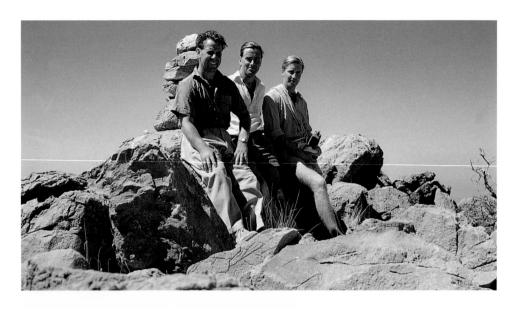

28 On Jebel Misht. Left to right; Sergeant Carr (Para), Julian Lush (PDO), the author.

29 The Wali of Ibri, Sayyid Sa'oud bin Harib after lunching at PDO Representative's House at Eid al-Fitr on 2nd March 1963. In foreground his son Harib bin Sa'oud; Stayun bin Kharboush, Rep's factotum behind. *By kind permission of A. J. M. Lush.*

*The mine incident caused quite a stir. A two-lorry convoy bringing up the donks [donkeys] and more petrol were the unfortunates. A rather ambiguous wireless message came through very indistinctly to me. I was commanding the company at the time. I had 2 scout cars from the 9th/12th Lancers with me at the time. I could not afford to leave the company myself as we were still on this rounding up of prisoners operation so had to send the armoured cars to investigate the mine incident. I was pretty relieved to see them back again as the rebels lay their mines in pairs so I had visions of the 9th/12th setting off a second.*

*The mine blew off the rear wheel of the lorry – luckily causing no harm to our donks – poor things. That it blew off the rear wheel implies that it was an old mine.*

*All this, plus the operation, occurred during the Consul General's visit to Ibri – so you can imagine the flap! However all seems to be over now – and normal peace and quiet restored.*

## A bargain with the Wali of Dhank

*February 22nd 1963*

*Back in Ibri again after 3 days of incident. Two days ago I went on a recce of some camel routes which are expected to be used by some rebels importing mines in about 10 days time. By then we had been out in the wilds for a few days so that transport was at best unreliable. Bernard was away elsewhere in the one remaining serviceable Land Rover so I set off in a 3 tonner – the newest and the best. What with the donkey truck mined and other 'dicky' vehicles I decided against taking a second vehicle with me. I had been pre-warned that the road would be GHASTLY – and had already seen it from the air in a Beaver the day before. This was my decision at the time – perhaps incorrect – but one lives and learns as you will see! Further to this I did not take a high powered wireless for had I done so it would certainly have been smashed to bits in the back of a lorry.*

In those days these 'high-powered' wireless sets (W/S 19 sets) were normally installed in a frame immediately behind a Land Rover cabin and suspended between two seats on either side. This left only one seat on either side, one for the wireless operator the other for the duty officer, complete with operational map, boards etc. Consequently installing such heavy and cumbersome radios in the rear of a three tonner with its rigid suspension was seldom attempted except on a route that was known to be 'good going'. This was thirty-five years before the communications revolution and the advent of the mobile phone.

*I set off at 9 o'clock as I was anxious for the return of a further patrol before I skidaddled myself. As expected, the road was unbelievably bad and I spent a lot of time out in front of the vehicle choosing the least precipitous route (57). To be truthful I am amazed that the lorry didn't pack up completely. I finished recceing the final gap at about 4 o'clock and got through somehow – out into the desert and started on my return route. I was just beginning to relax – and perhaps feel a little pleased with myself when one and a half hours (driving) from base the fan belt broke! Hamstrung! – for the Arab driver did not carry a spare. I nearly throttled him! Once again I suppose I should have checked spares before departure – but if one checks everything always – leaving no responsibility to drivers etc – they never learn.*

*By good fortune we were next to a tiny village which at least meant we wouldn't starve. Since passing through the final gap we had passed about an hour before breakdown, a largish village where to my amazement I spied a Land Rover and on asking the driver of my lorry about it he said it would belong to the Wali of Dhank. First however we tried mending the fan belt with pieces of wire. I then suggested an aghal – the black rope that keeps a shamagh[16] on one's head. This believe it or not worked for about 30 yards and then broke. So I then sent off two Arabs to walk to Dhank and ask the Wali for assistance. (I would have gone myself but still had a huge blister from mountaineering!) Three-and-a-half hours later (9 o'clock), having enjoyed some local hospitality sitting cross-legged on a carpet eating dates and rice from a central bowl by the light of a hurricane lamp, I saw two very welcome head lamps approaching from Dhank. It arrived, but to my dismay, the Wali had given express wishes that the Land Rover, which was lacking some ball bearings, should NOT proceed to our base. So all the assistance he had given was lifting our two tired soldiers back to the broken down lorry! He did, however, like all other walis since the emergency out here, possess a long-range wireless. But this was installed in the Wali's bait [house] in Dhank. Getting a little desperate for I knew how worried those at base would be, I got into the Land Rover myself and drove back to Dhank. At about 10.30 pm I arrived and was ushered into his 'palace'. Here I sat down on the carpet and went through all the customary greetings, perhaps a little hurriedly!*

Our Arab language instructors in Aden had taught us to enter into the spirit of these prolonged and florid greetings, regardless of circumstance. Indeed we practised them on each other with alacrity! We needed to understand that an Arab uses his language not only to communicate, but as a means of setting the tone, rhythm and temperament of the ensuing discussion.

'Very beautiful is the meeting of Arabs in the desert, with their greetings for each other – very formal, very long drawn-out and repetitive, for each member of each party exchanges the same friendly enquiries and assurances with each member of the other, until all have greeted all and they part or proceed to any business that may be in hand. 'Peace be upon you'. 'And upon you peace'. 'How is your state, oh Salih?' 'In peace; how are you, oh Ali?' 'In peace! May God give you health'. 'May God improve your condition'. 'How are you?' 'In peace'.'

H. St John Philby, on the Bedu, *Arabia of the Wahhabis*, 1928

*February 22nd 1963 (continued)*

*However it is extremely rude not to go through this rigmarole. More plates of fruit, dates, rice and cups of coffee were brought. This was all delicious but I was still anxious and impatient to put 'my own house in order'! After three quarters of an hour I broached the subject of using his wireless set upstairs to which he agreed. But no – try as I did, I could not get through onto our radio frequency. My only method would have been to send a morse coded signal, but because I did not have a wireless set in the lorry, I didn't have a radio operator with me either. And like the majority of British Officers I didn't know my morse code sufficiently well to send a message!* [Morse had long before been dropped from skills training in the British Army.]

*By now I was becoming increasingly desperate but at the same time seeing the absurdity of the situation. 11.30 pm and still no further on! I was ushered down stairs to some tea this time proudly produced out of full size teacups! I 'got round' to Land Rovers and said that if he would lend me his Land Rover to get to base I would ensure he got some new ball bearings etc. through the Army. He also took a liking to my map so I promised him one. At last after an hour's bargaining he agreed! In the end we seemed to get on very well indeed. Perhaps I am at last learning to be less impatient out here!*

Unless the reader has first hand experience of Omani lifestyle he or she may wonder at my apparent impatience with the lack of urgency in all matters. In retrospect I was young and typically intolerant of time wasting. However I was gradually coming to terms with an incredibly laid back lifestyle where time does not dominate. The Arabic 'Insh'allah' (If God wills it) – usually accompanied by a shrug of the shoulders – makes the Spanish 'mañana' (tomorrow) seem urgent!

*Two and a half hours later – I suppose about 3 o'clock in the morning – I got back to base in the Wali's Land Rover. It was then a matter of getting a new fan belt out to the lorry. Actually the vehicle that was delivering the fan belt met the lorry half way! The lorry driver had tried a fourth aghal and it had proved strong enough! . . .*

*Evidently the Commanding Officer is annoyed that I didn't take a second vehicle. Had I done so none of those available would have stood the pace and the recce had to be done that day to fit in with other things. All extremely unfortunate, but valuable experience. I really had to use my Arabic!*

## Climbing Jebel Misht

*February 25th 1963*

*Can you please send me some sheets and pillow-slips? – two sets to be precise. There's next to nothing here. Get something quite strong if you can – it will have to stand up to some pretty indifferent laundering. Also could you run a bed cover to earth – something to brighten up my room?*

*February 28th 1963*

*I want to tell you of another climb which three of us did the other day – a mountain called Jebel Misht. About 6,500 feet – pretty steep on one side with sharp and loose rock. Sergeant Carr from the Parachute Regiment, Julian Lush from Shell and I went off to climb it together. It took 6 hours up and down. As you may imagine the climate here is not ideal for climbing, but while we are still in our winter it is by no means a mad venture. It was a pretty rugged climb up and we all got very warm and sunburnt. From the top it is possible to see a long way – but oh so different from the Alps! Once you have climbed there – even as little as I have – you are spoilt for scenery.*

*The way down was extremely unpleasant – very sharp rocks on the hands and extremely brittle underfoot. We all cut our hands quite badly and I had 16 blisters on my feet! I wore chukka boots, which are ideal, but my feet are not really hard enough yet, though for two days I have been padding around without any sort of sandals so that I should soon be all right! However for 48 hours after Misht I genuinely hobbled like never before. I suppose I have some satisfaction in knowing that we were the second group of Europeans to have climbed the mountain. But I must admit that those sharp loose rocks have dampened my ardour for climbing out here (28).*

In retrospect it may appear strange that we climbed in chukka boots instead of climbing-boots. In truth very little proper climbing took place in Oman in those days. Nobody possessed climbing boots while the normal footwear on the Jebel was chukka boots, with or without socks, depending on the time of year. The sharp and brittle rock faces, unlike the granite of the Alps, would often fracture when pierced with pitons. Consequently climbing in the true sense of the word was unsafe. Nevertheless, careful route selection was possible making climbing something of a risky scramble. The sharpness of the rocks was hard on the hands (which need gloves) and the rubber soles of chukka boots wore out after constant use within a few weeks.

### Feasting at Eid

*February 22nd 1963 (continued)*

*I have mentioned Eid. This is a great period of rejoicing and giving fudhls (parties) in the Muslim world. I wrote to you of the fasting during the daylight hours of Ramadhan. Well, Eid is the blow-out at the end of it!* [Ramadhan occurs during the ninth month of the Islamic (lunar) calendar.]

*February 28th 1963 (continued)*

*Eid starts when the moon appears after a certain number of days. When this moon appears everybody fires off rifles into the air – village cannons are let off and rejoicing begins. As many Arab soldiers are sent home as possible during this period of festivity which lasts about a week.*

*This has meant that we have had little work to do for the last few days – but socially we have never stopped! Up to 5 fudhls a day seems to be about normal. The local walis and sheikhs invite British officers as honoured guests. As with my visit to the Wali of Dhank, you are ushered into the majlis [meeting place] where you sit cross-legged on the floor. This I find extremely difficult! My legs are too long or something. It is very rude to show the soles of your feet to your host (you take your shoes off before entering a house). I try to kid myself that I am getting more supple and use a camel stick to help get up again after a long session! The Arabs who are wonderfully supple have considerable amusement in watching the British officers trying vainly to sit comfortably!*

*Very soon huge trays (3 ft in diameter) are brought in mounded high with rice and meat. It is easy to pick out the goat's head which invariably sits snugly on the top. Very often there are other highly coloured tin bowls filled with curry and other types of meat. The feast begins with about six people sitting around one tray. Another tray a few yards of carpet away will have the same number of feasters. The right hand only is used – the left being considered unclean (being reserved for cleaning one's 'private parts'!). The sheikh will tear off a choice piece of meat and place it in front of you on the side of the mountain of rice opposite you. This you must eat – regardless of whether it is goat's eye or brains. Otherwise you take a piece of meat, wrap it in rice, squeeze it into a ball of food and eat it. All this procedure is quite simple and takes no time to get used to. The difficult part is the sitting and the conversation! I had my first goat's eye and brains three days ago – the eye was quite reasonable – the brains too sweet! Neither bore thinking about too much. Very often flies are a real menace and hum round the trays of food. In such cases a servant with a fan waves them away.*

*After everybody has had enough to eat, the trays and tin bowls are removed. Then a servant brings round a kettle of water to clean your hand. He pours water into a bowl while you put your hand under the spout of the kettle. A towel is usually provided. After this a servant brings round very small cups before serving coffee. The servant will wait over you pouring the coffee from an ornate Omani or simpler Saudi Arabian coffee pot – only filling your handle-less cup (finjan) a quarter full. It is usual to take about 3 cups – no more – and it is quite delicious! To show that you have had enough coffee you jiggle your cup from side to side.*

With five such feasts a day for up to a week the consequent discomfort from overeating can be crucifying. Being one of only two British officers within a large operational area, you are viewed as a prestigious guest. To refuse such invitations could cause grave offence and could easily stem the flow of useful intelligence concerning the movement of rebels in the area.

To make matters worse there were quite long journeys in the heat of the day to each celebratory feast. While such journeys over rough tracks helped shake things around a little, I recall this being an acutely trying time! Moreover a sheikh's harem would compete in providing the best and most sumptuous meals. You, being the honoured guest, sat next to the sheikh or wali, who would persist in passing you endless morsels which it was bad manners to refuse. Many of these 'wise men' knew full well your predicament. With a scarcely discernible glint in the eye they would pile up further agony!

*February 28th 1963 (continued)*

*In May we leave Ibri and go to Rostaq, a very much more isolated station in the foothills, though much closer to Muscat. I gather that this is a popular company camp though one of the most uncomfortable ones in the hot season (June, July, August). It has tents and barusti huts – not buildings, as there are here – and no electricity. More like a camp to my mind. The shooting is reputably excellent in the winter. Also because it is so difficult to get to, few people make the effort. This is again good, as we seem to get endless 'swanners' visiting Ibri.*

*Yesterday after the final fudhl I went swimming in the oil company pool, which is small, but very pleasant. Their camps are certainly plush – tennis court too. No such camp at Rostaq I gather.*

*John Cook and I went shooting yesterday evening. We got into position near some water in a wadi – peacefulness was unbelievable. It was a simply lovely sunset and not until John had fired did I realise that a duck was heading my way. I missed it with my first barrel, but recovered to get it with my left. Unfortunately it was getting so dark that I could not pinpoint where it had landed although it had hit the water. Mistakenly I did not attempt to retrieve it for we were still awaiting some sand grouse. Result the sand grouse never came – and despite Land Rover lights and wading thigh deep in filthy water we never retrieved the duck. Great pity for I have never shot a duck before. It is also quite unusual to get duck so far inland.*

*March 5th 1963*

*It's so warm here now that I am just plain thirsty. It's 90° each day now with precious little temperature drop at night. And it is only spring . . .*

## A sandstorm shortens a patrol to Yanqul

*March 8th 1963*

*I am just off to Yanqul again for 4 days. I don't suppose there will be a great deal of activity – we are merely there to put the fear of God into the wali there, whom we suspect to be against the Sultan. This means that I shall have a rather hot but idle time.*

*March 12th 1963*

*The 4-day patrol to Yanqul turned into a 48 hour affair because of a sand storm. However I did have two nights out – both of which were surprisingly cold (58°) – presumably before the sand storm. Sand got everywhere and Bernard and I broke down in our LR on the return convoy. I am beginning to learn a little about engines – it's expedient here. I had a go of Muscat tummy – same symptoms as the Aden variety – and had visions of being stuck out in a sand storm all night. Fortunately all was well after 3 hours and we limped home – finally juddering to a stop outside Ibri camp gates.*

*Since then there have been no more 'ops' and we have got on with some much needed administration. Neither of us likes doing it – but once again everything comes to a grinding halt without it.*

*I played tennis yesterday at the oil company. First game of any sort that I have played since I arrived. We thoroughly enjoyed ourselves.*

*Generally speaking things are looking up – perhaps I am at last settling in. It is very different from any previous experience – and my non-comprehension of Arabic is very frustrating at times. The good book says don't lose your temper or raise your voice with Omanis. I find that they don't take you seriously unless you do raise your voice – then they scamper! The language is still a very real problem – and always will be for they will not speak slowly, even if you ask them to!*

## Ibri

*March 15th 1963*

*For Muscat and the Oman, Ibri is quite a large town (30 – 32, 38 – 42). Mud huts, houses and forts are partially hidden amongst a mass of palm trees. A falaj or water course runs through the centre of the town with a well close at hand. Dusty and "corrugated" tracks lead their way to the market square which is a 'taxi rank' for donkeys and camels. Invariably the camels sit right in the middle of the road and merely gaze disdainfully when a Land Rover wishes to pass. Up one end of the town there is a certain amount of cultivation made possible by an ingenious but simple method of irrigation. But I would have said that this cultivation is considerably less than at other towns in the area.*

*The Wali of Ibri, Sayyid Sa'oud bin Harib, is a truly grand old man with a magnificent face and a long white beard (29). He has great charm, speaks slowly (thank goodness) in excellent classical Arabic. He is one of the Sultan's most staunch supporters and despite his years has a very firm control of Ibri. He is a well-educated man but speaks no English. Moreover he has scant respect for any British officer who cannot speak Arabic! Untypically of most Arabs, he is interested in world affairs and according to Bernard he was always up to date with news during the Cuban crisis.*

*The inhabitants of Ibri are very friendly. Whenever I or Bernard go to visit the Wali they turn out from their houses and shout greetings to us. The children go mad with excitement so that there is a deafening noise to warn the Wali of our arrival. This is an advantage for he then gets his best coffee set out!*

*The women folk are unveiled in Ibri but veiled outside the town. They appear to work hard collecting wood, water, food – and have few perks to life. They eat and gather in a separate room from the men, though occasionally they are present in the majlis [meeting place] of a Sheikh's house so you meet them quickly before they retire to leave the men to talk! I wouldn't know how much influence they have on their menfolk – no doubt quite a lot!*

*The litter which exists in the town is pretty excessive. Cats, dogs and chickens have a high old time. But in these surroundings it doesn't seem to matter – though in Aden it did.*

*The company camp is outside the town – 10 minutes away from the airstrip. Many of the barrack rooms are concrete buildings which have been built during the last year. The officers' mess has been made by previous officers to look quite nice – there is even a small garden. Cotton plants and sunflowers grow here, though we are shortly planting a vine! A generator gives us all electricity. A water bowser brings round water to the tank every day and we have a shower. When the need for hot water is extreme we visit the oil company, who are very accommodating, thank goodness.*

**30** The barber at Ibri suq attends a client from the desert. *By kind permission of A. J. M. Lush.*

**31** Three sheikhs walk down the street in Ibri. *By kind permission of J. R. Darbyshire.*

**32** Outside Ibri suq. *By kind permission of J. R. Darbyshire*

**33** A father reassures an uncertain son.

**34** A radio operator sends a morse code message.

**35** Commanding Officer, The Muscat Regiment, Lieutenant Colonel Clive Chettle, MC, inspects the guard on a visit to Rostaq. *Photograph courtesy of* Soldier, *The British Army Magazine.*

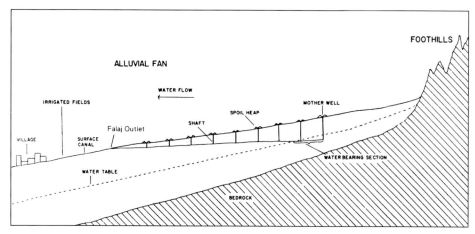

**36** Cross-section of a falaj. *Reproduced from* Oman 1972 *by kind permission of the Ministry of Information, Sultanate of Oman.*

MESSAGE FORM

**37** Copy of an original signal from HM Sultan bin Taimur, congratulating John Darbyshire on arresting a leading rebel. *By kind permission of J. R. Darbyshire*

*Furniture is practically non-existent but we now all at least have beds! We are gradually getting more furniture from Nizwa.*

## Searching for rebels in the Balad Sait region

*March 20th 1963*

*Since my last letter we have been on a 4 day operation at a place called Balad Sait. Intelligence reports that three rebels were in the area. Unfortunately they were supposed to be in the mountains to the west of the town. This meant that the NFR [Northern Frontier Regiment] and Muscat Regiment had to cordon and search a huge mountainous area. To my mind, with only two regiments, such an operation is practically impossible. Anyway an attempt was made to do this though many things went wrong and as a result, it can only have been partly effective and by no means thorough. Nobody suspicious was found.*

*As 2 i/c of the company I did very little climbing for which I was not sorry because it was very hot. I was responsible for supply of food and water – mostly packed on donkeys – to all separate sections of the company. There were few hitches here but how bored I get with administration only! Still it has to be done and the Omanis seem incapable of comprehending the abstract, ie thinking ahead for future contingencies.*

I recall emphasising to drivers of vehicles of the need to take sufficient petrol for the return part of a long patrol. In those days the usual response to running out of petrol would be 'Allah karim' (God is generous and will provide!).

*March 20th 1963 (continued)*

*However, I was not entirely a 'base wallah' for I had a couple of new experiences. During the slow advance towards the mountains to the west of Balad Sait there was a continual air reconnaissance going on – SOAF doing their stuff. A couple of pilots spotted a suspicious looking traveller hoofing it as fast as possible from the Balad Sait area. This person had somehow slipped through the ring before the cordon was in place. This person was reported to be approaching my area. A strange looking ground-to-air wireless was thrust into my hands by an Omani corporal. Then, over the command set (wireless permanently installed in my Land Rover) I was ordered to drive as quickly as possible to the outskirts of Aisha and arrest the suspect before he reached the safety of the village. I then established contact with both pilots whose job it was to direct me to the suspect who was some distance away and out of sight. This was a new experience for me for I had never before used a wireless set which gives ground-to-air transmission. The procedure is very simple and I enjoyed myself enormously!*

*I reached a defile on an approach to Aisha that the suspect had to use. Five minutes later SHE appeared walking extremely fast. When my two soldiers approached her, she tried to avoid them – and when caught just screamed and screamed. She had to be manhandled into my LR where she continued to scream, so that she had to be gagged in case she raised sympathisers from the outskirts of the village. By now I was beginning to hope that she really was guilty and that I was not terrifying an innocent woman.*

*I took her to Battalion Headquarters for questioning by the local sheikh. As I had feared, she was quite innocent, had been frightened by all the soldiers in the Balad Sait area and was fleeing for her life (kidnapping is still prevalent here).*

*I am afraid to say that the next part of the story does not flatter the set up for dealing with prisoners. After the sheikh had found her to be innocent no attention was taken of her – nor any attempt made to deliver her home. I would have done this but I was immediately sent away to a further arrest, this time of a donkeyman. Women seem to be afforded scant respect in this part of the world – generally speaking – but none the less, having frightened the poor creature out of her wits, at least some effort should have been made to set the matter right.*

*A couple of hours ago a further operation was put under way down on the Batinah Coast – the result of some illegal immigrants in some dhow. Being at Ibri we are too far away to be called in but we are affected in that all the SOAF aircraft are required which means no mail for another week – miserable!*

## Impressions of Omani people

*March 28th 1963*

*I want to give you my impressions of the Omani. I suspect that you may know most of this already, but some of my early impressions may have been wide of the mark.*

*The Omani on meeting him for the first time is a shy, extremely well mannered person. As previously described, every conceivable form of introduction is used – but depending on his attentiveness or otherwise, can be either charming or a meaningless rigmarole.*

*In time the initial shyness gives way and the Omani greets you warmly, looking you straight in the eyes.*

Unlike the firm and sometimes rigorous handshake of westerners the Omani handshake was a limp-wristed affair. Often this was supplemented by the left hand being held above the heart to show sincerity.

*I have sometimes found this warm friendly greeting almost disconcerting in its apparent sincerity. My experience so far has led me to use the word 'apparent' – for two reasons. Firstly, there are a number of Omanis who are undeniably charming, but not wholly trustworthy. Secondly, the lack of western materialistic way of life does dictate that the meeting, greeting and social life of the Omani is of paramount importance. It is a perfected art.*

*Generally speaking Omanis are poorly co-ordinated where sport is concerned. This, together with some degree of laziness, means that they show little interest in any game. However they can walk incredibly long distances in the heat of the day with little effect save recurring headaches. While some degree of sunstroke may cause these headaches the endemic diet deficiencies in their early years are also thought to have some bearing.*

*The Omani is prone to mood swings. Small instances can make him uncontrollably happy and excited whereas the next moment he can plunge into the depths of depression. I am beginning to fathom the type of thing which affects him in this way.*

*His mind seems to act in the present only. He seldom seems to reminisce or talk of past experiences – although he is a great discusser of the 'latest news'. As for looking into the future, this really does seem to be an effort for him. He has little comprehension of the abstract. He drives on in his Land Rover – runs out of petrol – and only then does he see the problem. He finds it difficult to forecast such simple problems and to prepare himself accordingly.*

*Furthermore discipline is very new to him. As you know B Company is all Omani. I find that the Omani NCOs cannot enforce their will. Soldiers will do anything "the Major" or "the Captain" says, but often flatly refuse to do what their platoon sergeant tells them to do. This results in the sergeant running to one of us for assistance in his problem. In fairness, none of them has known 'discipline' for longer than 5 or 6 years, so this situation is hardly surprising. But you can imagine that this continual running for advice or support over the minutest problems can be a real test of our patience.*

*Similarly the inability to look ahead constructively means a vast amount of checking by us beforehand. Although we would like to put the responsibility for such minor things as checking vehicles completely before leaving on an operation – none of us dares take the risk yet for we would undoubtedly come unstuck as I did in Wadi Dhank on my first patrol out here.*

*So all in all the Omani with his disregard for time has much to learn as a soldier. However, having highlighted his military shortcomings – all of which stem from his culture and environment, I would like to sing his praises.*

*The Omani has an incorrigible sense of humour; he is very respectful towards us as British officers. Many Omanis have tremendous charm. Some officers out here in the past have allowed themselves to get hopelessly attached to the Omanis – for which there is no return save a broken heart. For they do not know loyalty as we do and as a result unintentionally and unknowingly they will let you down.*

*As a climber of hills the Omani is quite superb and leads us a merry dance in this way. Having always carried a rifle with him since a very young age he takes a far greater pride than any British soldier in his valuable service rifle. When he has nothing to do he will reclean it. Furthermore his handling of the rifle is entirely natural.*

*To western minds he has a very different attitude towards general cleanliness – but in turn he laughs at our fussiness.*

## Sickness in the Company

*March 31st 1963*

*I have been commanding the company for the last 2 days during which there have been a number of typical incidents. One of the prisoners in the guard room has appendicitis and has reached the vomiting stage. I've signalled for a casevac Beaver to get him to Muscat. I've also sent a vehicle to his village to warn his wife that her husband will be operated on in Muscat – and that she can fly down too. This truck has broken down – as has also the recovery vehicle. There have been 5 more cases of mumps in the camp. I have had 3 sheikhs to visit me today – all on the scrounge. Furthermore the Commanding Officer visits tomorrow!*

Apart from an Indian paramedic in charge of the oil company clinic nobody had medical training other than in first aid. The only hospital within Muscat and Oman was the American Missionary Hospital in Muscat some 160 miles away as the crow flies. The Force Medical Officer was Major Mohammed Qureshi who was based in SAF HQ at Bait-al-Falaj in Muscat.

*April 2nd 1963*

*I heard yesterday that my Matterhorn article has been accepted by The British Army Review – I'm flabbergasted.*
*Letters missing – never received.*

## Combined operations

*April 21st 1963*

*The operation has ended. We came in yesterday. The ghost dhow supposedly carrying 50 rebels was not seen by air reconnaissance – nor by the 3 Royal Navy frigates in the Gulf. We have been called in to rest and are at 8 hours' notice to move should the RAF Shackletons spot the dhow after all. I must say I have enjoyed the last 10 days. The wadi al Waqba was a lovely spot. Did I tell you there was enough water in the wadi for a swim after dark? How wonderfully refreshing it was.*

*I took out a few patrols during the last few days. We climbed several jebel – from the highest one it was possible to see the sea.*

*I hope to get off to Buraimi or Sharjah on a 'swan' soon – but clearly cannot get away at the moment. It is certainly warm today – 105° – so it's warming up for the hot season.*

In retrospect it was a pity that the letters I wrote between April 2nd and April 21st went missing, because combined land, sea and air operations during a time of limited resources tested everybody's ingenuity. For example SOAF's four Beavers and five Provosts, fully stretched anyway on supply and support duties within Oman, had to be reinforced by RAF Shackletons, while the Sultan's Navy's two motorised dhows needed the help of those three RN frigates.

The Sultan's Navy was then something of a classic 'Pirates of Penzance' enterprise. Ex-RAF Wing Commander Jasper Coates with the rank of Major, resplendent in naval white rig, was in command. Both motor dhows patrolled nearly 1,000 miles of coastland to intercept craft bearing recruits, weapons, ammunition and mines destined for Talib's rebels. Jasper, a former Sunderland flyingboat captain who had previously sited Muscat's coastal airfields, commanded HMS *Nasr al Bahr* and had his personal supply of Glenfiddich. The ship's log when on routine coastal patrol always had five regular daily entries of 'All hands to Prayer' (43).

*April 25th 1963*

*Welcome to Kenya!*

Charmian had flown out to Nairobi to visit and stay with her cousin Anne Joyce who farmed at Kilima Kiu. We were in the process of planning a mid-tour holiday whereby we would meet up on the Nile and having visited Luxor, we would fly to Kashmir for a holiday on a houseboat.

Sadly her grandfather, Guffin, was to die three weeks later and she returned to Ireland for the funeral.

*April 27th 1963*

*I've just returned from Nizwa by road and for once was not driving. This meant I had six hours with little to do but look at the country and small villages through which we passed. The last hours were lovely as the sun was setting behind the dark jagged mountains.*

*One shilling and sixpence to Kenya. Monstrous isn't it. You have become six times as expensive overnight!* [Forces airmail from Muscat and Oman cost threepence while airmail to Kenya cost one shilling and sixpence.]

*We went down to Nizwa for a live firing demonstration called 'a light scale battalion'. Interesting for soldiers, but hardly a best seller otherwise. SOAF made a nonsense by rocketing the wrong target. Many rude remarks floated about.*

*Have just come back in from a shower. This is a home made affair consisting of a spray tap running off from a large drum of water. Really excellent, because the water is quite pleasantly warm from the sun during the day and while showering you look up at the stars which are fabulous in Oman. Thoroughly recommended – you must try it sometime!*

*We are still at 8 hours' notice. I gather we are likely to be for at least another 10 days. We are expecting a United Nations visitor shortly and my personal view is that we are on standby to impress him. I wonder how wide of the mark I am!*

## Leave transport and monsoon rains

*May 3rd 1963*

*No news from Ibri except that our move to Bid Bid has been put back a month. Eid starts tomorrow (Allah willing!) and we have an influx of visitors today. Fudhls galore will follow – but how I hate overeating. I would settle for cheese any day!*

*May 6th 1963*

*Eid is well under way now and all waistlines are bulging.*

*The weather has been incongruous lately. It should be the hot season with temperatures about 110°. Instead there has been a huge drop – and three days of monsoon rains. This has caused its problems as before Eid, transport is laid on to take soldiers to their homes if humanly possible. At Ibri we are central so we organise most of the leave transport for the force. Because of the monsoon rains (which are freak) numerous lorries have been bogged down in the sand miles away from their destinations. Soldiers have been wet through (no covering on any vehicles) and two Land Rovers were actually submerged in a raging torrent in a wadi. John Cook and I have spent long hours day and night going out and recovering overdue lorries. The whole thing is a complete paradox – the soldiers have little experience of driving vehicles under such conditions and are hopeless at it. Furthermore, once the vehicles are bogged down they wave their hands in the air, say 'Allah Karim' (God is generous) and have not the slightest idea as to how to set about extricating their vehicle! Fortunately John and I have had a wealth of experience at this – so we find ourselves not only directing but physically digging the vehicles out ourselves. To start with this was all rather fun (in a school boyish sort of way) but after the umpteenth time such tasks lose their attraction and become a bit of a curse. This is particularly so when long distances are involved before the stricken truck can be reached. However despite all, I thoroughly enjoyed myself – generally speaking – though I cannot remember ever being so wet for so long in my life before!*

*Luckily the day before yesterday the rains washed away the track bringing a mine into view. Fortune sometimes smiles when the sun doesn't.*

*However we now have managed to get all the soldiers we can to their homes – and have all the vehicles back too. Only a few of the forecast visitors from other outstations have arrived in the mess for which I am truly grateful. The weather has now turned fine and the temperature is slowly climbing again. The weather prophets forecast a 'sizzler' hot season after all these rains. Several barusti huts have been swept away – and the Bedu must have had a pretty rough time. One camel stuck firmly in the mud – and had to be dragged out. Many roads have been made impassable by these rains and no aeroplanes have landed in Muscat airport because it is flooded.*

*John Darbyshire managed to get here – so this has been great fun. Yesterday morning, the start of Eid was greeted with rifle shots of jubilation over the Camp. We then had Eid breakfast with the soldiers (those who are still in the camp on standby). The rice was cold but the goat was very tender and well cooked. At 11 o'clock we went to visit the Wali of Ibri where we had coffee, peaches and hulwa (quite like marzipan but more like jelly – delicious).*

*At 2 o'clock we all went to a fudhl a couple of miles outside Ibri at a Bedu encampment. Here we had more goat, rice, peaches, dates, hulwa and coffee – a really excellent feast. We were sat down for so long that I could hardly stand up and walk away when the meal was finished. How glad I was of my camel stick! (45)*

*We have a tame gazelle in the mess – he is utterly charming and loves to play about. The garden in front of the mess which once looked colourful is gradually being eaten away. However I have no doubt 'Dubby' is considered more important than the garden – temporarily anyway (44).*

## Leave transport

*May 9th 1963*

*Eid leave is now behind us thank goodness. Organising the return of the soldiers from their homes to their companies had its moments too. Time, as I have said often before, means nothing to the Omanis. We lay on trucks to collect them from their villages and houses dotted all over the country. We attempt to make the process not too long and drawn out by asking them to be near the track used at a certain time, allowing plenty of time for all previous stops. Not having enough British officers or indeed local officers to roust them out, one is forced to send a sergeant or corporal. What happens? The soldiers are not ready when required so to avoid further delay the truck is driven to the house. As hospitality is the byword in Oman, the sergeant is bidden in for coffee or a meal. Meanwhile all the others who have already been picked up are invited to other nearby houses. And this happens in every village! Whereas this is really very pleasant it does mean that the hospitality time far outlasts the travel time despite the long distances between villages. Also it is very difficult to gauge when a truck is overdue just because of an extra fudhl or whether it has broken down or perhaps even been blown up on a mine. On an average out here, you need to allow very nearly 4 times the length of time that you might expect to take to do most jobs in England, Germany, Kenya or any other country under Western influence. As you can imagine I am rapidly becoming more patient and also more tolerant.*

*May 15th 1963*

*It's really brewing up now. It was 95° at 8 o'clock this morning. The sun is incredibly strong. I have just completed a patrol to a place called Hail in the Wadi al Ayn (47). The monsoon rains had played hell with the road so that we averaged 1 mph in the wadi for three hours. Two vehicles broke springs.*

*My patrol was purely routine – showing the flag in a place the Army had not visited for some while. However during the time that I was out the whole Muscat Regiment was called out to a place 10 miles south of my position. Two rebels were captured and one gave himself up a while later. Of those reported to be there (result of interrogation) only one is still at large. There was much excitement, some shots were fired and a few people were wounded but not seriously. Those wounded were not soldiers but men from a tribe called the Awlad Zahr, who had been previously loyal to the rebel cause but have now come round to the Sultan's side seeing that the rebel cause is a lost one. It was annoying not to be in on this little excitement but there it is.*

*May 21st 1963*

*Very weary after 2 days patrolling.*

*May 24th 1963*

*No worthwhile news I'm afraid. I did go out shooting last night – returning with only two pigeons. Today is Jumma (Friday) the Muslim Sunday so we have a rest.*

*May 26th 1963*

*A lot of shooting the last few days – both in the early morning and evening. It is the greatest fun. I have just returned from a visit to the oil company where I drank only two whiskies but am well away! They had a visitor from Nigeria with a real drawl of a voice – my whisky and his mood seemed to go perfectly!*

## A visitor from the United Nations

*June 1st 1963*

*At present we have a visiting representative from the United Nations. He has been doing a tour all over Muscat and Oman and is 67 years old. He comes from Stockholm and is a highly intelligent and charming man. I could tell you the reason for his visit but there is a degree of secrecy about it all so I shall refrain from doing so just yet. I certainly don't envy him at his age for temperatures are between 115° and 120° at the moment and he seems to have a very full programme. Unfortunately, it is not possible for him to fly everywhere so he has to travel by Land Rover over our shocking roads. I sat next to him at dinner last night when we were guests of the oil company. He was very much a man of the world with great experience.*

As mentioned in Chapter Four the three small campaigns of 1955, 1957 and 1959 had been exploited to the full by Cairo Radio's 'Voice of the Arabs' as 'savage and overwhelming use of British force'. Since then radio propaganda continued to champion the 'Omani Freedom fighters' under Talib and Ghalib by making absurd and unsubstantiated claims of 'heroic victories' and the killing or wounding of thousands of British soldiers. Because the Sultan chose to ignore rather than deny these nonsensical claims, radio propaganda persisted with its tissue of lies. By placing an embargo on press reporting he not only surrendered the opportunity to discredit this malicious propaganda but presented scope for further rumour and embellishment.

Nowadays it is customary to issue denials instantaneously but, in the late '50s and early '60s there was a school of thought that the best way to discredit absurd reporting was to ignore it. However, it would be interesting to know whether the Sultan ignored or followed the advice of his British advisors at the time.

Inevitably over time the combination of radio propaganda, rumour, inquisitiveness and Britain's waning influence in Middle Eastern affairs forced the 'Oman Question' high on the agenda at the United Nations. The Sultan's refusal to attend the General Assembly personally to respond to other Arab delegates was bad enough. Sending a British spokesman to represent his country and respond to charges of 'colonialist aggression' was incendiary!

In 1963 U Thant's special envoy, Mr Herbert de Ribbing, was invited to visit Muscat and Oman on a mission of inquiry. This was the impressive man I had the privilege to sit next to over dinner on May 31st 1963. In his report[17] to the United Nations' General Assembly later in the year he did find a few signs of discontent here and there in the Sultan's kingdom. He also found the Sultan to be stubborn which had been well known for several years. He confessed to having some difficulty in evaluating all the evidence he collected, which, bearing in mind the conditions under which he was working, let alone the prevailing feudal attitudes, was hardly surprising. However, most importantly by far, he was able to dismiss the principal claims of the 'Free Omanis' about the size and nature of 'the war', the legal and historical independence of the 'Oman State', and the existence of a 'British military occupation'.

### Rising temperatures and a visit to the Sheikh of Yanqul

*June 4th 1963*

*It's 115° today in the shade. I am alone at Ibri. John Cook has gone on a 5-day patrol up the Jebel Kaur (9,000 ft). He is lucky for this is something I would like to do. With temperatures as they are at present it is impossible to try to climb it entirely in daylight so he will do 4 hours by moonlight tonight if he is lucky. He is taking 12 men and 6 donkeys with him (48).*

*June 17th 1963*

*No sooner had I written Ibri and the date at the top of this page than a Baluch signaller knocked on my door clutching an 'Op Immediate' signal from Nizwa. I am to go to Yanqul to question the sheikh about some rebel information which he is supposed to have. It says go today.*

*It is Jumma (Muslim Sunday) – and I am damned if I am rushing off this very moment for anybody. I shall finish writing to you, have lunch and then go. Quarter of an hour ago an unheralded convoy arrived with an officer very ill with flu – having decided he was not strong enough to make his original destination.*

*I shall let you know how I get on with the Sheikh (of Yanqul) who is scared stiff of the Army.*

*June 10th 1963*

*It gets hotter everyday – 117° today. I put a thermometer in the foot space in my LR the other day. This part gets the hot air rushing through as well as the sun and it registered 154°.*

*What of my visit to the Sheikh of Yanqul, Saif bin Armagh? It was a hot drive there for 2 hours. He, an Arab staff sergeant and I sat under a large lumi (lime) tree by the falaj, conversing in low voices so that nobody might overhear us. He was not forthcoming about the information which he was supposed to possess but did produce, when pressed, quite a lot of information about one of Talib's rebels who landed by dhow a month ago with 24 mines from Damman. He said that this rebel had been seen in a certain area and gave further details, all of which tie in with one other similar report from another source. I am therefore hoping I was not palmed off with a pack of lies. In all it was not a wasted trip for a small girl produced, on orders from the Sheikh, a basket full of mangos.*

## Teaching Arab soldiers to play hockey at Bid Bid

*June 15th 1963*

*We leave Ibri today at 6 pm and we are driving through the night to Bid Bid.*

*Subsequently from Bid Bid*

*No news from here worth relating. I have been teaching the Arabs hockey in temperatures of over 100° in the early morning. They are unbelievably uncoordinated as far as sport is concerned but get very excited, enjoying themselves tremendously. Trying to explain the finer points of the game is no mean task for they ALL want to strike the ball at the same time so that they ALL move about the ground – 22 of them in 10 sq yds – just like a flight of sand grouse. However my efforts are not being entirely wasted for they now stay in their positions but I'm afraid that once I am gone they will ALL swoop on the ball once more!*

*June 17th 1963*

*A quick note in the midst of upheaval here. I look like being here another 2 days at least before moving on to Rostaq and 'A' Company. Bid Bid is a very palatial camp. Air conditioning, basins and showers in each officer's room. I am making the best of it before moving to the other extreme at Rostaq.*

# Chapter Seven

# A Baluch Company
# in the Jebel Foothills

## A Company, The Muscat Regiment, Rostaq,
## June to September 1963

Rostaq – The falaj system of water channels – Working with Baluch soldiers –
Second-in-command to John Darbyshire – John Darbyshire captures a
leading rebel – A brief respite in Bait-al-Falaj and a four-day patrol –
Excited donkeys and a scrounging sheikh – Philosophic and other
observations – Rostaq Officer's Mess – John suffers from heat exhaustion –
A welcome break at Saiq – Mortar cadre in Rostaq and a mutiny at Saiq –
Saying goodbye to A Company – A visit to a fort in Hazaam –
Retrospective on Rostaq – A proposal for an early release

## Rostaq

Rostaq, a village in the foothills to the jebel, has enjoyed a reputation for being at the centre of events in Oman's history. Its fine fort, which predates the Islamic era, has been the subject of constant embellishment ever since. It was the residence of Imam Saif bin Sultan of the Ya'ruba dynasty when Rostaq enjoyed capital seat status. He, and later Ahmed bin Said Al-Said, founder of the Albusaidi dynasty, are both buried here.

In the 1950s the fort once again became the centre of attention during the Jebel conflict. When the Sultan was persuaded of the need to deploy his forces in company camps within Oman, Rostaq's history and dominant position made it an obvious choice. Rostaq's old suq and hot springs are further remarkable assets of which residents are justifiably proud. However the extreme heat of the summer months – often referred to as "the 100 hot days" – posed a real challenge to those used to a temperate climate (49, 50).

*June 21st 1963*

*What of Rostaq? It is (censored) hot. I have four pieces of paper under my wrist while I am writing to you, and I am still in danger of smudging everything. It is too hot to lie down in my tent this afternoon (120°) – the metal bedsteads are too hot to touch, the mattress too hot to lie on – so I am in the mud-walled office with a large thermos of iced water to hand. One of the two fridges has given up the unequal struggle (both are paraffin) while the other just works if we keep putting wet blankets around it every hour or so!*

*The coolest place is the falaj – which is 15 ft underground with a staircase of stones down to it. The water, as it flows underground for the majority of the time, is refreshingly cool (70°–75°). John Darbyshire and I visit this fairly frequently to cool off. If it gets any warmer I shall moor my lilo down there and sleep there at midday. I am grateful that we only have two more months of this hot season for it is very tiring.*

## The falaj system of water channels

The falaj system, often referred to as aflaj (the plural), is a system of water channels introduced in pre-Christian times to conserve water and to convey it to where it is most needed to irrigate and increase crop production – and generally to serve the needs of local inhabitants. This is achieved by locating an underground water source or 'motherwell' in the foothills of the jebel (36). A path is then marked on the surface below which the underground channel will conduct the water to the area to be irrigated. At regular intervals along this path 'spoil heaps' are marked to indicate where vertical shafts are to be dug down to the underground channel or falaj through which the water will flow down a gentle gradient until it reaches the surface at the falaj outlet. At this point a series of surface canals then channel the water to irrigate fields and supply villages. While the water is underground loss due to evaporation is minimised and it remains refreshingly cool.

Unfortunately, construction and maintenance of Oman's two-thousand-year-old falaj irrigation system is labour intensive, expensive and hazardous. For both construction and maintenance purposes vertical shafts, often at least twenty feet deep, need to be dug at twenty- to fifty-yard intervals along the path of the falaj. The bottoms of these shafts are then connected to form a long tunnel between the falaj outlet and the 'motherwell'. At any stage in this process shafts and tunnels can and do collapse so frequent maintenance is essential. Where channels have to cross a wadi bed an inverted siphon is constructed (53).

However, the reward for such hard work is the absolute reliability of water supply to fields and villages. Even in the longest period of drought the flow of water never fails though it may slacken. No wonder the aflaj is regarded as one of the oldest and most important of heritages in Oman.

Best use of water has always been central to Omani culture. It is literally a matter of life and death. Whatever strides have been made to increase the availability of water in recent times, it will always be a sin to waste it in Oman.

'Of all the gifts with which God has blessed us, water is the greatest. It must be cherished and husbanded. Every effort must continue to be made to develop this resource. If extravagance is forbidden by Islam, it is even more applicable to water. Indeed, Islam emphasises in its teachings that it is our duty to conserve it.'

His Majesty Sultan Qaboos, from his National Address, November 18th 1991.


*Working with Baluch soldiers*

*June 25th 1963*

*Rostaq is a little cooler at present which is a blessing. The last two nights have been down to 85° and not sticky – making sleep a very pleasantly simple affair. I am quickly getting used to this place and enjoy it more every day. By various means we have made ourselves pretty comfortable. I even listened to the test match last night after the feverish hoisting of wireless aerials. I also heard news of that incident on the Yemen Border. Heads will roll there. General Sir Charles Harrington was visiting Bid Bid and Nizwa last week and I believe was flown back to Aden at great haste.*

*My Baluch orderly is terribly keen – quite unlike my idle, dreamy Arab in B Company. He washes everything he claps eyes on and spends hours pressing my shorts and so on. He has already expressed a wish to go with me when I leave A Company for either the Training Centre or B Company.*

As A Company was a Baluch Company whose soldiers spoke Baluchi, further steady progress in improving my Arabic was put in jeopardy for the next three months. However, by then Arabic had become the Army's universal language so the Baluch were expected to speak it more and more.

As far as I can recall no seconded British officers attended language courses in Baluchi, although many contract officers spoke the language fluently. Some had served previously in the Indian Army.

In practice the Baluch soldiers spoke better English than Arab soldiers so we managed to make ourselves understood using a combination of Arabic, Baluchi and English.

For my part I persisted whenever possible with Arabic, interspersing this with occasional Baluchi words or phrases and when 'stranded' resorting to English.

### Second-in-command to John Darbyshire

*June 28th 1963*

*Little goes on here at present. This is just as well for it is really too hot to be ambitious. Most of our time has been spent getting the Company properly administered.*

Somewhat in contrast to my arrival at B Company in Ibri in February, when I needed to get to know Bernard Mills, I was now second-in-command to John Darbyshire, who was not only a Light Infantryman, but also an old friend. We had both been to Heatherdown Preparatory School in Ascot. After attending school at Winchester and then officer cadet training at the Royal Military Academy at Sandhurst he was commissioned into The Somerset Light Infantry. In 1960 he was cross-posted to the 1st Battalion The King's Shropshire Light Infantry then stationed in Roman Way Camp, Colchester where he became affectionately known as 'Zarb'. While his reasons for volunteering for secondment to the Sultan's Armed Forces were similar to mine, I do not recall that collusion played a part in our respective decisions. However, having preceded me to The Muscat Regiment, he did ask that I should become his second-in-command. This was fortunate for both of us as of all postings during the hot season, Rostaq was known to be the most trying.

*June 28th 1963 (continued)*

*John and I are off to a fudhl today with a contact in Rostaq who gives information to the DIO (District Intelligence Officer) David Erlam, here. This Omani contact has only one arm, is too cloak and dagger to be true and I would think quite untrustworthy. I fixed him the other day with quite a piercing stare – he became shifty-eyed and promptly invited us to dinner!*

*After two days of relatively low temperatures (108°–110°) it seems to be stoking up again. John was involved in shooting down a leading rebel high on the jebel a fortnight ago.*

## John Darbyshire captures a leading rebel

Some thirty-six years later John, now a retired Solicitor, describes what happened.

'In June 1963 an informer had told the DIO that the rebel was hiding out in a cave high up on the Jebel between Nizwa and Birket al Maus. The CO (Clive Chettle) asked me to lead a small patrol to capture this rebel for interrogation. I set off after dark with two soldiers and a guide/informer who was to locate the cave. We left the vehicles short of the Jebel and set off on foot after midnight for the approach under cover of darkness.

'The ascent probably took about three hours moving cautiously. It was stifling hot and I particularly remember foxes barking around us. Just before dawn we laid up as we were close to the cave and didn't want to alert him.

'At dawn we crept closer and soon saw him lying out on a slab of rock on which he had spent the night. I shouted to him to surrender, but instead he slipped off the rock and, out of sight, rushed back to his cave and grabbed his rifle. As he took aim on us I fired a burst from my Sterling which hit the rock just above his head and at about the same time he fired at me, his round hitting the ground a few inches from my feet. I and the others took cover and at the next sighting he was making off across the Jebel. I therefore fired again, this time at his legs and was successful in hitting him; one of the soldiers with me also fired a round (possibly without orders) and hit him in the shoulder. At this point he surrendered and we took him back to the cave and tied up his wounds.

'I left one soldier to guard him and returned to Nizwa with the other soldier who was guarding the guide and reported to the CO. Meanwhile the soldier who had returned with me led a stretcher party to collect the injured rebel. I believe that he provided valuable information under interrogation in Bait-al-Falaj and he recovered from his wounds relatively quickly. Subsequently I received a message of congratulation from the Sultan (Said bin Taimur) through CSAF (Commander Sultan's Armed Forces).' (37)

*June 28th 1963 (continued)*

*He will spend the rest of his life in Jellali Prison. This is the first shooting incident for 9 months – and is certainly a setback for the rebel cause.*

## A brief respite in Bait-al-Falaj and a four-day patrol

*July 1st 1963*

*In this hot season I am finding it very difficult to concentrate on anything for long. I get tired of what I am doing exasperatingly quickly. I have plenty of things to see to but they take me twice as long as usual. This is maddening and makes me irritable with myself – and equally so with others.*

*July 5th 1963 (Bait-al-Falaj)*

*I am down here in Muscat for 2 nights. I have a number of things to see to for the Company. It also gives me 2 nights of air conditioning. Perhaps a good thing as the heat in Rostaq is pretty wearying just now. John will be down in 2 weeks time.*

*July 6th 1963 (Bait-al-Falaj)*

*Tomorrow I am off on a 4-day patrol – most of the movement by night. It should be interesting – I will let you know how it goes.*

*July 9th 1963*

*To date all has gone well – no mishaps except the wireless has broken so I have no contact with John. All 8 donkeys seem to be doing their stuff nobly. A few soldiers have a blister or two as I do. One soldier was very sick early on but a course of my aspirins seems to have done the trick. I felt for him, but having no wireless to call for help, I just told him to keep going. He did.*

99

*This is really no more than a routine patrol, having little tactical significance · save generally showing the flag, and keeping an eye on various sheikhs, who could be valuable to us by producing information.*

*We left Rostaq at 7 o'clock last Sunday morning arriving at Zahir by 1 o'clock. As you can see from the map that distance is not great, but it took 6 hours in vehicles, which gives you an idea what the track is like.*

*Midday in the hot season is pretty desperate so we made ourselves as comfortable as possible until 6.30 pm and then started marching up the Wadi beni Ghafir reaching Al Haibir by 9.00 pm. Only two and a half hours but temperatures of over 100° soon make one tired on the march.*

*We found some water and shelter from the sun for the donkeys and handlers for the next day – whereupon we bedded down for the night.*

*At about midnight a fantastic wind got up so that when I raised my head from the pillow to see that all was well, the pillow and my sheet were blown 20 yards away. For 4 hours the wind blew making sleep impossible.*

*At 6.30 am the following morning I left the camp with about 15 men, not taking the donkeys with us. By 8.00 am we finally reached Murri after a little difficulty in locating it. I visited the Sheikh, Zahir bin Salim, a nice old boy who seemed surprised to see the Army in his village – and expressed a wish to fire our machine gun!*

*He gave us coffee and dates for an hour.*

*During this time I was able to get some photos of the coffee roasting and grinding, which I hope will be fun to look at later on.*

*We then left Murri, arriving back at camp at about 10.30 am – very hot indeed for the sun is pretty high by then. Everybody rested for the remainder of the day (must have been 120°) except 'muggins' who went to visit a sheikh (pure duty and not much enjoyed).*

*At 6.30 pm we left Al Haibir marching down the wadi towards Rostaq. By 9.00 pm we reached Zahir again. By now we were a little weary for there was no moon so that hundreds of toes were stubbed on rocks in the wadi bed.*

*We stayed last night in Zahir – out in the wadi[18] away from the trees, for it is cooler like this by night. At 6.15 am we set off again reaching Difa (here) by 9.00 am. I felt rather weary despite a good night and am experiencing not being the fittest man on patrol for the first time. This I suppose is due to the Baluch being used to such heat and I myself having done most of the patrols in vehicles up till now.*

*Difa is really very pleasant, plenty of water and shade – but it is still too hot to sleep midday. I visited one sheikh this afternoon whom I liked a lot. He is getting me some camel rugs.*

100

*July 10th 1963 3.00 pm (continued)*

*Left Difa at 5.30 pm yesterday evening – earlier than usual as we had no moon to help us night marching during the two previous nights. The first half-hour was hell, my blisters proving particularly painful. In the end I lost patience and stamped my feet down, dashing up and down the line of donkeys like a madman! By 8.30 pm we reached Ghatadi which is what I had hoped to achieve. I slept the night alongside a 4 ft deep pool, which was very refreshing to bathe in last night and first thing this morning.*

*Owing to lack of firewood the soldiers could not have their breakfast early so, as I also had to visit the Sheikh, but not too early, we did not leave Ghatadi until 8 o'clock. The Sheikh is only a boy of 15 but is incredibly mature. He rules his askars with a rod of iron, is immaculately dressed with a lovely hunjah and carries a magnificently kept 1883 model of a Martini Henry rifle. We got on very well and he understood my Arabic better than most.*

*Starting out at 8.00 am to march anywhere is far too late particularly during the hot season. However we had little choice this morning so we had a fairly hot time of it arriving here at Dahaz soon after 9.30 am. The rest of the day we have spent in the customary idle fashion – resting and drinking water.*

*About a couple of hours ago I heard the sound of vehicles coming up the wadi. John, not having heard from me over the wireless, sent out some vehicles to bring us back as originally planned for the fourth day. In a way this was a pity as I had hoped to surprise him this evening by marching into Rostaq Camp – knowing that his parting words had been – 'Get to Murri if you can and see how far back down the wadi you can get, before calling for transport.'*

*Perhaps I have been a little ambitious in the last few days, but I now know what donkey and man patrols can do in the heat. It is as well to discover these things for yourself.*


## Excited donkeys and a scrounging sheikh

*July 12th 1963*

*Could you read my last epistle on that patrol? I forgot to tell you of a special moment. While on the march all 8 donkeys were well laden with rations, equipment etc. A couple of female donkeys came in sight from the opposite direction. All of our 8 went quite mad. It was complete chaos. Loads were virtually tipped off and the honking was unbelievable. It took us a good half-hour to restore control, re-secure their loads and get under way again. How we laughed.*

*I wouldn't trust him further than I could throw him. I have seldom seen such an evil bloated face. Who am I talking about? A visiting sheikh who has just left the camp! I would have loved to have seen your reaction to him. Even more expressive – probably! In Rostaq these sheikhs continually visit the camp – more often than not on the scrounge. What makes me smile is the way they lead up to their request saying all manner of good things (quite untrue) about the Army, probably whispering a piece of information (at least a week old) in confidence to you – and then – only then – asking for two gallons of petrol for their Land Rover. This is just what has happened.*

*This one had a particularly nasty glint in his eye. Unfortunately it is part of the Army's policy to be polite to these scroungers or I should be infinitely less tolerant. He even asked for ice in his drink – obviously having been treated to some here before. I saw his evil eye alight on the fridge (which does not work in this heat) and blatantly ask that his orange squash be filled with ice. I believe this was his only reason for coming over to the mess instead of talking to the Local Officer (Omani) in his tent. Please do not think this is bitter talk – it is unquestionably true.*

*John is away on patrol and I am therefore more busy than usual. It is wretchedly hot today.*

## Philosophic and other observations

*One of the things which I am grateful for over coming out here is the time available for thinking. By normal western standards there is relatively little to do during the hot season – no mad rushes hither and thither, one eye on the clock etc. The relative solitude helps you to learn to live with yourself.*

*John is away in Bait-al-Falaj this weekend so I am holding the fort here. Today is Jumma (Friday) so it is a holiday.*

*I see General Lord Freyburg recently died. What an unbelievably brave man he was. He ranks with Carton de Wyart as far as decorations and wounds are concerned.*

*I also see we won the test match – great news. 'Tis too hot to ramble on. I am retiring to my lilo in the falaj.*

*John has since returned and is not well. I am not much good at symptoms – but it looks a little like jaundice to me. Let's hope it is only a mild go of heat exhaustion.*

*July 24th 1963*

*It is much cooler – 98° today. We even had some rain yesterday. John is now under observation at Bait-al-Falaj where they cannot make up their minds if he has a slight go of jaundice or merely heat exhaustion. I run the Company and am thoroughly enjoying more responsibility.*

*A recent joke amused me. Christine Keeler's newspaper order: 1 Daily Mail – at least I Observer – 2 Mirrors and as many Times as possible!*

## Rostaq Officers' Mess

*July 26th 1963*

*John does not have jaundice and is returning here in 2 or 3 days' time. They do not seem to be able to diagnose him – and I gather he is still not quite himself. I am rather worried about him especially as I am at present due to leave Rostaq in about 3 weeks' time. If he is then here he will be on his own for this is a peak leave period. And one officer here in the hot season needs to be fit and strong to cope with everything. Still, we shall see.*

*I am quite busy at the moment. Unfortunately the clerk (Baluch) is on leave so I have to do my own typing.*

*The Sultan has coughed up some money which has been spent on producing some furniture. This arrived a little while ago and I have had a certain amount of enjoyment in putting what we have to good advantage. I think you would approve.*

Rostaq Officers' Mess was a grandiose description for a simple mud- and stone-walled building with a barusti roof. Most of the internal space was taken up by the company office with desks, chairs and filing cabinets. There was just enough open space to 'march in' escorted soldiers on disciplinary offences when conducting Company Commander's orders.

At the falaj end of the building there was a small verandah with relaxed seating for three or four people, a low table, a bookcase and a paraffin fridge. As there was no electricity evenings were lit by Tilly lamps (52).

At the other end of the building, but under an open-sided barusti extension, was the cook's galley manned by a pair of Goanese cooks. Although these cooks did their level best to keep the galley area clean it was a beacon to local rats. When chased from the galley area rats would climb up and onto the beams of the Company Office. Many was the time that John and I took pot shots at rats scampering along the beams with our 9 mm pistol. Small wonder that most British officers contracted jaundice after a Rostaq posting.

103

Sleeping-accommodation was tented, extremely basic and of course oven-like between 8 am and 6 pm throughout the hot season.

John describes our normal diet in those days:

'For those camps which had air conditioning, European food could be bought from the cold-store in Bait-al-Falaj and flown to the company on the routine weekly flight. However, during the hot season at Rostaq, where there was no air conditioning, we soon discovered that European-style food was less appetising than soldiers' rations. Consequently our diet was usually:

At Reveille: 'The working day started at 5 am and finished at 10 am, when it was too hot to continue. At Reveille, our orderly brought us tea and piratha. The tea tended to be very strong and the piratha like a greasy chapatti.

Breakfast: 'A dry chapatti and dhall. The dhall, which was made from lentils and fried onions, was wrapped within the chapatti. Fresh lime juice squeezed over the dhall made this a delicious warm breakfast.

Evening Meal: 'We had fresh fish four days a week and fresh goat on the other three days, both eaten with rice. The fish was bought from fishermen on the Batinah coast, an hour's drive away. For the goats, we kept a supply of Maria Theresa dollars locked up in an ammunition box in the Company office.

'On goat days a local goat owner would arrive with three or four goats, of varying misery, for a bargaining session at which a colour sergeant would assist. Once the luckless goats had been purchased they were led away for almost instantaneous execution according to Muslim custom. I never really watched the throat slitting being rather squeamish. The goat was cut up and put in a pot to stew with various spices for several hours and in due course eaten with rice. It was always tender and delicious.

Other Supplements: 'Apart from local hospitality, this included the best dates in the world, mangoes, oranges (usually sour) and hulwa (from the suq). On occasion we enjoyed peaches, figs and fresh vegetables supplied from the Jebel.'

*July 26th 1963 (continued)*

*Other than the odd bit of inside information requiring investigation, the operational scene remains relatively quiet. One of the hard-core of rebel mine-layers was arrested in the Ibri area the other day, so the list dwindles still further. Most of the rebels are making concerted efforts to get their wives out of Muscat at the moment, so it really does*

**38** Some cultivation at the outskirts of Ibri. *By kind permission of J. R. Darbyshire.*

**39** Donkey, foal and handler. *By kind permission of J. R. Darbyshire.*

**40** The covered suq at Ibri. *By kind pemission of A. J. M. Lush.*

**41** Looking down on an Ibri house and garden. *By kind permission of J. R. Darbyshire.*

**42** A narrow Ibri street with a boy aloft. *By kind permission of J. R. Darbyshire.*

**43** His Highness's Ship Nasr al Bahr on coastal patrol 1972. *By kind permission of C. R. Butt.*

**44** Dubby at Ibri mess.

**45** Luncheon, courtesy of the Duru (a Bedouin tribe from the Fahud region) at Ghaibah in 1963. Left to right; Major Malcolm Dennison, Captain John Cook and Desert Intelligence Officer, Michael ffolliot-Foster. *By kind permission of A. J. M. Lush.*

**46** Well scene between Sunainah and Hafeet.

**47** Inquisitive children at Hail, Wadi al Ayn.

**48** Two Omani shepherds on the Jebel Kaur spinning sheep wool on spindles. *By kind permission of J. R. Darbyshire.*

**49** Rostaq village from the wadi bed. *By kind permission of J. R. Darbyshire.*

**50** Remarkable scenery in the Rostaq area. *By kind permission of J. R. Darbyshire.*

**51** Curry up. *By kind permission of J. R. Darbyshire.*

**52** Falaj view of Rostaq Officers' Mess.

**53** Falaj syphon system crossing the wadi at Izki, 1963. *By kind permission of A. J. M. Lush.*

**54** View down from Saiq.

**55** The donkey lines, Rostaq.
*By kind permission of*
*J. R. Darbyshire.*

**56** The seven-hour climb to Saiq with donkeys. *By kind permission of J. R. Darbyshire.*

**57** Threading a three-tonner 'through the eye of a needle'.
*By kind permission of J. R. Darbyshire.*

**58** Officer Commanding B Company, The Northern Frontier Regiment, Major Christopher Ballenden, at Saiq with a saluki. *By kind permission of J. R. Darbyshire.*

**59** Saiq fort. *By kind permission of C. G. Ballenden.*

**60** The Commanding Officer, The Northern Frontier Regiment, Lieutenant-Colonel Dougie Dalglish, MC, at the wheel of 'the Beast'. *By kind permission of J. R. Darbyshire.*

**61** Jebel Puentry. *By kind permission of C. G. Ballenden.*

**62** Patrol on Jebel Heel. *By kind permission of C. G. Ballenden.*

**63** Terracing on Jebel Poundjry. *By kind permission of C. G. Ballenden.*

**64** Mortar cadre 'bedding in'. *By kind permission of J. R. Darbyshire.*

**65** Hazaam fort.

**66** Ghalla village.

**67** John Darbyshire, Officer Commanding B Company, The Muscat Regiment, with our bag.

**68** The author (left) as Training Officer with Major Jim Sheridan, who commanded the SAF Training Centre. *By kind permission of J. R. Darbyshire.*

**69** Volleyball at Izki.

**70** A typical beach scene on the Batinah coast. *By kind permission of J. R. Darbyshire.*

*sound to be a lost cause. I wonder where they will go from here – perhaps to Iraq to train for another better equipped coup?*

## John suffers from heat exhaustion

*July 31st 1963*

*John is back. It was heat exhaustion. He is much better. I am not sorry to see him back for life here in time would have proved a strain. I go up to Saiq this weekend for 2 days' leave. Saiq is very high and therefore cooler. I do feel like a bit of a rest I must admit. Chris Ballenden (also KSLI) commands an NFR Baluch Company there (58). It looks like being a bit of a party. I gather I am going to play poker. I shall lose hopelessly – always do at cards (but lucky in love).*

Recently (July 2000) I asked John whether he could recall this bout of heat exhaustion and perhaps shed some light on why it may have happened. His account follows:

'In July 1963 I took a patrol from Rostaq up the Jebel to Saiq. It was the usual affair of a platoon of 15 to 20 soldiers plus donkeys. We went by truck to Awabi and then walked up the Wadi Fara to the track up the Jebel Akhdar. I remember an enormous mango tree at the top of the wadi.

'It was the hottest time of the year and the climb was continuous and steep and took about 5 hours to the top from where it was another 2 hours to Saiq – obviously it got cooler as we ascended. We were carrying rifles (9 lbs) and full webbing packs (56).

'I think we only spent one (or two) nights in Saiq before returning. In many ways descending jebel tracks is more exhausting than climbing as one's thighs object strongly. Anyway, two day's marches with only a short break were too much for my constitution and shortly after returning to Rostaq my body lost control of my temperature which soared, and I began shivering and feeling so awful we felt it necessary to contact HQ SAF. As a result, a Beaver (light aircraft) was sent to collect me and I was put in a spare air-conditioned bedroom (at Bait al Falaj) for 4 days which got my temperature under control and enabled me to return to Rostaq.'

Although we were all extremely fit at the time there was a tendency, which my letters to Charmian seem to bear out, to test our stamina and fitness to the limits. While this is typical of young people of any generation, the exceptionally high temperatures experienced during the hot season in Rostaq made it essential to take sufficient rest time after long climbs up or down to allow the body temperature and energy reservoir to readjust and recuperate. Many of us learnt this lesson the hard way.

*July 31st 1963 (continued)*

*Scorpions are a bit of a worry at the moment. Five have been killed in the camp during the last 2 days – shook one out of my chukka boot yesterday morning. We have anti-scorpion serum but it is none the less very unpleasant. The soldiers walk around barefoot most of the time so we are expecting the worst.*

*I have spoken to the CO during John's absence and it seems that I shall be running the 3 inch mortar cadre here instead of at Bid Bid. This will mean I shall be here in Rostaq until mid-September to help John out. This is a much better solution.*

## A welcome break at Saiq

*August 3rd 1963 (at Saiq)*

*I don't suppose that this letter has more than a 50/50 chance of being completed here – for this is quite a wild and thoroughly enjoyable weekend.*

*It is now 12.30 – almost time for lunch and all except Alistair Cummings and myself are sleeping off a 5.30 am poker session. I am writing this to the intermittent snores of Chris Ballenden whose 'bait' (room) I am sharing.*

*I think if I had not had this welcome two and a half day break here I might well have followed in John's footsteps and would have had a 'go' of heat exhaustion.*

*Saiq is a wonderful station – right on the top of the Jebel Akhdar (Green Mountain) – the site of the camp being somewhere between 5,000 and 6,000 ft. The climate here is wonderfully invigorating – very many degrees cooler and less humid than Rostaq. One even feels cold mornings and evenings – a novel experience at this time of year. The many views are quite wonderful and the sunsets are lovely (54, 61 – 63).*

*August 3rd 1963 (continued)*

*The camp overlooks the village of Saiq which is a small well-gardened and cultivated village – amazingly green, but surprisingly flat and unterraced for a mountain village. A few houses and one fort show obvious signs of the bombing which took place during our action against the rebels in 1957. The people seem very friendly and are wonderfully fit-looking in comparison with those in Rostaq where trachoma is rife.*

*The camp is essentially unmilitary looking and is well spread. The fort which overlooks the camp is occupied by many of the Baluch soldiers. It is straight out of P C Wren and I long for a coloured photograph of the Sultan's Red Flag being lowered at 'Retreat' on the mast high on the main tower. A typical sunset behind (59).*

*There is a small mess which is very pleasant but really ought to face a different way. A generator plant exists so electric light and air conditioning are on the menu though I do not really see the need for air conditioning.*

*Wild donkeys roam around at night and mosquitoes can be unpleasant at times especially in the wadis. Fruit – particularly peaches, grapes, figs and dates seem to be in mouth-watering abundance. The peaches are very small and green to look at, but are quite delicious. Corn-on-the-cob is another Saiq boast.*

*I left Rostaq by LR at 6.00 on Thursday evening arriving at Bait-al-Falaj by 9.00 am in time for breakfast. After a rapid visit to Muttrah suq to buy some things for the canteen I flew to Saiq in a Beaver calling at Nizwa en route. I had a quick glimpse of Colin McLean there. We arrived here at Saiq at about midday, not before I had felt dreadfully air sick, something which I never feel in light aircraft so put it down to being slightly under the weather.*

*Within an hour I was beginning to feel more invigorated with life than I have for months, the cooler climate having a deliciously refreshing effect. However, I retired to bed and slept solidly for 3 hours. In the evening after a threatening of poker, we mixed a powerful martini and got quietly fuddled!*

*This weekend party consists of 7 of us. Chris Ballenden and his 2 I/C Donald Clarke, Alistair Cummings, Anthony Witheridge from the 15th/19th (a recent addition to the Northern Frontier Regiment) two very pleasant SOAF pilots and myself – the only member of The Muscat Regiment.*

*After a thoroughly idle lie in on Friday (Jumma) morning we all went to a coffee party in Saiq given by the Sheikh. The usual thing, cross-legged contortions, sitting on the carpet eating figs, peaches and dates from a central tray – followed by the inevitable coffee, which you see being ground beforehand. I never lose my taste for these delightful forms of hospitality – save when the flies are really bad.*

*August 4th (on return to Rostaq)*

*As predicted earlier I was unable to finish! I am now back at Rostaq feeling much better for the break.*

*To continue from where I left off at Saiq! After lunch on Friday an idle couple of hours reading and writing was followed by an outing in the 'Beast'. This is an old Land Rover with no bodywork except for two seats (60).*

Because Saiq was inaccessible by road, this Land Rover was shed of all inessentials, dismantled and cut into sections at Bait-al-Falaj. It was flown by Beaver to Saiq where it was welded together and reassembled. It was used for conveying stores from Saiq airstrip to the camp. No other wheeled transport existed in Saiq area at the time.

*August 4th 1963 (continued)*

*The exhaust is thrown out from the engine sideways – no silencer. She is the most extraordinary four-wheeled machine I have ever seen. The petrol tank consists of a 1 gallon can tied by rope to where the windscreen would be. They have fashioned a small circuit, the record lap time being 1 min 28 seconds. We each had a real go at breaking the record, the best time being 1 min 29 seconds (mine was 1 min 32 seconds). The noise and dust were unbelievable. We all behaved like small boys and thoroughly enjoyed ourselves.*

*Friday evening was clearly going to be a poker session. As you know, I do not like cards particularly – probably because I have not played often and am quite hopeless. However, knowing Christopher Ballenden of old, I knew he would insist on making up a five. So before I left Rostaq, John gave me 5 minutes instruction on the art of poker. Luckily 5 of the 7 of us were keen to play leaving Alistair and myself free. However, I did watch and picked up the game so that when Donald Clarke had to leave to visit the loo I was able to take over – and in the space of two hands I won 12 shillings. Fortunately he then returned, so I retired to rest on my first and probably last poker winnings. The session went on to 5.30 am, whereas I slunk off to bed at 2.00 am, as did Alistair.*

*Yesterday you know about – all that intense activity in the morning! After lunch 4 of us walked for an hour to the most lovely mountain pool and had a swim. The pool must be 15 ft deep, is surrounded by rock faces of 100 ft on all sides and boasts very green vegetation on either side of the falaj which fills it. A very romantic spot indeed.*

*This morning 'Butlins' was due to break up and visitors to return from whence they came. The aircraft took off at 6.30 am only to return 10 minutes later because there was a sea of thick cloud covering the whole of the country beneath the jebel. We waited 2 hours, during which time we sent various signals to our respective destinations asking for reports on the cloud situation. After the cloud thinned we flew to Bait-al-Falaj. I then drove by Land Rover back here arriving early afternoon.*

*John had left on patrol so things are back to normal again.*

### Running a mortar cadre in Rostaq and news of a mutiny at Saiq

*August 13th 1963*

*John is away in Bahrein on a course. Things are more mad than usual just now. Much to say but no time to write.*

*August 14th 1963*

*The two parcels arrived safely, thank you. The Wilkinson's blades are a blessing and should last me many years.*

*August 16th 1963*

*I told you that John has left for Bahrein for 10 days so I am on my own here. Without making a tall story, this naturally means more work especially as the 3 inch mortar cadre which I am running in 2 days time, is being run here, so another 30 assorted Omanis are descending on Rostaq. Running this cadre is going to be a considerable challenge for I have to teach what is recognised in English as being something of a test to start with, in Arabic and Urdu. I can see myself getting into hopeless knots of self-expression and I daresay going mad with impatience. However I shall attempt to take everything very slowly indeed – and have prepared a number of gimmicks which will appeal to their minds – and help them to learn. Another problem is the quickness of the Omani versus the painstakingly slow Baluch.*

*Patrol-wise we have been unable to arrest these two suspected murderers I told you of. Being alone I am forced to remain in Camp. A patrol has been out, but failed to find the two men mainly as Baluch, having little idea of Arabic, have difficulty in questioning the locals. When not supervised they tend to be rather inexpert despite being fit and strong.*

*Another reason has been that one of the NFR companies – the Baluch Company in Saiq – has had a mutiny of a bloodless nature. A couple of soldiers struck a Baluch colour sergeant who reported them to Christopher Ballenden, the Company Commander. Christopher punished the soldiers but the whole company came out in sympathy for the two punished men.*

*The company marched down the jebel with its arms and ammunition and refused to return to Camp. They complained of overwork. Mutinies of this nature do occasionally occur in forces like these – more often than not from a religious problem.*

*As you can see, you have to be very careful concerning soldier management – far more so than in a British battalion, where disciplinary rules and procedures are well understood and respected. The Baluch seem worse than the Omani in this way for being in what to them is a foreign country, they stick together through any difficulty and continually do things 'in sympathy'. This can be very stupid at times. The Omani by nature is more of an individualist. Omanis do not gang together in the way the Baluch do – they are quicker-witted, less easily led and less cause-conscious. For the most part the Omani has had to learn to survive as an individual so that the well being of himself and his immediate family is paramount.*

*I have not heard whether the company has "marched up to the top of the hill again"[19] (per the Grand Old Duke of York). But this has been a serious worry for the force requiring careful attention to avoid other Baluch companies coming out in sympathy. You can understand why I have refrained from going out on patrol. I think the crisis is now over. The Baluch are very loyal to their British officers – the Omanis rather less so. This Baluch mutiny was against their own NCOs and not against us. It will be interesting to hear in due course how the Force decides to deal with the mutineers.*

One initiative taken at the time to reduce the likelihood of this mutiny spreading to other Baluch companies was for each commanding officer to address the troops in every company under command. John Darbyshire, as Company Commander, recalls receiving a message from the CO (Clive Chettle) saying that he was coming to address 'A' Company.

'At his arrival the whole company was formed up for the CO's address. I cannot remember what he said but it was to do with his being able to rely on their loyalty. When he had finished the soldiers gave him a spontaneous cheer (unrehearsed!), thus allaying any possible anxiety he may have had.'

*August 18th 1963*

*The mortar cadre is under way. Somebody has had compassion on me and I am getting an interpreter to help with my language problems! He arrives tomorrow.*

*August 23rd 1963 (at Bait-al-Falaj)*

*Why am I here? On his return from Bahrein John insisted that I should have 2 days' leave. I arrived last night and certainly revelled in the air conditioning to catch up with some sleep. This morning I spent swimming in the sea and lying on the beach.*

*August 26th 1963*

*Rostaq is at last getting cooler which is welcome. After that break in Bait-al-Falaj I am feeling really well again. My mortar cadre continues – this morning I managed to get myself into difficulties trying to explain angles, degrees etc. I still don't know who really looked the most worried – the Omanis, the Baluch or the interpreter!*

Some thirty-six years later I recall this mortar course as being the most difficult period of instruction in my life – in or outside the services. I had been wonderfully trained at the Support Weapons Wing at Netheravon and was keen to convey these mortar line and fire control skills simultaneously in Arabic and

Baluchi. Most of this month's tuition took place in the early mornings and evenings under one of the few large trees in temperatures in excess of 100°.

To this day I have absolutely no idea how successful I was but I do recall much humour and enthusiasm. (A little knowledge can be a very dangerous thing!) However, you have to start somewhere and I believe that this was the first mortar course in the Sultan's Armed Forces. Perhaps it was not a disaster after all because my next appointment – somewhat to my dismay – was to be SAF Training Officer (64).

## Saying goodbye to A Company

*August 30th 1963*

*It is still hot at midday but the mornings and evenings are getting cooler. John and I have been truly wearied by this summer in Rostaq but it is a marvellous feeling to think that it is all but over.*

*I finish this mortar cadre in a fortnight's time after which I suspect that I shall go to the Training Centre. But considerable strings are being pulled to keep me in The Muscat Regiment, while the Commander of the whole Force wants me to become Training Officer. Contrary to what many people seem to believe I suspect this is what will happen.*

*It seems unlikely that I shall be allowed to serve on with John in A Company, for it is not the policy to leave 2 officers from the same parent regiment in the same company for overlong. In principle I agree for you come out here to gain new experiences. I believe they are terrified we shall teach the Baluch Light Infantry drill!*

*September 1st 1963*

*After dinner by Tilly lamp – and after 3 strong whiskies! I suspect this will soon be obvious so I will keep it short. John is off to Bahrein on his promotion exam to Major. What better postman?*

*I report to the Training Centre on September 19th – so that saga is finally settled thank goodness.*

*No other news except that much to the amusement of all concerned I was stung by a hornet when in the falaj yesterday. No effect to start with – but then I had an hour's worth of giddiness, swollen face and chronic itching. Little sympathy I can assure you. All well now.*

While I made light of this in my letter to Charmian at the time I recall the incident being a little alarming. When stung and beginning to itch, John gave me a glass of brandy which I have since discovered would have made matters much worse. Having been stung on the neck, my whole face puffed up so much that my eyelids closed and I could not see. Fortunately I refused further alcoholic stimulants and after several hours the swelling gradually subsided.

Subsequently we discovered that there was a hornets' nest on the side wall of the underground section of the falaj several yards downstream from where we moored our lilo to cool off at midday. Using the longest pole available we attached a struck thunderflash, which blew the nest off the wall and its senseless inhabitants disappeared downstream.

*September 3rd 1963*

*The coolness of the evenings now is wonderfully refreshing and some lovely sunsets make Rostaq the romantic place it can be save for 3 months of the year. It is peaceful sitting out of an evening looking at the reddish glow behind the jebel and listening to the frog chorus from the falaj not 15 yards away. I shall now be sorry to leave!*

*September 6th 1963*

*John returns from Bahrein in 2 days time. All eyes are now on the forthcoming administrative inspection while my mortar cadre finishes on September 12th. I shall then have 5 days to do all I can for John before I leave for the Training Centre on September 17th.*

*Having banished the junior leader subaltern to Bait-al-Falaj on leave and being alone I sat outside this evening listening to some lovely music and looking out across the jebel not far away. It was amazingly cool, so much so that I felt I ought to have worn a shirt. You have no idea how pleasant it is to feel cool again. As the heat haze is less I might even get brown by the time I see you in December.*

*September 8th 1963*

*Things are going 'hammer and tongs' with all kinds of inspections due when the inspection team arrives. With John being delayed I am pretty busy with the cadre and preparations for the inspections. Worst of all, every vehicle is being tarted up and none go anywhere so that our mail line is plugged this week.* [As Rostaq was only three hours' drive from headquarters in Bait-al-Falaj there was no need for an airstrip for resupply. Hence no mail.]

*September 12th 1963*

*John is now back so I can now hand over various things to him. As the cadre has finished perhaps I may be able to get a couple of days to relax before I leave. He passed his exam.*

*We have an inspection today – the first of many. This force is trying too hard to emulate the British Army. Paperwork is growing.*

*September 14th 1963*

*Two nights ago the whole Company had one of their dancing evenings. The Baluch love dancing and do so given any excuse, my imminent departure being a heaven-sent opportunity.*

*First of all we were invited along to the sergeants' mess for a curry supper. This was, as usual, excellent, but the amount of food you are expected to eat is phenomenal. We sat at tables eating from plates, using spoons and forks. After dinner the dancing group approached and sat itself down in a circle a few yards away. They then started hitting empty jerry cans with the palms of their hands, working up a catchy rhythm. One sings, while the others act as chorus, mostly repeating the singer.*

*Then the chief dancer bounds on to the scene stripped to the waist and dances around adopting pornographic attitudes. He has tremendous energy and he dances long after the sweat is pouring off him. But his attitudes and postures tend to be repetitive and what had promised to be exciting at the outset, due to lack of progression, becomes rather comical. However, I would not have missed it for the world – especially as the chief dancer seemed to "serenade" me with his suggestive poses (a compliment, so I was told) until I had to slip him 5 rupees in the hope that he might leave me alone! Quite fatal – and very short sighted of me for he then proceeded to "serenade" me all the more violently. Finally, I had to hold a lit cigar to dissuade him from landing in my lap!*

## A visit to a fort in Hazaam

*September 15th 1963*

*Yesterday was very interesting. John and I visited a very old fort in Hazaam. The sheikh of this village is continually scrounging petrol from the Army so we decided that it was high time he gave us some hospitality. We suggested he should show us around his showpiece fort. He then invited us to lunch.*

*Unfortunately, as all vehicles have been tarted up for inspection, we could hardly take a shining LR for such a joy ride the day before inspection. During the recent period of restricted vehicle movement we have been using the DIO's LR, which is not an Army vehicle, during his absence on leave. However this broke down on the "fish-run" to the Batinah so John and I crammed ourselves on to an Omani taxi LR, which was really rather fun.*

*We arrived at Hazaam Fort two hours late for lunch so did not get a goat killed but instead had relays of coffee, fruit and dates which were delicious. The Sheikh produced a table for us in a vain hope to impress, but suddenly, forgetting its existence, got up quickly and knocked it and its contents flying.*

*The fort is huge – at least 200 years old and covered with ancient cannon. It is literally falling down for no attempt has been made to repair it. It has the most complicated system of passageways which are low and arched. It was obvious that conducted tours were unusual for we managed to lose our way often. As everything was pitch black, this had its moments. There were bats everywhere – literally thousands of them. There was a dear old boy in a pink dish-dasha who took a liking to us and led us everywhere long after the Sheikh had clearly had enough. He went off in a huff for he really is a rather unpleasant man. John and I got some photographs but I stupidly ran out of film (65).*

John and I had no idea at the time who had built Hazaam Fort but according to Peter Ochs's *Maverick Guide to Oman* it was built by Imam Sultan bin Saif in 1711. Its design structure and defensive characteristics were regarded so highly that it became a model for many other forts and castles throughout Muscat and Oman. Not only did it contain living-quarters and stores for prolonged occupation but a falaj runs through it providing a constant water supply. It also contained three dungeons and two escape tunnels, one of which was believed to lead to Rostaq some twenty miles away.

By the early 1960s the majority of these forts had fallen into disrepair as well as being hazardous and in need of wholesale refurbishment. Sultan Said had set aside some meagre funds for this purpose but this was only a drop in the ocean. Nothing more was affordable at the time. The reader should remember that the discovery of oil was not until 1964 and it would be several years after then before oil revenues would enable Sultan Qaboos to embark on a series of five-year infrastructure plans.

*September 15th 1963*

*The broken down DIO's LR eventually arrived at Hazaam to pick us up having been partially repaired. I drove it back to Rostaq which required a sense of anticipation for the steering had 2 ft of play.*

*It was in all a welcome day out after being confined to camp for a hot month during the cadre.*

## Retrospective on Rostaq

When reading through these transcribed letters thirty-six years later I do wonder on reflection, as the reader may, whether I was exaggerating the heat and humidity of that hot season in Rostaq. Was I being a wimp? It was therefore reassuring to read the following paragraph in Peter Ochs's *Maverick Guide to Oman*:

> 'In Oman, some of the highest temperatures on earth have been recorded (over 50° C or 123° F). It is hard to imagine how some of the interior tribes survive in the oppressive heat, but survive they do.'

Rostaq is where these highest temperatures have been recorded. Small wonder that John and I and others like us who emanated from a temperate climate, found those one hundred hot days such a trial. Unlike nowadays, our only escapes were short breaks to Bait-al-Falaj and Saiq.

## A proposal for early release

Just as I was leaving Rostaq en route for the training centre at Ghalla there was some pressure from my regiment in England to complete my secondment in December, some seven months early. The reason for this request was that I had been told that on my return from Muscat and Oman I was to take over as Adjutant, 1st Battalion King's Shropshire Light Infantry, then stationed in Plymouth. David Pank, who was adjutant at the time, would have been an abnormally long period in post if I served my full secondment.

While naturally delighted that I had been selected to become adjutant, the next extract from my letter to Charmian shows that I was not convinced that it was right to cut short my secondment. This was a difficult stance to take bearing in mind that I could forfeit a key appointment (which both my father and uncle had held) and that come December I would have not seen Charmian for fourteen months.

*September 17th 1963 (passing through Bid Bid)*

*To talk over again an early release from here next year: if I finished here in December, I would be delighted from one point of view but I hate not completing something which I voluntarily started, however difficult it may be. The fact that I am now going to the Training Centre weakens my resolve considerably but I suspect that the final decision will be taken by the Force Commander. Time will tell.*

As things turned out the request for my early release was refused. Fortunately for me David Pank[20] agreed to remain as Adjutant until my secondment finished, so I, like a number of my contemporaries, returned from Muscat and Oman in July 1964 to become adjutant of my parent regiment.

# Chapter Eight

# Training Recruits
# on the Batinah Coast

## Sultan's Armed Forces Training Centre,
## Ghalla, September to December 1963

Ghalla – An enforced rest at Bait-al-Falaj – The political situation –
Enforced rest continues – More news of the mutiny at Saiq – Life in the
Training Centre – Shooting sand grouse at Khor Dthyan –
A taxi crash – Omani recruits – President Kennedy is assassinated –
Brigadier Leask's visit – A weekend at lzki

# Ghalla

September 20th 1963 (SAF Training Centre)

*I am now ensconced here and am enjoying having a room to myself, air-conditioning and an easily available hot shower. To be able to read in bed (by electric light) is another luxury which I missed in Rostaq. All in all I think you would find me more civilised.*

*I have only been here 24 hours now so cannot tell you a great deal yet. Ghalla is a small village about half an hour's drive up the coast north of Muscat port. The Training Centre camp is half a mile away from the village on a flat open plain 15 minutes' drive from the sea. The camp is not unlike Ibri but more spread. White walled buildings with aluminium roofs comprise the barrack rooms and mess building.*

*A few miles inland the jebel rears up out of the sand making a relieving background – for without the jebel this part would be characterless. Around the camp there is sand – plenty of it – though occasional tufts of sparse grass and scrub dispel any suggestion of real desert.*

*The village of Ghalla looks very small though the green of the palm trees provides a marvellous contrast to the reddish jebel behind (66).*

*On our 15-minute drive to the sea is another village called Azaiba which is virtually on the coast. This is larger than Ghalla but consists of a few mud buildings – most of the houses being rigged from barusti. I am told – though I have not seen it yet – that there is a small Shell Oil community just outside the village. Mostly Dutchmen I expect, but I haven't a clue whether they are drilling there or if it is a staging point. I gather they have one film a week so I shall not be quite so wild, woolly and out-of-touch when I return home in December.*

*The Training Centre is reliant to a large degree on junior leader sergeants – on detachment from battalions in Kenya and Aden – to train the recruits here. Obviously they don't speak Arabic or Baluchi, so considerable difficulties arise in instruction. This means that most of the instruction consists of demonstration and imitation plus considerable inventiveness and ingenuity on both sides. Because the Sultan's Army is still relatively new and untrained, the need for the right calibre sergeants as instructors is acute. Relatively few local sergeants are sufficiently experienced or can be released from the Muscat and Northern Frontier Regiments to train their countrymen.*

*Those currently on the strength of the Training Centre are 1 subaltern and 2 sergeants from the Staffordshire Regiment, 1 sergeant from the King's Own Scottish Borderers, my boss, Major Jim Sheridan (now a contract officer, but formerly SAS), who commands the*

*Training Centre and myself (Training Officer) (68). There is one mess for the six of us.* [An essentially practical but unusual arrangement in those days.]

## An enforced rest at Bait-al-Falaj

*September 25th 1963 (Bait-al-Falaj)*

*Perhaps, like my gramophone, I rather packed up a few days ago. I suppose it must have been reaction after a Rostaq summer – and being faced with a fair amount to put right at Ghalla.*

*Anyway I am here for a week or 10 days of enforced rest which I am enjoying immensely. I sleep and sleep. I am also undergoing a course of penicillin injections, so that my backside is like a pin-cushion.*

*Yesterday I finished a book called 'Orde Wingate' by Christopher Sykes. He was the most amazing man imaginable – certainly the most controversial and legendary of the last war. Christopher Sykes has written a wonderful book and has surely got closer to giving an unbiased character study of Wingate than any other man. Orde Wingate, a sort of genius, possessed the magnetism of 'personality leadership' and a ferocious temper. His introspective nature seemed to bar the door to love and affection. A sense of spiritual endowment possessed him for his lifetime – his fear being that the Army and politicians might suppress its expression. He must have been the most fascinating yet frightening man to meet. He must certainly have been a little mad too.*

*I am delighted that being under the weather has given me this opportunity to read this book for my knowledge of the Chindits, Burma and Palestine was previously very limited. However it is the study of the man which really absorbs me.*

## The political situation

*September 26th 1963*

*I should like to tell you a little about the political situation here as it is really quite interesting.*

*As you know, rebel activity has been practically nil during the summer inside the country. The occasional courier has managed to get his way into the country, and various rebel wives have been collected and taken out of the country. Does this mean that the rebel cause is now a completely lost one – and that Talib is now not interested? I believe the answer to be no although I do not believe that the rebels in exile are anywhere near ready to mount any kind of revolution against the Sultan – nor will be for some time.*

*But time does not matter for these people – as long as they get their way in the end. They know that the people in Muscat are generally content with the peaceful life they*

**71** Training Centre Shooting Team, 1964.

**72** Training Centre awarded Winner's Cup at the annual rifle meeting in 1964.

**73** An Omani squad.

**74** The author, as Training Officer, en route to a passing-out parade at the Training Centre, Ghalla.

**75** Sergeant Naseeb bin Hamad (left) and family. He was to become the first Omani Commander of the Sultan of Oman's Land Forces (CSOLF) twenty years later in 1982.

**76** Corporal Ali Saif going on leave.

**77** Camel convoy at Seeb.

**78** Women at Seeb well.

**79** An Omani girl with a necklace of Maria Theresa dollars. *Reproduced from* Oman 1972 *by kind permission of the Ministry of Information, Sultanate of Oman.*

**80** A sheikh in typical Omani dress.

**81** Charmian on board MTB 219, Cheyne Walk, Chelsea, soon after our engagement.

**82** Our wedding in 1965. The author and Charmian with their best man, John Darbyshire, bridesmaids and pages (left to right) Julian Birley, Anna Birley, Elizabeth Connyngham-Greene, Rachel Carson and Richard Connyngham-Greene.

**83** Bedouin boy, Wahiba Sands. This boy belonged to the Al Wahiba, a Bedouin tribe who elected to remain in their coastal desert rather than settle in a town. *Source: Marianonietta, Peru.*

**84** Bedouin succumb to Westernisation. *Source: Robert Azzi, Woodfin Camp, New York.*

**85** Major Malcolm Dennison chats with some young recruits he has brought in from the villages.
*By kind permission of C. A. S. Hinton.*

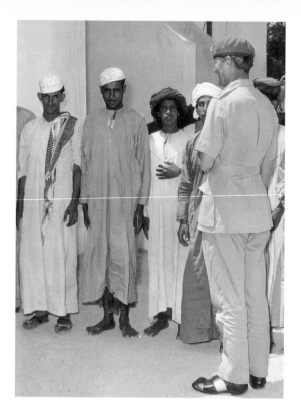

**86** His Majesty Sultan Qaboos bin Said who succeeded his father on July 23rd 1970.
*Reproduced from* Oman 1972 *by kind permission of the Ministry of Information, Sultanate of Oman.*

*now lead. Always there will be grouses – mainly over the rights to dig wells – but the people are glad of a rest after 4 years of non-stop rebel fighting. Many innocent people were killed in the bombing of the jebel villages – and the enforced military law which has meant continual searching of villages, hostage taking and so on has made everyone war-weary. The people do not want another rebellion with its resulting bloodshed. They want to be left alone by the Army and to lead a peaceful existence improving the fertility of their gardens, strengthening and building their houses and improving their water supply by digging new wells and constructing new aflaj. There may be grouses over education (Sultan's policy) but none of their grievances merit another rebellion at the moment.*

*Talib and his followers realise this and are prepared to bide their time. It suits them that this should become a war of words now. As you know, the whole of the Arab world is against the present rule in Oman. Saudi Arabia and Radio Cairo have produced an enormous amount of propaganda on the subject – all implying a cruel dictatorship in Muscat and Oman. The most unlikely stories are given over the radio including daily situation reports as to how the 'war' is going, the use of rebel aircraft, countless rebel ambushes and British casualties. The whole thing is quite ludicrous but the Arab is extremely gullible to reports from Radio Cairo. Such propaganda has, of course, invited UN investigation (do you remember my telling you of De Ribbings' visit to Ibri?). Needless to say these UN reports bear no resemblance to what is churned out over Cairo Radio each day but unfortunately the UN reports do not get any coverage out here at all. They are taken back to New York, Stockholm and London and brought to the notice of various committees of enquiry (U Thant, of course) and probably given one column's coverage in a national newspaper. Most people have not heard of Muscat anyway.*

*But, UN report or not, the mass anti-Oman feeling is being stirred up. Nasser has his hands somewhat full in Yemen at present or he would be giving more active support still. But despite this Talib has been seen close to Nasser at various rallies making it clear that he is very interested in Oman. Also, reports say that more financial backing is now being given to the rebel cause than at any time during the war. A fair amount of troop training is going on in Iraq. Its plans for the future are anyone's guess – but here is one. Sometime in March or April is the next UN Assembly on the 'Oman Question'. By then Nasser will have stirred up sufficient feeling about the subject to demand a further investigation and report. How soon he will start threatening, if ever, seems dependent on the Yemen situation, which may keep the limelight yet a while. If he can glean any information detrimental to the Sultan, he will – and, of course the Sultan is open to criticism of some of his policies. In the end Nasser will be forced to take action, but being the brilliant man he is, he would not support any revolution until the ideal opportunity arose. This time, having had his fingers badly burnt in the Yemen, he will be unwilling to give more than financial support. But how soon he will be prepared to support a rebellion in Oman, only time will tell. In the meantime, he is clearly keen to make the exiled rebels feel that they have a cause and that they should trust in him for fulfilment.*

*The next vital attraction in the Oman is oil. There is little doubt that this part of the world is very rich indeed with oil. Kuwait has never known such wealth – but there is only a limited dome there which may dry up inside a number of years. Bahrein and Abu Dhabi are again likely to have a limited life. Like any mineral deposit its production needs to be planned so as to win the best possible market. In short, if there are two oil domes gushing oil enough for the world market, why produce a third at the same time? Oil prospecting has been going on in Muscat by Shell for a long time now. There is oil here, but the question is – is there enough of it to make a profit over the development costs?*

*Reading in between the lines – no more – there is more than enough here. The Empty Quarter is forbidden to drillers. Consequently few prospectors really know how far these oil domes stretch into the Empty Quarter. On the face of it the strata of rock is said to be much the same but uncertainty remains.*

*I realise these comments are hopelessly general for as you know this is hardly my field of expertise.*

*However, if I am right – which is quite possible – this country will be unrecognisable inside the next decade or so. The British, through aiding the Sultan, have a better claim for a share of oil rights than any others. But Nasser realises its mineral promise – and has a very watchful eye on things. Much depends on the UN which fortunately seems to be gaining in stature. The Foreign Office are certainly keen to play this as deftly as they can. America is beginning to take an unobtrusive interest too. What will happen? I wish I knew – but it is certainly going to be fascinating to watch.*

*In the meantime, the Omani people want peace and quiet and are, to all intents and purposes, apparently oblivious of the involved situation which is arising in their country. It will be a tragedy if this beautiful country is opened up to western civilisation in a compressed period of time. The people will be utterly lost and their essential charm a memory.*

*The Sultan is an astute man, but he needs to be more than this to weather the next few years.*

Seven years later in 1970 the Sultan's son Qaboos overthrew his father in a coup and succeeded him as Sultan. Sultan Qaboos, encouraged by the prospect of oil revenues, embarked on a carefully prioritised programme of five-yearly infrastructure plans designed to bring Muscat and Oman into the twentieth century. Chapter Ten describes this in more detail.

*September 26th 1963 (continued)*

*Sultan Said bin Taimur does not want his country to open up to westernisation for he sees that this will mean his end.*

*I think I have said enough! It is doubtful whether I should have said all I have for this could be read by the wrong person en route to you. However, it is only very general and the vast majority is conjecture. But please let me know if it arrives with you untampered.*

In retrospect it seems that many of my concerns in 1963 were well founded and that some of my predictions turned out to be correct. However, far from being clairvoyant at the time, I suspect that most thinking people would have conjectured a rather similar outcome. Perhaps the only surprise was that it took as long as it did.

### *Enforced rest continues*

*September 28th 1963*

*As you can see, I am still at Bait-al-Falaj resting. I am beginning to feel something of a fraud. Injections have finished. The doctor (Mohammed Qureshi) has discovered a slightly low blood count which he wants to put right before I return to Ghalla. Nothing to worry about – I did much the same in BAOR once so I must be prone to anaemia. I suspect this whole thing could have been avoided if I had been sensible enough to take vitamin pills in Rostaq. Many people do out here.*

*September 30th 1963*

*The weather is getting so very much cooler that I find myself really appreciating this country all over again. The summer was hell and I tended to forget the attractions of the country. The evenings are now quite lovely with the red glow of the setting sun. The villages and palm trees have taken on a freshness too even though we have had virtually no rain for 6 months.*

*I am now sea-swimming again in the half-mile long Turtle Bay all to myself – only the crabs for company – millions of them. I walk up and down the beach several times and they rush away in their hundreds to their little holes in the sand when they see me approaching. Or if they cannot make the holes in time they rush into the sea for all they are worth. They are quite a big variety – some even as big as a handspan. They seem to get up on their hind legs, their eyes on the end of stalks, and run so fast sideways that you need to walk very fast to catch up with them. They are mostly sand coloured, although at the end of the beach there are some rocks where the black and brown-shelled ones rule the roost. The hermit crabs are more attractive and are minute and favour setting up house in any suitable sized shell they can find. If they see you coming they take refuge well inside and refuse to be drawn out.*

*October 3rd 1963*

*Mohammed Qureshi still will not say when he is going to let me return to Ghalla but it cannot be long now. I went for a 3-hour walk yesterday – to the sea for a swim and back. I feel much more myself again and even climbed a little.*

*October 4th 1963*

*I really do feel a waster. He must let me go soon or I shall go mad. What a thoroughly bad patient I am.*

## More news of the mutiny at Saiq

*October 6th 1963*

*Do you remember the mutiny at Saiq I told you about? All the mutineers – Baluch – were shipped back to Baluchistan yesterday having been sacked from the Sultan's Army. A bold but correct step I think. Thorough explanations are being given to all other soldiers who were not involved. Let's hope all will be well now – and that these will be the firm steps required.*

Being on sick leave at the time I was not present when these thorough explanations were conveyed to all members of the Sultan's Armed Forces. While there is no doubt that such firm disciplinary action was essential to restore cohesion, pride and respect this step had far-reaching and costly repercussions. The mutineers had lost their livelihood and were returning home in disgrace. They were barred for life from re-enlisting in the prestigious Sultan's Armed Forces. Moreover the loss of nearly one hundred trained soldiers represented about 7 per cent of the infantry. The time and cost of recruiting and training soldiers to replace them were considerable. Demands on the Training Centre inevitably increased.

*October 6th 1963 (continued)*

*The send-off did have its problems as it was bound to. The mutineers refused to get on the trucks, refused to be vaccinated, demanded to go to Muscat where they would have stirred up local feeling – and goodness knows what else. The escort was quite a problem because other Baluch would have been useless and the use of Omanis could have been provocative. This meant the use of all available British – and as there are so few in Muscat, it meant flying in some paratroops from Bahrein. Anyway after some pretty awkward moments when anything might have happened, they were finally shepherded on to the launch to deliver them to the boat and then to Gwarda across the other side of the Gulf. I was not present at any of these happenings but have just heard the full account from a friend in the Northern Frontier Regiment.*

*October 10th 1963*

*Please don't worry about me. I am well. I know it. My blood count has risen by 10% and in 2 days' time, if it has risen a further 10%, I shall be back at Ghalla inside the next week. My response to treatment has been excellent – far better than the doctor anticipated. It seems that through diet deficiencies I allowed myself to get run down. Entirely my own fault – and I shan't make that mistake again.*

*October 11th 1963*

*Wanted you to know I'm all right again and am returning to Ghalla tomorrow. The doctor is very pleased with my reaction to treatment – in fact amazed. He gave me a fearful rocket for not having come to him earlier than I did. Justified, I'm afraid.*

### Life in the Training Centre

*SAFTC Ghalla, October 16th 1963*

*I am well settled in now. It is good to be doing something again. I am putting on weight and am forbidden spirits until Christmas. I have started taking exercise again which is the best sign imaginable for I feel I want to. I run along the beach for a couple of hours each day much to the amusement of the fishermen who clearly think I am mad.*

*Another weekend is here and I am on my own, the others having gone in to Bait-al-Falaj for the highlights. These consist of a film and a change of menu.*

*Life is very different from being in a company outstation. I can see already that it is going to take a considerable effort on my part to see this posting through. It is fine at present for it is new and I have to get it running the way I would like. But I cannot believe that this will take very long. Later on, come May, June and July will be the test. I shall need to get myself absorbed in something to take my mind off the humdrum repetitive nature of things at a Training Centre.*

*Now that I have been told that I have been specially selected for this job (not certain that I consider this a compliment) and that there is no chance of returning to a company I am naturally disappointed. I like Jim Sheridan, it's just that the job prevents me seeing* more of this marvellous country which I find so difficult. What a pity I could not have taken over the Arab Company in January as Colonel Clive Chettle had planned. That would have been invaluable experience.

As I am here, far from being sorry for myself, I shall give my best. Things have been allowed to slide here so that I find myself with 20 recruits on my orders this morning. This is more than has happened in the last 3 months. No, I am not a sadist, but these Omanis and Baluch do understand firmness. If they are told what is required of them and shown what will happen unless they comply they will respond.

*October 24th 1963*

I have just returned from an evening swim. It really was a lovely evening, nobody in sight – miles of sand to myself and a gorgeous glowing sunset. The sun sets in this country at about half past five – with little change throughout the year.

This beach by daylight is, I suppose, uninteresting in that it is miles and miles of sand with no break. In the distance there is a headland which seems to glint yellow in the evening sun – and about 2 miles out there is a small island which appears unexpectedly from a calm dark sea. Sometimes you can see the white sail of a dhow not far from the island – its destination most probably Muscat or Gwarda.

In the evening light the beach itself becomes beautiful and the outline of a dozen or so fishing boats, often covered by their nets, makes a dark silhouette against the outline of the jebel far inland. Seagulls – black-headed and white-headed gulls – fly low over the small waves. Sand plover scrounge where the waves lap the sand and dash around, their tiny legs moving so fast that you can hardly see them. It is wonderfully peaceful. I took my camera along, but knowing my ineptness, I doubt whether I shall have any success in photographing this beauty (70).

I have had a letter from Brian Lowe who was previously adjutant of 1 KSLI. He writes to congratulate me on being chosen as David Pank's successor next September. This means it is now out of the bag.

John Cook is back from Kashmir. I met him off the boat from Gwarda yesterday. He had a wonderful time – shot 2 bear – a red and black one. One was 6 ft 2 inches from spine base to nose – which is how you measure them. He did a lot of hill walking, driving a LR up to 14,000 ft. He stayed in a houseboat for a fortnight and caught 150 brown trout in 3 days. The biggest was 3 lbs. The mountains, as you can imagine, were breathtaking and he has fallen for the Pakistan side in particular. Surprisingly it was not expensive for his six week mid-tour leave.

Next week looks like being busy. I have 3 recruit exercises one after another which entails being out and sleeping out all week. When I am home I must get a book on astronomy for the stars are superb here.

126

*I was on patrol last night leading 3 British sergeants acting as enemy to a Baluch defensive position. We got within 5 yards of them.*

*November 6th 1963*

*Little news here though 120 recruits passed out this week whereupon a further 120 new recruits arrive next week for their basic training. The pressure is on to compensate for the loss of the mutineers. Not the most exciting sort of soldiering, but nevertheless it is important to give every recruit the best start that we can.*

*Do you know what is going to be a pretty high priority during mid-tour leave? You've guessed it – good food! Goat does wear very thin after 10 months. The occasional scraggy chicken does make a change. At Ghalla the fish is delicious, particularly the crayfish!*

*John Darbyshire and Tony Woodward are coming down tomorrow. We are all going shooting tomorrow evening and the following morning to a couple of waterholes, frequented by sand grouse. I am looking forward to meeting up with kindred spirits again.*

## Shooting sand grouse at Khor Dthyan

*November 10th 1963*

*The shooting weekend was great fun. It developed into a large party – 7 of us in all. We drove about 100 miles up the Batinah coast to a fresh water pool called Khor Dthyan. The road was abominable – parts being so bad that clouds of dust came over the LR bonnet, when moving at less than 5 mph. We arrived tired and filthy at 5.30 pm in the evening, had a swim in the pool and pitched camp. No tents, but camp beds and a table to eat on. We had roast chicken, and sat talking and drinking whisky (unfortunately not me) until the early hours.*

*We were up early ready for the pintail sand grouse to wheel in to the water. Their 'gutter-gutter' call alerted us as they approached at about 7.30 am (later than we had expected). It was a lovely sight – and we must have seen nearly 1,000 in the next hour. Unfortunately a couple of crack shots[21] in the Oman Gendarmerie had been down 2 days previously so the birds flew very high. The bag was small – under 50. I shot with John's gun – like a drain to start with but bagged more than my fair share eventually for I was well placed. I thoroughly enjoyed myself – it was just the fillip I needed after a month at Ghalla (67).*

*Some of those shooting loosed off their pieces at the most phenomenal range – more or less at anything in sight. John and I came to the conclusion that we had come to shoot sand grouse and nothing else. John has kindly lent me his gun and I have since discovered some water not far from Ghalla where Lichtenstein sand grouse fly in of an evening.*

I recall that these evening trips from the Training Centre to this waterhole as being rather special. I needed to ensure that I was in position and ready just before 6 pm. It never ceased to amaze me that some sand grouse wheeled in at precisely the same time every evening. They added variety to our rather limited menu in the mess. However, they were small birds and you needed four on your plate to make a reasonable meal.

## A taxi crash

*November 10th 1963 (continued)*

*On our way back from our shooting expedition up the Batinah Coast we came across the aftermath of a crash by a heavily overladen Omani taxi. The steering must have failed for it had hit a palm tree at about 40 mph. A British sergeant from the Training Centre was first on the scene. He did a wonderful job, making splints for broken limbs and getting the very seriously injured to the American Missionary Hospital in Muscat* [the one and only hospital in the country at the time.] *Three passengers have died so far and the hospital staff are trying to cope with many horrific injuries. The families of those being operated on got completely out of control, stormed the hospital, climbed on to the roof. From here these poor overwrought relatives tried to climb through the skylights and side windows into the operating theatre. Soldiers had to be used to restrain them and escort them to a waiting area so as to allow emergency operations to proceed. Further relatives arrived bringing food for their injured. They screamed their insistence on giving it to their loved ones, however dangerously ill they might be, and had to be restrained from doing so.*

In the early 1960s health care in Muscat and Oman was almost non-existent which meant that the inhabitants had absolutely no idea of what hospital treatment meant. Furthermore, because education was actively discouraged, there was little opportunity for the majority, who did not travel abroad, to discover what was happening in the outside world. It is no wonder that in such an emergency these poor people behaved like traumatised children.

Happily, since Sultan Qaboos's accession in 1970, enormous advances have been made in health and education. By 1998 there were fifty hospitals, ninety clinics, maternity and preventive care centres and mobile units throughout the

Sultanate. By the early 1990s there were 823 schools. Within a single generation the Omani Government has succeeded in virtually eradicating illiteracy. (See 'Some Facts and Figures' at Appendix 4.)

## Omani recruits

*November 10th 1963 (continued)*

*I must stop because I have several reports to write and there's another passing out parade tomorrow. I interviewed one of the (Omani) recruits today and asked him what he wanted to do now that he had completed his 7 months' recruit training here. His first choice – pilot; second choice – Commanding Officer of the Northern Frontier Regiment. I have included this in my report which will go to Colonel Dougie Dalglish (CO, NFR)!*

During the 1960s, the Sultan's Armed Forces, by then deployed throughout Oman, had begun to alert the local inhabitants to the need to improve standards of health and education. Consequently the potential to improve young men's health and education by joining the Army made their successful recruitment the opportunity of a lifetime. On arrival at villages, the Force Recruiting Officer, Major Malcolm Dennison,[22] would be besieged by excited young men, determined to enlist. Unfortunately the chronic poor health of many of them barred them from selection. Many failed their medical due to poor eyesight, enlarged spleen due to malaria or branding[23] on the stomach. Inevitably this meant that the healthier young men joined up leaving many villages with fewer healthy specimens except when soldiers were home on leave. However, the net effect of such qualified progress was to stir a formerly dormant ambition for improvement which was destined to remain largely frustrated by a lack of money and resources. Not until the mid-1970s did the combination of oil revenues and Sultan Qaboos's inspired five-yearly infrastructure plans introduce wholesale improvement to the health and education of everyone.

*November 18th 1963*

*It is raining for the first time (properly) for 6 months. Everywhere smells fresh and damp – an amazing contrast to the recent sand storms. Last week I had to wash my hair every day of the week to clear it of sand.*

*I have a military paper to write before I leave here – 5,000 words, so I had better get started.*

*There seems little point in writing epistles with only 20 days to go before I see you. Time really doesn't go fast enough.*

*November 22nd 1963*

*I have just this moment returned from Muscat where I sent you a telegram. Just hope their 'tomorrow-will-do' attitude will not delay its dispatch because tomorrow will most certainly not do for you are off to Berlin.*

*Anyway in case you don't get it (which would not surprise me) I leave Bait-al-Falaj on December 7th arriving at Bahrein an hour or so later. I leave Bahrein at 4 am on Sunday arriving at Gatwick Airport at 7.20 pm that evening. By the time I have cleared customs etc it will be 8 pm at the earliest.*

## President Kennedy is assassinated

*November 23rd 1963*

*I only heard about the Kennedy assassination this morning. I must confess it has made me feel sick with disgust and worry over repercussions. News is slow to reach here but from what I gather he was killed by a member of the Communist Party who has a Russian wife. If true, what a ghastly situation. I just pray to God that America will not be so roused as to retaliate in a way to start a world war.*

*Kennedy has always had the firm backing of the British people for we looked to him for a lead against the ever-spreading influence of Communist Russia. And how well he was beginning to make his presence felt in the Eastern and Western world. He, with his charisma, will be incredibly difficult to replace. I just hope that the United States have other men of his calibre to put forward in his place.*

*What a world we live in. Exciting, yes – but incidents like these and the Cuban Crisis which we lived through last year – make one realise how close we ride to the precipice at the moment. It is sobering and unnerving.*

## Brigadier Leask's visit

*November 23rd 1963 (continued)*

*Brigadier Leask,*[24] *the Deputy Military Secretary at the War Office, visited Muscat yesterday and today. He must have seen my name, realised that I was my father's son and asked to meet me. During the war he was Brigade Major to my father's brigade in Italy. I was sent for at 6 am this morning to drive to Bid Bid for breakfast to meet him. I did so, but through a tropical rain storm in an open LR, getting soaked to the skin. Anyway the storm was too much for SOAF so he could not land at Bid Bid but flew straight on to Azaiba which is the oil company base camp near Ghalla. So I had to turn round and drive back – this time in sunshine. I met him at Azaiba looking extremely scruffy and worse for wear. He was very charming and was full of praise for my father and spoke very good sense indeed.*

My father had been killed while commanding 36 Infantry Brigade in Italy in 1944 when I was seven years old. Naturally such reports from those who had served with him meant a great deal.

## A weekend at Izki

*November 28th 1963*

*I am just off for the weekend to Izki – my final swan before leave. What a wonderful thought. John Darbyshire has invited me up for the weekend and Christopher Ballenden is coming down from Nizwa. It will be a 3 KSLI Muscateers party! We all go on leave inside the next 2 months so it might be quite an evening.*

*November 29th 1963*

*The drive up to Izki was much as I expected but rather slower as I had a new LR to run in. This meant I hit every little rut in the road (which you skim over driving fast) and with the springs as rigid as they always are when new – made for a pretty bumpy ride.*

*The dinner was excellent:*

*Soup (du jour)*
*Smoked Salmon*
*Duck a la Bigarade*
*Something on Horseback*

*We sat and talked and laughed to the small hours – oh yes – we drank too. John really did us proud.*

*This morning was fresh, sunny and picturesque. There was a volleyball match between 'A' Company The Muscat Regiment (my old Company) and 'B' Company The Northern Frontier Regiment. We naturally won. I took a few photographs, we drank black coffee and took to Pimms before lunch (69).*

*I came back this afternoon – this time in an old LR and in half the time. John, Chris and I have made a date to have dinner together on the roof of the Hilton on January 11th 1964, as our leaves overlap then.*

*November 30th 1963*

*If I write again I may arrive before the letter –*

On reflection it is a little surprising, bearing in mind the number of letters I wrote from Ghalla, that my first period at the Training Centre lasted only seven weeks. If you deduct my two and a half weeks' sick leave at Bait-al-Falaj, this reduces my useful time as Training Officer to four and a half weeks. I seem to have used my 'under-the-weather' time to write frequently and at some length to Charmian. During the remaining four and a half weeks, work pressure and my imminent mid-tour leave reduced both the time available as well as some of the incentive for letter writing.

# Chapter Nine

# Memories without Letters

# Training recruits on the Batinah Coast, Sultan's Armed Forces Training Centre, Ghalla, December 1963 to July 1964

Mid-tour leave in England – At the birth of a training manual –
Some memorable episodes in recruit training – Limits on photography –
Omani dress – A bout of jaundice and leave in Kenya –
Return of the white oryx – Christian soldiers in a Muslim world –
Specialities of the day – Sailing and water skiing –
A subaltern's induction programme – Differing perceptions of loyalty

## Mid-tour leave in England

As I remember, my flight from Bahrein to Gatwick Airport was on time and the aeroplane touched down at about 7.30 pm in pouring rain. A polo-necked sweater helped keep the chill off a damp winter evening. After passing through passport control and customs in something of a haze I hugged my mother and Charmian, both of whom had come to meet me. We were soon on the road to Farnham in Surrey, our family home, where happily Charmian would be staying for the first part of my leave. Thankfully, Charmian was at the wheel for I was already slightly overwhelmed by the sheer numbers of people, volume of traffic and wet roads. Seeing one another regularly over the next six weeks of precious leave after such a long absence was going to take some getting used to. As I recall, we agreed not to talk too much while Charmian drove us expertly homeward through the pouring rain.

Thirty-five years later and with the benefit of hindsight it is perhaps easier to understand how difficult it was at the time for Charmian and me to pick up the threads of our special relationship again. Naturally, expectations were high that we would become engaged. As we had written regularly to one another for fourteen months, we were reluctant to accept that our differing experiences had changed our outlook on life. We were both miserable at our disappointment. Looking back, we suspect that our difficulties were similar to any couple after a prolonged period of absence. It became clear that we both needed more time to continue our separate careers. By mid-December Charmian had returned to London and then spent Christmas with her family in Suffolk. By then we had agreed to no further letter writing during my remaining six months in Muscat and Oman and to see what the future held for us both on my return.

During my leave I can recall two other events before returning to Muscat later in January. The first was being able to afford to buy myself a second-hand Coggswell & Harrison 12 bore shotgun in London. The second memory was of having dinner as planned at the Hilton with fellow KSLI Muscateers John Darbyshire and Christopher Ballenden on January 11th.

This explains why my remaining six months in Muscat and Oman, most of which were spent at the Training Centre at Ghalla, are not chronicled using 'Letters from Oman' sent home to Charmian. Indeed, the lack of such letters not only makes this final period more difficult to recall but requires a change from the letter and commentary style of Chapters Four to Eight. Instead, I have used some photographs taken at that time, together with my subsequent reflections, to illustrate and comment on some of the more interesting episodes during the period January to July 1964. I have also included some observations which on reflection were surprising omissions in my earlier letters.

## At the birth of a training manual

At this stage in the development of the Sultan's Armed Forces all training was based on British Army training manuals. Because the greater part of our Army was based in Germany and England during the Cold War of the early 1960s, these training manuals tended to have a European flavour but were spiced with experience gained in Korea, Malaya, Kenya and Aden. They were used as no more than a point of reference by British junior leader sergeants on short attachment to the SAF Training Centre at Ghalla. As explained earlier, training in weapon handling, fieldcraft and platoon tactics was largely a matter of demonstration, sign language and imitation.

That no Arabic training manual existed at this early stage in the development of the Sultan's Armed Forces was hardly surprising. Indeed, the abysmal standard of literacy at the time made this omission apparently unimportant. However, as Training Officer I had come to the conclusion, shortly before going on leave, that in the interests of both consistency in training methods and the need to prescribe tactics suitable to Oman's terrain, a training manual was urgently required. My own experience on operations in the Radfan in 1958 gave me a good insight into what was now needed.

Consequently, on my return from leave I volunteered to draft SAF's own training manual and get it appropriately translated into Arabic. Much of my spare time over the next six months was devoted to drafting this manual. Unfortunately a combination of my training officer duties and a bout of jaundice made it impossible for me to complete the task by the time my secondment finished in July 1964. However, by that stage I had nearly finished my original draft and had embarked on arranging for its translation into Arabic. At Appendix 2 I show extracts from my original English version.

## Some memorable episodes in recruit training

My recollections of training recruits are probably similar to those involved elsewhere before and since. Intakes usually comprised 120 recruits split into two Omani and two Baluch squads of about thirty soldiers. Each squad occupied one of the four barrack rooms for the duration of their seven months' training before 'passing out' and posting to either the Northern Frontier or Muscat Regiments. It was a carefully programmed period of concentrated basic training designed to prepare recruits to become riflemen (73, 74).

Each platoon or squad was nursed through the early stages of induction into army life. From hereon there followed a steady learning curve of all the necessary weapon training, fieldcraft and platoon tactics skills. Much emphasis was placed on cleanliness, healthcare, physical fitness and military discipline, as well as the culture and 'esprit de corps' of the Sultan's Forces. There were also daily education classes for all recruits under the direction of Mahmoud Ibrahim, the chief teacher.

Much time was spent on becoming skilled with all platoon weapons and live firing. Indeed, so enthusiastic and proficient was the training staff at the time, that the SAFTC Shooting Team won a number of competitions at the Forces' annual rifle meeting (71, 72).

Although there were occasions when new recruits became homesick or took longer to adjust to army life I recall that most recruits settled in remarkably quickly and were infectiously enthusiastic towards their military training. They took great pride in learning to cultivate an immaculate turnout. In spite of language difficulties the bond that existed between British junior leader sergeants and their eager-to-please recruits was invariably strong. A sense of humour, inventiveness and pride played a major part in achieving this success. There was a noticeable difference in the style of performance between the quick, independent-minded Omani recruits and the slower, methodical, loyal, but cliquey Baluch.

There is little doubt that despite linguistic and training manual shortcomings of the time, let alone the shortage of Omani or Baluch instructors, the quality of training was good and morale high. However, I do recall one barrack room incident which, like the mutiny at Saiq, was a sharp reminder of the dangers of Baluch inter-family feuds. As far as I can recall a Baluch recruit while at home on leave in Baluchistan had molested a married woman but had returned to Muscat before being discovered or incriminated. Sharing the same barrack room were at least two recruits from the same family as the molested woman. Late one night the platoon quietly conducted its own Shar'iah trial, found the recruit guilty and administered its own justice. This was done by retaining a live round from range practice, wrapping a rifle in several blankets to muffle the shot and shooting the recruit through the thigh. The recruit had been gagged and strapped to the bed beforehand allowing remaining members of the platoon to retire to bed, leaving the recruit to bleed to death.

By something of a fluke a British sergeant who happened to be returning to the Mess at the time heard the muffled shot and wisely decided to investigate matters thus probably saving a life. I forget the outcome of the subsequent investigation but the injured recruit, after a period in hospital, was discharged from the Army and sent home. However, this was another example of intolerable behaviour provoking a group of Baluch soldiers into taking the law into their own hands. While this may seem alarming behaviour, it does highlight both the intensity of inter-family feuds and penal immediacy of Shar'iah justice.

## Limits on photography

In the early 1960s the camera was still an object of wonder to the Omanis while in the duty free port of Aden it was commonplace. Most contract and seconded officers had brought their own cameras into the country but due to the Sultan's distaste for publicity and his refusal to grant entry permits to press reporters, photographic coverage of the country and its people was minimal. Indeed part of our induction briefing when joining the Sultan's Armed Forces was that we should take great care not to distress Omanis by taking photographs without first having obtained their permission.

The reason for this reluctance to be photographed stems from a mixture of religion, modesty and decorum. Not only did the glorification of imagery sit uncomfortably with complete obedience to the Prophet Mohammed, but the Omani people are by nature a modest people, who favour tasteful decorum and abhor the brashness of self-indulgence. In those days it was absolutely forbidden to photograph Muslim women. But children in colourful attire and with mischievous smiles would allow themselves to be snapped – charming subjects caught twixt shyness and inquisitiveness.

Even nowadays it is considered improper for a woman to allow someone to keep a photograph of her, particularly if she is married. To do so would run the risk of inviting adverse comment. Nowadays photographs of anyone on posters or in brochures appear stage-managed with the subjects' permission, and lack the spontaneity of western intrusion on privacy.

In the early 1960s some photographs were taken of feudal scenes of Omani people by seconded British officers or oil company managers. Nowadays, the opening up of the country to tourism has put pressure on Omani people to become more camera-friendly to the growing number of visitors. Nevertheless the need for a measure of respectful circumspection remains. Fortunately no such restrictions have ever applied to those wishing to capture Oman's great variety of scenic beauty.

## *Omani dress*

A surprising omission in my letters to Charmian is any attempt to describe Omani dress. Omani men wear either a white or off-white ankle length garment with long sleeves and no collar. It is known as a dish-dasha. In early days this garment had a breast pocket but nowadays this has been replaced by side pockets hidden within each seam. It is fastened by buttons ascending to the neck line (80).

On formal occasions a man will wear a traditional khanjar (or dagger) attached to a belt so that it sits exactly central, like the buckle of a westerner's belt. Its sheath is decorated with ornamental thread while the hilt is made of wood, metal or bone depending on the region or tribe. Next to the khanjar there may be a small silver container of kohl, an eye shadow used by desert travellers to reduce glare and a pair of tweezers for extracting thorns.

On strictly formal occasions Omani men wear an outer cloak called a bisht over the dish-dasha. This is usually black or some dark colour to offset the white dish-dasha and is embroidered with gold thread along the edges. It is worn across the shoulder and is fastened at the neck but drops away to reveal the khanjar at the waist (99).

The headdress is either a kumma or a massar. The kumma is a flat-topped brimless cap embroidered with ornate bright floral and geometric patterns. By contrast the massar, which is the more formal of the two headdresses, is a square head shawl made of either cotton or wool with ornate patterns woven into the material. The shawl, often from Kashmir, is folded into a triangle and placed over the head so that the ends drop down on either side. Then each end is wrapped round the head so that the final appearance is similar to a turban. Different ways of wrapping, tucking and tilting the massar identify the origin of the wearer.

Underneath the dish-dasha a man wears a wrap called a lunghi. This can be plain or printed cloth and is wrapped around the body from waist to below the knee like a sarong. Omani dress is designed to cover the body, reflect the sun rays and yet provide the maximum of natural ventilation. Omani men take great pride in their national dress and are immaculately turned out.

During the early 1960s Omani women's dress was vivid in contrast and reflected a woman's origin. Apart from Bedu women, most town and country women in the interior wore brightly coloured clothes with headscarves in public. When unexpectedly confronted by a man in the street they would pull their headscarf across their face. When introduced at home they would shake hands through the folds of the cloth they were wearing.

In contrast, Bedu women wore black in public and still do so nowadays. I recall feeling sympathy for the Bedu women of the Wahiba Sands, who instead of a black veil, wore a rigid black mask which covered most of the face except for large eye holes exposing the cheeks and forehead. This mask, which is called a birqa, was usually shiny black but occasionally indigo blue or gold. From a distance and to western eyes, the birqa appeared raven-like and seemed to us to symbolise repression.

However, contrary to our impression at the time this was not the case at all. While the practice of wearing black in public was thought to emanate from other regions, the Bedu men were far from requiring their womenfolk to wear black in public with their face covered. It was the Bedu women who chose to do so out of modesty and a sense of morality. Indeed they consider their public attire alluring and seductive. Even nowadays young girls look forward to wearing the mask when they reach puberty.

Few of us serving with the Sultan's Forces at the time were privileged to meet Omani womenfolk in the privacy of their own homes except fleetingly on introduction when first entering a sheikh's majlis. Within a matter of moments they would retire from view leaving their menfolk to get on with the serious business of conversation, coffee or a meal. Consequently our recollections were a mixture of amazement at their colourful and attractive clothing and disappointment at their premature departure.

So during our time on secondment in the early 1960s we knew virtually nothing about women's dress. We had a job to do in leading and training the Sultan's Army. It was not only none of our business but more importantly Omani men would have been deeply offended had we breached convention by expressing our interest in such a delicate subject. Moreover, the opportunity to discover more – however ill-advised – was restricted to distant scenes of Bedu women shrouded in black drawing water from a well or colourful glimpses of Omani women during visits to villages in the interior (78).

Since the 1970s, the country has made steady and increasingly rapid advance from feudal times through oil revenues and tourism. This has encouraged Omani women to come out from behind screens to show themselves in all their colourful finery to an inquisitive world.

Although Omani women's clothing varies according to region there are essentially three elements: a loosely fitted dish-dasha that falls just below the knees; a surwal, which is baggy trousers gathered at the ankle, and some form of headdress. All fabrics are very bright and colourful, often using exotic prints or ornate hand-stitching with silver and gold thread. The trousers are richly embroidered at the ankle in floral and geometric patterns which extend to the knee. Embellishment of the dish-dasha starts from rectangular panels around the bodice and continues along all borders. The colour combinations are wildly innovative and are topped with either a patterned shawl or wiqaiah, an even more colourful and richly embroidered headdress, reserved for special occasions. If this were not enough, the womenfolk adorn themselves further with rings, necklaces, anklets and bangles. Silver jewellery, sourced from melted down Maria Theresa dollars, was preferred. Young children often wore anklet pods containing pebbles that rattled to denote their whereabouts (79).

While we had fleeting impressions of such colour during the early 1960s few of us would have been able to describe Omani women's dress with real confidence. Thanks to Peter Ochs's *Maverick Guide to Oman*[25] I am at long last able to do so.

## A bout of jaundice and leave in Kenya

During my final six months at the Training Centre in Ghalla I succumbed to a bout of jaundice, a condition that often prevailed after a tour in Rostaq. Perhaps it was showing signs of doing so when I complained of being 'under the weather' soon after my arrival at Ghalla the previous September.

Fortunately for the reader I have little recollection of this period other than the need for me to be flown to RAF Muharraq Hospital in Bahrein for treatment before being discharged on sick-leave. Like a number of previously smitten colleagues I was determined to escape from Bahrein to spend my sick-leave in Kenya.

After helpful discussions with 'RAF Movements' I soon found myself to be the only passenger in the boom of a RAF Beverly transport aircraft conveying freight from Bahrein to Aden. I was in a bucket seat with the heavy drone of four engines for company – strangely reminiscent of earlier parachuting from Abingdon. My flask of cold lumi was a welcome refreshment and a timely reminder that I was once again 'on the wagon' – this time for six months.

After one night in the mess at Aden I was fortunate to get a seat on a passenger flight to Eastleigh Airport Nairobi, arriving at midday on a Saturday. By then it had dawned on me that my Muscat cheque book and some small change would not be sufficient for a couple of nights accommodation anywhere.

I telephoned Rosemary Knocker, recently married and a family friend from childhood days, explained my predicament and asked her if I could stay for a couple of nights. Despite having David Shepherd, the wildlife artist, staying with them at the time they kindly picked me up from the airport, gave me time to sort out my cash problems and then lent me their Land Rover for a fortnight. This kindness and generosity enabled me to drive up the Rift Valley and revisit all those places I had so enjoyed when serving with my regiment during 1958. To cap it all I was invited to join Rosemary and Christopher for waterskiing at Malindi.

I remember some robust competition with Christopher as to who would be the first to mono-ski. How fortunate I was to be made so welcome and what a marvellous recuperative leave this turned out to be, before returning to Ghalla.

## Return of the white oryx

At some stage during my remaining months in Oman I recall being prompted by an Omani soldier to lift my binoculars to see a white oryx on the horizon. These Arabian antelope were hunted by the local Bedu, mainly for their meat but their skin and horns were also used to decorate rifle butts and as part of camel saddles. Later however, outsiders with modern weapons came to hunt them for their exotic value until they were nearly extinct.

In 1962, the Fauna Preservation Society (FPS) took the initiative to try to save the white oryx from extinction. Collaboration between scientists and tribesmen in Operation Oryx led to the capture of one male and two females from the Hadramaut in the East Aden Protectorate[26] which borders Oman. They were transported to Phoenix Zoo, Arizona, where the climate was considered ideal. Soon other donations from Kuwait, Saudi Arabia and the London Zoo brought those in captivity to nine. A captive breeding programme was established in the hope that this magnificent creature could be successfully bred in sufficient numbers to be reintroduced to its natural native habitat.

When His Majesty Sultan Qaboos heard about the success of Operation Oryx, he pronounced in 1976 that the point of their reintroduction to the wild should be Jiddat Al-Harasis, the spot where the last wild oryx had been seen. The Harasis tribes were delighted at the opportunity to restore a piece of their natural heritage.

In 1980 a group of descendants from the original captive herd had been dispatched to Oman where they spent several months in the White Oryx Project enclosure at Jaaluni. In January 1982, twenty years after Operation Oryx, the original capture, the doors of the enclosure were opened by the head ranger, Said bin Dooda al Harsusi and the white oryx was home again. The Arabian Oryx Sanctuary was established by royal decree in 1994 and by 1996 there were approximately 315 oryx roaming the 16,000 square kilometre reserve (98). Later the same year, the World Heritage Committee of UNESCO declared the

Sanctuary a world natural heritage site. After such a success story it is disappointing to hear that during 1996 there was such a resurgence of poaching that by 1999 there were less than one hundred oryx left in the wild. A number of breeding females and a herd bull have been brought into the Jaaluni enclosure again for safety. These are now breeding well and thriving. As new rangers are being recruited from neighbouring tribes it is very much hoped that when the next lot of oryx are released into the wild, their safety will be assured. Let us hope that the Arabian Oryx Sanctuary will once again become a popular venue for visitors from all over the world and prove that reintroduction projects can succeed.

## Christian soldiers in a Muslim world

Looking back over my letters to Charmian thirty-six years ago I cannot understand why there is so little reference to Omani religion and the law of the land. Perhaps I was fearful that I might bore her with an earnest appraisal of a culture which I did not completely understand. Maybe, like many of my generation, I fought shy of detailed analysis of differing religions which nowadays are discussed more openly. Lack of confidence in the relative depths of each other's beliefs may also have had a bearing. Moreover I probably doubted my ability at the age of twenty-five to write a reasoned comparison between Islam and Christianity.

The reader will be relieved to know that I have no wish to rectify this omission now. Instead I shall summarise the main principles of Islam and recall some of my earlier impressions.

The principal belief of Islam is the existence of one God, the same God worshipped by Jews and Christians, known to all Arabs as Allah. A Muslim means one who submits to Allah, whose words were given to the Prophet Mohammed (AD 570–632) who proclaimed them in the Koran. This book is not only a spiritual guide but specifies laws and rules of conduct. Muslim worshippers approach Allah directly and simply and must perform five practical Pillars of Faith. Each must pronounce publicly that 'I bear witness that there is no god but Allah and Mohammed is his prophet'. Each must pray five times a day (salat), give alms (zakat), fast from dawn to dusk during Ramadhan (saum) and make a pilgrimage to Mecca at least once in their lifetime (Hajj).

In addition, Muslims are urged to practise virtue of the highest order, refuting pride, calumny, vengefulness, avarice, prodigality, adultery and the taking of intoxicants. Each is urged to put his trust in Allah, to understand his will of

143

patience and modesty, forbearance, sincerity, love of peace, truthfulness, frugality and benevolence.

During his lifetime the Prophet Mohammed proclaimed that the Islamic faith was focal to both spiritual and temporal law. Consequently religion and secular law were fused together into Shar'iah law. Hence the concept evolved that all law proceeds from religious law. This means that Church and State are one, a concept now foreign to western thinking. In this way a western visitor to the Middle East soon becomes aware that religion plays a more fundamental role in life than in his own country.

The most immediately visible of a Muslim's five Pillars of Faith is prayer. This takes place in any place that will allow worshippers to prostrate themselves in the direction of Mecca. Every practising Muslim must perform this allegiance to Allah before sunrise, at noon, in the mid-afternoon, at sunset and in twilight. As a Christian soldier in Oman during 1963–64 I recall being a respectful bystander while Omani and Baluchi soldiers were called to prayer:

> 'God is most great. I testify that there is no god but God. I testify that Mohammed is the Prophet of God. Come to prayer! Come to salvation! Prayer is better than sleep. God is most great. There is no god but God.'

There followed an ordered but completely natural ritual that I found strangely compelling to watch and to which I gradually became accustomed. This invariably involved the washing of face, hands and feet. There followed the sucking of water into nostrils, putting wet fingers into ears and the passing of wet hands over the top of the head. Each soldier, who might choose to pray singly or in ranks, would sweep the ground before him, place his rifle down and then pray facing towards Mecca. After standing upright, each would bend forward placing his hands on his knees, before kneeling with head bowed until his forehead touched the ground. This sequence of movements was performed several times, simply yet in measured fashion, while reciting the formal prayer. On occasions after they had finished their prayers some would intone long passages of the Koran.

In my earlier days with B Company at Ibri I recall having mixed feelings about these devotions. On the one hand I felt an intruder on a simple yet compelling example of devotional prayer. On the other I soon discovered that the frequency of daily prayer varied from the required five calls to sometimes only twice a day. Prayers at dawn and sunset seemed to be sacrosanct while the others were often neglected. It also seemed to me sometimes that there must be some subterfuge in calls to pray which so often seemed to occur just when time was short or at some critical stage on patrol. But to suggest that they should wait for a more convenient moment would be denying their religious rights and would be doomed to failure.

The next most visible of Muslim devotions is fasting during Ramadhan, the ninth month of the Islamic (lunar) calendar. As mentioned in my letters to Charmian this requires all practising Muslims to fast from dawn to dusk for the entire month. Exceptions are made for travellers, the weak and sickly, those on medication, young children, pregnant women and mothers breast-feeding their children.

Once again, as a Christian soldier, I was torn as to what I should do. Should I fast in sympathy so that I could experience what they were going through? Should I do so out of respect for their culture and to ensure that I did not harbour unrealistic expectations of their stamina while fasting? But if I fasted the Omanis would naturally expect me to pray with them. Or should I eat and drink during the day and by so doing undermine their resolve for fasting? Or did it simply not matter what I did so long as I was capable of commanding them? Clearly there were diverse opinions on the subject and seconded officers tended to rely on their best judgement. If we decided that it was completely unnecessary for us to fast for both religious and practical reasons it was incumbent on us to refrain from flaunting our non-compliance and to make reasonable allowances for their lack of energy.

Omanis are predominantly Ibadhi Muslims, a tiny sect of Islam claimed to be the oldest of the Islamic orthodoxies. Being geographically isolated from the rest of the Arabian Peninsula by the Empty Quarter and the Hajar Mountains has helped to preserve an independent communal sense of Ibadhi self sufficiency.

Looking back to the early 'sixties, we were indeed privileged to be Christian soldiers in a Muslim world. Not only were we able to acquire some understanding of Omani Muslim culture but in spite of our Christianity, we were made to feel welcome in their midst. Providing we respected their Islamic culture – and we had been well briefed on this beforehand – we were accepted without hesitation and with good grace. Our abiding impression of Omanis was of a people who were devoid of prejudice, intrigued by our presence and who genuinely wanted to like us.

Although few if any of us thought to analyse it at the time this generosity of spirit was rather remarkable in the context of medieval history. After all as a nation we had played a leading role in instigating a series of brutal holy wars against the Muslims of the Near East. Subsequently most Christian scholars depicted Islam as a violent and intolerant faith. In contrast to this trend, longstanding historical relationships between Britain and Muscat had helped to reduce such prejudice. Muscat's first treaty with Britain in 1798 had paved the way for the first resident British political agent in 1800. During the next one hundred and fifty years much progress was made towards achieving a greater understanding of each other's needs and aspirations. By the early 1950s this had been translated into financial and military assistance in developing the Sultan's Armed Forces and some support in overthrowing internal rebellions. By the early 1960s, a good measure of mutual trust and respect had been established.

However, not all of Omanis' generosity of spirit towards us was due to history. We were soon to learn that Muslims respect the Prophet Mohammed as a man of great humanity with a passion for justice and equity. In particular the Koran is emphatic in its condemnation of coercion in matters of faith. Indeed in the past Muslim scholars have insisted on the sacred right to freedom of expression as vehemently as any Western liberal. Therefore much of the reason for Omanis' generosity of spirit towards us stemmed from their Muslim culture.

Nowadays people throughout the world are beginning to research and discover the richness of other religions without necessarily abandoning their own faith. Others may choose to adopt a different faith. The Internet provides speedy access to information on many religions for those questioning their own faith or seeking greater fulfilment in another. This relentless search for religious nourishment has had some interesting consequences. More Christians read the Jewish philosopher Martin Buber than Jews. Jesuits learn meditation from Buddhist monks; people of all faiths seem drawn to the teachings of the Dalai Lama.

However, despite the more tolerant climate of today's world the Muslim religion seems to be excluded from this circle of goodwill. For nearly a thousand years the Western world has cultivated a distorted vision of Islam which bears little relation to the truth. Even now western media seem intent on prolonging these flawed prejudices. Those of us who served in Oman find ourselves embarrassed by such distortions. When we speak up to counter them, we invariably invite disapproval. When westerners can learn to welcome Muslims with the same generosity of spirit as Omanis welcome us, a proper respect for each other's culture can follow. Once trust has the opportunity to take root, peaceful enterprise can prevail.

## Specialities of the day

If I were asked to choose three specialities of the 1960s which typified Oman and which to this day remain vividly reminiscent they would be limes, dates and crayfish. Many of my contemporaries might beg to differ but few I suspect would omit dates.

Before I went to Oman my experience of dates was limited to the dried variety served up in oblong boxes after Christmas pudding. Dates were a once-a-year sticky treat which by then most people were too well fed to enjoy.

However, once you have had the privilege of visiting Oman, dates are elevated from a somewhat sickly afterthought to a deliciously fresh and restorative centrepiece. For centuries dates have been Oman's main crop and are renowned the world over. Every oasis, large or small, boasts a cluster of date palms. There are more than two hundred varieties, of which twenty are considered commercially viable. Nowadays the annual production exceeds 150,000 tons. My abiding memory is of tin dishes of this succulent light brown fruit, accompanied by coffee or lumi.

To me the cool sharpness of fresh lime juice (lumi) on arrival at a sheikh's bait in the heat of the day was a perfect welcome. Made from freshly pressed limes well stirred with sugar, it seemed far sharper than the lime juice cordials of the nineties, good though they are, and infinitely more refreshing. Limes, which are Oman's second largest crop after dates, have thin but tough skins, are light green when ripe and are seldom larger than a squash ball. Somehow the offer of lumi in well-worn tall glasses seemed to bestow a genuine favour on any guest.

One of the compensations for being posted to the Training Centre at Ghalla or for that matter for those on the staff at headquarters in Bait-al-Falaj was the nearby marine life of the Batinah Coast. This coastline which stretches for over a thousand miles is home to crustaceans and shellfish. Omani fishermen have sought their livelihood from these waters for centuries. The coastal shelf around Muscat in particular teems with fish. During my ten months at Ghalla I remember the abundant deliciousness of crayfish, an expensive delicacy elsewhere, which could be bought over the boat-side from fishermen for next to nothing. Indeed I fear I may have overindulged at the time for in later life I seemed to have developed an allergy to all shellfish.

## Sailing and water skiing

As well as enjoying fresh fish we were also fortunate enough, when time permitted, to indulge in some water sports. During my time in Ibri and Rostaq these opportunities were limited to occasional weekends, usually acting as crew to a helmsman like John Darbyshire or John Hutton, sailors far more experienced than I. However, having learnt to mono-ski at Malindi while recuperating from jaundice in Kenya I was keen to practise these new skills on my return to Oman.

Once again we were fortunate to be able to use oil company powerboats and water skis, usually for the price of fuel consumed. Over time I remember becoming a much more confident and proficient water skier and powerboat helmsman.

Such ski trips would involve beach starts from sheltered coves without wetsuits. During long trips out to sea it was not uncommon to see the fins of basking sharks. Despite their reputation for being harmless few of us were keen to put this to the test. Much more dangerous were shoals of jellyfish and in particular Portuguese men-of-war. Sometimes water skiing trips would be called off because of their presence. At other times when the risk seemed marginal we would proceed. Most of us were stung at some time or other. While clearly wet suits would provide protection, the wearing of them in such a climate was considered intolerable.

## A subaltern's induction programme

This episode is not a good example of Christian soldierly conduct but nevertheless deserves to be told because of the unexpected outcome. It also leaves the reader in no doubt as to the nastier side of human nature personified by the author and his two fellow KSLI muscateers.

On January 11th 1964 when lunching with Christopher Ballenden and John Darbyshire at the Hilton Hotel during our mid-tour leave we learnt that on our return to Oman we were to play collective host to a KSLI subaltern called David Hallett. This would involve us in devising an induction programme for a couple of weeks to give him a taste of life in Oman.

Unfortunately our shared impressions of David during earlier service together was of a bumptious subaltern who needed to be taken down a peg or two. So over lunch we decided to devise a rigorously testing programme that he would never forget. It was not difficult to agree some suitable tests of David's courage and stamina while he was a guest at our respective locations. Naturally it fell to me as Training Officer to co-ordinate matters and type up the final programme.

While sadly a copy of this programme no longer exists, our combined recollections are that David Hallett's induction programme included:

- donkey and foot patrol up the jebel;

- five-mile camel ride in the desert;

- aerial acrobatics in a Beaver light aircraft;

◆ attendance at a sheikh's feast renowned for passing honoured guests sheep's eyes and brains;

◆ an all-night poker session;

◆ water skiing over sharks and jelly fish.

Contrary to our anticipation David Hallett passed all these various tests with flying colours. Despite falling from one of the most ill-tempered of male camels who bit and spat with alacrity, David hung on gamely and survived without serious damage. When it came to being flown by one of our most intrepid SOAF pilots, 'Kiwi' Williams, through a series of loop the loop and rolls off the top, it was Kiwi who was airsick, while David grinned and asked for more. Indeed David remembers his taste of Oman as the most memorable time of his life. Our memory is of a ruddy smile that never disappeared from his face. It is no small wonder that David has since become a very successful businessman. His appetite for adventure training remains undiminished to this day.

## Differing perceptions of loyalty

During my ten months as Training Officer I made it my business to cultivate a good working relationship with a local wali. Although our prime role at the Training Centre was to train recruits for the Army, the GSO 2 (Int)[27] at Headquarters, Christopher Hinton, had stressed to all of us how essential it was, wherever we were stationed within Oman, to win the hearts and minds of the locals. By so doing, we would have our fingers on the pulse regarding attitudes and needs and in this process of building mutual confidence, we could obtain invaluable information regarding the movement of rebels or their supplies. Although the area was well away from the normal scene of rebel activity in the interior there were small coastal towns through which supplies of arms, ammunition and anti-tank mines might pass.

With this in mind I soon made a point of visiting the wali of a local village on most Jummas (Muslim Sundays) for a chat over morning coffee. Far from being a necessary duty, I discovered – somewhat to my surprise – that these visits were developing into a thoroughly stimulating exchange of views which we both much enjoyed. As well as making me feel a special guest over delicious coffee and dates he was patient with my less than fluent Arabic when discussing a wide range of subjects. He was an intelligent and discerning man who made it his business to be well informed on local and Middle Eastern affairs. Many of the topics we discussed stemmed from news bulletins on the radio. Separating propaganda from reality played a significant part in proceedings. While each of us held firm to our own counsel our discussions were laced with much pragmatism and good humour.

As a result of this respectful friendship I was able to arrange for the Army to help the village in small practical ways. In return I received some useful local information on rebel supplies to the interior. Most of this information proved to be correct and helped build a sound intelligence picture of this stretch of the Batinah coast.

Indeed by the end of my secondment in July 1964 I was beginning to be rather pleased with what had been achieved as a result of this positive relationship. During my final debriefing by the intelligence officer at headquarters in Bait-al-Falaj I told Christopher Hinton that the wali was an entirely trustworthy source of information and would always remain loyal to the Sultan and the Army.

At the time I realised how often similar assurances had been given before, only to be dashed to smithereens later. After all the Omanis' perception of loyalty had always differed from that of a British Army Officer. This is not to deride the Omani one jot but merely to recognise that the inherent instinct for survival in a harsh unrelenting environment transcends all other sentiments. It is an essential element of an Omani's existence to be able to respond to changing circumstances.

Despite all this I had convinced myself that the wali would be the exception that proved the rule. In retrospect I wonder whether my hope was born of an arrogance that I knew better or that like many other British officers before and since I remained an incurable romantic.

Some months after my return to England I received a short note from Christopher Hinton from Muscat. He reported that despite my earlier reassurances the wali had without doubt been actively involved in a mine incident involving an Army lorry. Christopher had been right and I totally wrong.

I later learned to my relief that this mine incident was not fatal and had its lighter side. The anti-tank mine had been laid without an anti-lift device on the track leading from the Training Centre to Muttrah. An afternoon leave truck was en route to Muttrah when the driver stopped to relieve himself. On returning to his cab, he noticed the mine in the track ahead and alerted the commanding officer. Whereupon 'Jungle Jim' Sheridan, who had defused it with his typical Irish phlegm, noticed some tell-tale signs and promptly rushed it by Land Rover to HQ Bait-al-Falaj, carrying it proudly on his knee.

In retrospect, thirty-five years later, it is difficult to excuse my error of judgement. In the 1960s the differing perceptions of loyalty between the Omanis and the British were more marked than they are today. After all, this was before oil wealth had modified the Omanis' instinct for survival. It was before the British Army's withdrawal from Empire had undermined our nation's confidence and rendered unquestioning loyalty a misplaced virtue.

While relative attitudes towards loyalty between both nations may have become closer neither should forget the role that environment and history have played in fashioning attitudes.

# Chapter Ten

# Oil and the Quickening Beat
of Change

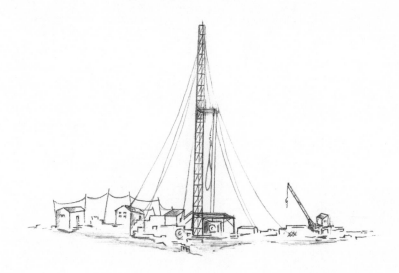

# 1964 to 1977

On a personal note – Discovery of oil June 1962 – Bedu succumb to the
twentieth century – Could the speed of change be governed? –
An Omani/British partnership to be proud of – Sultan Qaboos succeeds his
father, July 23rd 1970 – Oil revenues become a catalyst for renaissance –
Contribution of oil revenues to total government revenues –
Percentage of GDP – Omanisation of the Sultan of Oman's Armed Forces –
Dhofar war 1964 to 1975 – Massive changes to infrastructure –
Summary Reflections

## On a personal note

In August 1964 I returned to England and after a short spell of leave rejoined my regiment then stationed in Plymouth. I had some difficulty in adjusting from life in a Force that functioned satisfactorily without much paperwork, to my new duties as adjutant which demanded forests of the stuff. Walks with my yellow labrador Kim, helped to preserve my sanity and to readjust. Derek Clapham, my first Commanding Officer, was fortunately patient. By the time Neil Fletcher took over I had become a better adjutant and a happier man.

Much of this happiness was due to Charmian. In early 1965 I caught a glimpse of her in London and discovered she was living on a houseboat (MTB 219)[28] at Cheyne Walk. I rang her and arranged to call in after work the following evening. Rather than arriving with flowers or chocolates (they hadn't worked before) I walked up the gangplank with a bottle of Dry Fly Sherry. It was blissful seeing her again. Some weeks later we holidayed with her brother Richard's family at Birdstown, Burnfoot, Co Donegal. One afternoon we climbed the Gap of Mamore and before descending from this beautiful place we agreed to marry. We returned to Birdstown after dark, bubbling with our happy news. Richard and Caroline, who were relieved to see us, were delighted but not surprised (81, 82).

On May 25th 1965 we were married at St James's Piccadilly and established our first home at 18 Charlton Crescent in Plymouth. After moving the battalion from Plymouth to Singapore and then to the 28th Commonwealth Brigade in Malacca, I was posted to the Royal Military Academy, Sandhurst, as Company Instructor in 1967. Charmian gave birth to our first daughter Grania on August 11th 1968. After failing the examination for Staff College I decided to leave the Army in 1970. In retrospect those six years after returning from Muscat and Oman in 1964 had been typical of the time.

In contrast Colin McLean decided to remain in Muscat and Oman in 1964. This involved resigning his commission, leaving the Argyll and Sutherland Highlanders and becoming a Sultan's Commissioned Officer in the Sultan's Armed Forces where he continued to serve until 1977. Unlike me he had become a fluent Arabist. Over time, he was promoted Lieutenant-Colonel and commanded the Dhofar Force, the Oman Gendarmerie and Firquat Forces. He saw the effect of the discovery of oil, had first hand experience of the Dhofar War and was Military Secretary during the Omanisation of the Sultan of Oman's Land and Air Forces and Navy. He witnessed the early stages of change to

Oman's infrastructure and the stresses and strains of the people. Indeed it is he who has generously provided the information for the latter part of this chapter.

## Discovery of oil, June 1962

In Chapter Four I provided the background to the uncertainty which seemed to prevail regarding the imminent discovery of oil. When Colin McLean and I joined the Sultan's Armed Forces in February 1963 we had no knowledge of how the prospecting for oil was going. However, we did realise that there was a distinct possibility that Muscat and Oman could ultimately follow Qatar into the last throes of the Gulf oil boom. We naturally wondered whether an Omani strike would happen during our secondment.

During the next eighteen months, while learning about the country and its people, we became familiar with the sight of PDO's[29] mobile oil rigs towed by huge tractors. We also became aware of an intensification of prospecting activities in the interior. Try as we did to discover more from a handful of PDO friends, a blanket of secrecy prevailed. Meanwhile, as we became more knowledgeable about the country and its people, so we became increasingly concerned that exploitation of oil – when it came – would rape a beautiful country and blast aside the innocence of its remarkable people.

Despite this quickening pulse of uncertainty which reached a crescendo between 1962 and 1964, the prospectors managed to keep their discoveries top secret. Naturally rumour was rife, but few, if any of us were aware that oil had already been discovered at Yibal in 1962 and at Natih in 1963 (87–89). Apparently commercially exploitable quantities do not come all at once and further investigation was necessary to establish sufficient reserves. Not until oil was found in Fahud in 1964 could the decision be made to develop all the fields discovered. Since Fahud was in central Oman, a thirty-inch pipeline was laid to Saih al-Malih on the coast 173 miles away. A terminal at Mina al-Fahl was constructed. Three years of intense infrastructure development were needed before commercial exports began in 1967.

## Bedu succumb to the twentieth century

In the 1950s the word 'Arab' meant an inhabitant of Arabia, usually regarded as the Bedu. Relatively few westerners would have been able to draw the distinction between those Arabs who had opted to establish permanent roots within an urban community and the nomadic camel-breeding Bedu who roamed the Arabian Desert.

156

Unlike those Arabs who sought settled livelihoods as farmers, fishermen, merchants and businessmen, the Bedu preferred to turn their back on the certainty of a settled existence. Like their forebears over many centuries, the Bedu preferred to pursue a simple uncluttered nomadic and uncertain existence where customs and habits became ingrained by the acute harshness of their desert environment. Learning to survive under such circumstances made the Bedu intensely independent and fiercely loyal to each other. Not surprisingly their sinewy toughness and stamina were legendary.

Perhaps more surprising, on first impression, was their great generosity and depth of compassion. However when you began to understand that these two graces were essential ingredients to their collective survival, then they became entirely appropriate.

Moreover, because Bedu travelled for days without seeing anybody, it was easy to understand that in a featureless desert the art of discussion was cherished, almost as if thinking aloud.

Loneliness in such circumstances did not exist. When Bedu met this provided a heaven-sent opportunity to exchange greetings and enjoy swapping news and views while giving and receiving simple tokens of hospitality. When the situation merited, generosity prevailed over poverty. For example, if the livelihood of some Bedu depended on twenty goats they did not hesitate to kill one to feed a guest.

However, in those days the harshness of the Bedu existence, which was a matter of pride, was all-prevailing. Lawrence of Arabia and Wilfred Thesiger both bear witness to this fact:

'Bedouin ways were hard, even for those brought up in them and for strangers: a death in life'.

T. E. Lawrence in *Seven Pillars of Widsom*.

'In this book I have described a journey in disguise through Inner Oman in 1947 and I wrote: "Yet even as I waited for my identity to be discovered, I realised that for me the fascination of this journey lay not in seeing this country, but in seeing it under these conditions." The everyday hardships and danger, the ever present hunger and thirst, the weariness of long marches: these provided the challenges of Bedu life against which I sought to match myself, and were the basis of the comradeship which united us.'

*Arabian Sands* by Wilfred Thesiger.

During the early 1960s the Bedu continued to thrive but by then there was much talk of latent oil resources. It was of real concern to us how the Bedu would respond to the inevitable exploitation of Oman. We harboured real doubts as to how they could possibly survive such wholesale and traumatic change.

While only a very few of our number had entered, let alone crossed, the Empty Quarter, fortunately most of us had frequently met Bedu during our various postings within Oman. Some had been recruited into the Army. Without exception we seemed to enjoy an affinity with these people whom we much admired. After all, their incisiveness, courage, self-reliance, generosity and loyalty were all highly desirable and soldierly qualities. Had we fully understood that they were pragmatists rather than romantics we might have been less concerned as to how they would react to cultural change.

Our problem was that many of us were romantics, having fallen under the spell of this beautiful country and its charming people. Because we knew the western world and had chosen to escape from it for a while we genuinely feared what precipitous westernisation would do to Oman. Most of us knew how important it was to improve the standards of health and education but how could this be reconciled with the future of the Bedu?

It seems that our concerns in the early 1960s were consistent with Wilfred Thesiger's own concerns in 1950. On the final two pages of *Arabian Sands* he wrote:

'I shall always remember how often I was humbled by those illiterate herdsmen who possessed, in so much greater measure than I, generosity and courage, endurance, patience, and light hearted gallantry. Among no other people have I ever felt the same sense of personal inferiority.'

And when saying farewell to his two Bedu travelling companions before returning home in 1950 he wrote:

'Yet I knew that for them the danger lay, not in the hardship of their lives, but in the boredom and frustration they would feel when they renounced it. The tragedy was that the choice would not be theirs; economic forces beyond their control would eventually drive them into the towns to hang about street corners as unskilled labour.'

Yet on his return to Oman twenty-seven years later in 1977 to re-meet his former travelling companions, he wrote:

'I realised that after all these years and under these changed conditions, the relationship between us could never again be as in the past. They had

158

adjusted themselves to this new Arabian World, something I was unable to do.'

Despite his disillusionment with the changes which he saw in 1977, Wilfred Thesiger returned to Abu Dhabi in 1990 for an exhibition of his photographs. On this occasion in the Preface to the 1991 reprint of *Arabian Sands* he wrote:

'On this occasion I found myself reconciled to the inevitable changes, which have occurred in the Arabia of today and are typified by the United Arab Emirates.'

Somehow these remarkable extracts seem to epitomise the special and enduring relationship that westerners felt towards the Bedu at the time. While we have struggled to come to terms with our perception of the damage inflicted by the petroleum exploitation of Oman, clearly the Bedu have once again proved themselves to be resilient and opportunistic. According to Peter J. Ochs II's *Maverick Guide to Oman* (1998), the Bedu have become more absorbed into society yet still maintain their independent lifestyle. Many of their old traditions have fallen by the way. For example, camels are now kept for their milk, meat, wool and for racing; Bedu now travel by four-wheel-drive vehicles. Mobile telephones have shrunk their world. Despite these changes they are proud of their history and remain outgoing and generous. Apparently there is not the slightest trace of embitterment for the hardship and privation they formerly endured. Being pragmatic by nature, they know that in a land where few things in nature are forgiving, something or someone has to be. They remain devoted to life, their fellow men and to Allah (83, 84).

## Could the speed of change be governed?

Sultan Said bin Taimur had been in power for thirty-two years when the discovery of oil was announced in 1964. Throughout his reign Muscat and Oman had been a poor and feudal country whose health and educational standards were a disgrace. Yet by the late 1950s his countrymen and his neighbouring states realised that the discovery of oil within Muscat and Oman was a near certainty. To provide backbone to his precarious position he encouraged Britain to pay for and train his army in exchange[30] for a privileged position on pending oil rights. By doing so he satisfied earlier treaties and secured his country from external aggressors.

Long before oil was struck in June 1962 he had studied the experience of other Gulf states caught in the oil boom. He was determined that the speed of change should be governed more slowly. Then, with his advisors, he started to draw up infrastructure plans that he could gradually implement when the oil revenues rendered each stage affordable.

However, his perception of the speed at which each step should be taken differed from his advisors. Undoubtedly his judgement was influenced by many years of presiding over his country's parlous finances, when bargaining and thrift had been essential to survival. Due to advanced years his inbuilt reluctance to accept a quicker pulse of change was becoming an increasing cause of concern to his advisors.

By the late 1960s – some five years after oil had been struck – there was a discernible impatience with the apparent slowness of change throughout the country. Some of this stemmed from a lack of understanding that not only were the oil reserves relatively modest but also that they invariably take time to flow through to tangible improvements. But this impatience for change began to be directed towards the Sultan. Was he really the right person to lead them into the 1970s? Surely this was the dawn of a new era.

## An Omani-British partnership to be proud of

During the last twenty-five years of the twentieth century the British people have been striving for a fresh identity that can provide a renewed confidence on the world stage. Those born since 1945 have witnessed not only the British Empire in terminal decline but until recently an economy struggling to compete.

Perhaps it is no small wonder that our resilient nation, virtually bankrupted by the Second World War and then struggling to survive during a period of relentless withdrawal, has no wish to dwell on recent history. To succeed in such circumstances seemed to require a single-mindedness, unfettered by the past.

Unfortunately this reluctance to give any time or thought to history runs the risk that past achievements are not considered significant in the modern scheme of things. Such a blinkered approach flies in the face of enlightened future progress. Now that Britain is showing encouraging signs of regaining her self respect the time has come to recognise those past achievements which provide opportunity to improve our sphere of influence. Britain's contribution to the emergence of Oman as an enlightened nation state is just one such example. Between 1952 and 1970 Britain's leadership of the Sultan's Armed Forces was conducted with sensitivity and deference to a people still living a feudal existence.

There was little doubt that Sultan Said bin Taimur was well pleased with the quality of service provided by seconded and contract officers during these formative years. Invariably, those selected to serve made it their business to learn the language and understand the culture of the Omani people. Much of the success of this cultural partnership was due to some key personalities of the time who not only set an excellent example to us but who were also determined that we should be given the best possible advice. Colonel Colin Maxwell and Major Malcolm Dennison[31], both contract officers from the early days of the Muscat Field Force of the mid-1950s and fluent Arabists, seemed to us to understand the hearts and minds of the Omani people. In the early 1960s Colin was Deputy Commander and 'father' of SAF, while Malcolm seemed to combine the role of recruiter from the villages with Intelligence work (85). Each appeared to possess a brand of persuasive charm and tireless persistence that few of us had encountered before. We took note and did our best to emulate them.

During 1963 and 1964 we were fortunate in both the officers who held the position successively of Commander of the Sultan's Armed Forces (CSAF). Firstly Colonel Hugh Oldman[32], OBE (Durham Light Infantry) and from April 1964 Colonel Tony Lewis, DSO, MBE (Royal Marines) who, at the age of 24, had been the youngest lieutenant-colonel commanding a fighting unit (No. 6 Commando) in the British Army during the invasion of Normandy.

Within the two regiments, The Northern Frontier Regiment (NFR) and The Muscat Regiment (MR), we were equally fortunate with both commanding officers and their seconds-in-command. While Lieutenant-Colonels Dougie Dalglish and Clive Chettle were talented leaders seconded from their respective parent regiments (The Leicesters and The Devon and Dorsets), their seconds-in-command were also both highly experienced contract officers. Major John Clarke, formerly of The Household Cavalry, brought experience of the Sudan Defence Force and Malaya. Major Johnny Cooper was something of a Special Air Service legend, having been Colonel David Stirling's driver in the Long Range Desert Group in North Africa during the Second World War and later SAS Squadron Commander during the Jebel Akhdar Campaign in 1958. This meant that the Armed Forces were well led during the early stages of their development.

On the other side of this partnership, the Omanis possessed so many inherent qualities that with the right blend of opportunity, encouragement and discipline made them potentially good soldiers. Among these qualities was a thirst for knowledge which, during the 1960s had little prospect of being satisfied because few if any schools existed. Those hand-picked recruits saw the Army as an opportunity to escape from deprivation and to improve themselves. They also brought with them an indigenous knowledge of their country, a natural eye for the lie of the land and endemic rifle-handling skills. They possessed a well-developed judgement of people, a respect for others and an infectious sense of humour.

Consequently it was no surprise that those Omanis who took full advantage of the education, training and development provided by the Army became good soldiers. Indeed their privileged experience helped to alert their families to the need to improve the quality of their lives. When oil was discovered in 1964 and Omanisation of the Armed Forces followed in 1970 the Army had already provided some essential foundations from which to build and progress.

This partnership was based on trust and respect. Both nations were justified in feeling proud of what they had achieved together. Happily this mutual debt of gratitude still continues to this day. It is in the interests of both nations to perpetuate this good will and explore how to continue to work together.

## Sultan Qaboos succeeds his father, July 23rd 1970

In this final section Colin McLean has helped me to provide a snapshot of Sultan Qaboos's first seven years in power after succeeding his father, Sultan Said bin Taimur, in 1970. These same seven years were also the final seven of Colin's fourteen years of service to the Sultan. In 1977 he returned to England and, four years later in 1981, I was privileged to be present when he was ordained as a Roman Catholic priest by Cardinal Basil Hume at Brompton Oratory.

Since 1970 the Sultanate and the Omani people have undergone the steadily quickening beat of change. Neither Colin nor I has returned to Oman since we left, preferring to cherish our own memories of times past. Far from implying our disapproval for such inevitable changes, we, like so many other British officers, know how privileged we were to have served the Sultan but have since moved on to new chapters in our lives.

So often in life the demand for wholesale change highlights the need for fresh leadership. Oman was no exception. Qaboos had spent the early 1960s outside Oman, first undergoing two years officer training at the Royal Military Academy Sandhurst, which was followed by a tour with the Cameronians in Germany. After a course in local government and a world tour he returned to Oman in 1966 only to find himself excluded from government affairs. Virtually under house arrest in Salalah he had yet to visit Muscat. Suggestions by the Sultan's advisors that Qaboos should become involved in Oman's future development planning were ignored by his father. Consequently his increasingly impatient son spent much of his time studying Islam and Omani history.

By the late 1960s Qaboos began to express his desire for change to sons of the Sultan's advisors and expatriate visitors to the palace. These quietly supported his impatience for change which by then was rife throughout most of Oman. Qaboos decided that it was time to take the initiative.

After gaining pledges of loyalty from Buraik bin Hamud al-Ghafri, the son of the Wali of Dhofar, and Hilal bin Sultan al Hosni, who commanded the Hawasini contingent that formed half of the guard outside the palace, he approached the Defence Secretary Colonel Hugh Oldman for help in preparing and co-ordinating matters. Both understood that it was essential that no British officer should take a direct part in the overthrow.

On July 23rd 1970 Buraik led a group of the Sultan's bodyguard to the palace, followed by soldiers from SAF's Desert Regiment led by Lieutenant Said Salem Al Wahabi. After a series of sporadic but heavy fire fights through the palace corridors, the Sultan was finally cornered. However, this was not before an armed slave had been killed and the Sultan, being called upon to surrender, shot Buraik in the stomach and said 'I will not surrender to anyone except a senior British officer'. On being asked if he would surrender to the Commanding Officer of the Desert Regiment, he replied 'Yes' whereupon Colonel Turnill was called forward from the courtyard outside. And so Said bin Taimur, Sultan since 1932, finally relinquished power to his son and heir Sultan Qaboos (86).

After Said bin Taimur had received medical treatment for a gunshot wound in his foot caused by an accidental discharge, he was conveyed by RAF plane to London where he went into exile at the Dorchester Hotel. He died two years later.

Sultan Qaboos issued a press release on July 26th (Appendix 3) and took over the reins of government. The British Government formally recognised him on July 29th. The slowly emerging oil revenues allowed Sultan Qaboos to embark on a series of infrastructure plans to improve the quality of life of his people.

## Oil revenues become a catalyst for renaissance

Since 1967 many other fields have been found and developed by PDO. Between 1970 and 1998 production increased from 332,000 barrels a day from four fields to around 900,000 barrels a day from over 100 fields (90). During 1998 the Government decided to cut PDO oil production by 50,000 barrels a day in the interests of oil producing states, bringing the daily average down to 810,000. At current production rates oil reserves are guaranteed until 2050 and in June 1999 PDO discovered a significant new region of oil and gas fields in South Oman.

Revenues from the initial years of production set the scene for the rebirth of Oman in 1970 – the year of Renaissance – when His Majesty Qaboos bin Said succeeded his father. He immediately embarked on the first of a series of five-year plans. These included acutely needed reforms in health services, education and economic development, largely funded from steadily increasing oil revenues.

### Contribution of Oil Revenues to Total Government Revenues

| Five year plans | | Oil revenues (million Rial Omani) | Oil revenues as % of total revenues |
|---|---|---|---|
| 1st | 1976 – 1980 | 3125 | 92.2 |
| 2nd | 1981 – 1985 | 6649 | 88.4 |
| 3rd | 1986 – 1990 | 6016 | 80.2 |
| 4th | 1991 – 1995 | 8571 | 84.5 |

Source: *Oil and the Transformation of Oman 1970–1995*
by Mohamed bin Musa Al-Yousef.

Bringing the classically underdeveloped Sultanate of Oman into the twentieth century within twenty years was a remarkable feat. To achieve this meant that Oman's Gross National Product per capita needed to grow by more than 6 per cent per annum between 1965 and 1990. This demanded a blend of dedicated leadership and a substantial degree of state intervention to sustain a rate of growth that surpassed every other country in the world.

The Ministry of Petroleum and Minerals now restricts production to a level that does not exceed 6.5 per cent of the remaining reserves per annum. At 'The Vision Conference: Oman 2020' held in 1995 it was decided that by 2020 Oman's economy should no longer be so reliant on oil. A 25-year forecast for diversification towards the non-oil sectors was agreed and expressed as percentages in relation to GDP.

### Percentage of GDP

| Sector | 1996 | 2020 |
|---|---|---|
| Crude oil | 41% | 9% |
| Gas | 1% | 10% |
| Industrial | 7.5% | 29% |

Source: *Oman '99* page 89.

It is an inescapable fact that oil revenues have been the catalyst for transforming Oman from feudalism to modernity within a single generation. Yet reliance on a resource which may not exist in fifty years' time is no longer an option. Recent volatility in crude oil prices emphasises that any nation's over-reliance on oil revenues is an economic policy fraught with risk. Diversification is now the planned and prudent route towards consistency in balancing Oman's books.

## Omanisation of the Sultan of Oman's Armed Forces

During the early 1960s the first carefully measured steps were taken towards Omanisation of the Sultan's Armed Forces. A select handful of young Omanis was promoted from senior non-commissioned officers and awarded a Sultan's Commission in the Army. This transition, which was entirely on merit, was watched with interest. At this stage Sultan Said bin Taimur who feared the possibility of a military coup, stipulated that no Local Officer was to be promoted above lieutenant.

By the mid-1960s this early experiment towards Omanisation was seen to have been successful. A policy was agreed to encourage the talent of local troops by identifying potential leaders from enlistment onwards and also by seeking trainees for technical posts. This was achieved by a combination of education, training-courses and early independent responsibility. Care was taken to offer equal opportunities to all Omanis. Every step taken was based on a strong sense of mutual trust.

At the Pay Review Board of 1969–70 chaired by Colonel Hugh Oldman, a refreshingly bold and far-reaching decision was made to introduce equal basic pay for each rank regardless of nationality. This was supplemented by an expatriate allowance and flying and technical incremental pay.

This ground-breaking decision paved the way to the amalgamation of officers' messes. Sultan Said in the meanwhile gave his authority for local officers to be promoted on merit and in due course to the rank of captain.

In 1970 a combination of increased threat in the southern province of Dhofar and a need to exercise greater control there prompted Sultan Qaboos to bring the Dhofar Force (DF) into the Sultan of Oman's Forces. At the same time the command of the Dhofar Force passed from Pakistani to British officers.

Two years later, in 1972, the National Firquat Forces (FQ), who were based in Dhofar by tribes under their own appointed leaders, became uniformed and began a process of gradual regularisation.

By this time Brigadier Colin Maxwell had established an Omanisation Office at HQ in Bait al Falaj (91). With the Dhofar War at its height, there was a fresh impetus from British and Omani sources to speed up the process of localisation. Accordingly, in 1974, the Omanisation Office became Military Secretary's (MS) Branch. Lieutenant-Colonel Colin McLean was appointed Military Secretary to the Minister of Defence and was responsible until 1977 for the selection, training, appointment and promotion of local officers in all three services.

One of the first things which Colin did on taking up his appointment was to borrow his father's[33] 'Notes on MS Matters'. Using much the same principles Colin adapted these to suit the Sultan of Oman's Forces. In 1975 the Sultan, as Minister of Defence, gave his approval for these 'Notes on MS Matters' to become the textbook for the career planning of local officers of all three services.

By 1976 newly established Regular Commission Boards selected candidates for officer training in Oman and abroad. The Sultan's excellent relationship with King Hussein led to Jordan becoming an alternative venue for officers' courses to those in the UK. Promotion boards met regularly taking particular note of seniority, education qualifications in Arabic and English and course gradings. The first local lieutenant-colonels were then promoted.

By mid-1977 multicoloured flowcharts on wallboards and in talc books[34] traced the planned career of every officer. The aim was that all officer posts in the Sultan of Oman's Land Forces should be localised by a named officer by 1981. The first local Commander Sultan of Oman's Land Forces (CSOLF) was to be appointed by 1982. I was delighted to hear that he was none other than the Deputy Commander, Naseeb bin Hamad, whom I remember as a young and promising sergeant in 1963 (75, 92). Inevitably, the planned progress achievable in relation to the Air Force and Navy was slower due to their later formation and the longer technical training required.

## Dhofar war 1964–1975

Unlike the three small campaigns of 1955, 1957 and 1959 that took place in the Northern Region where the rebels established isolated strongholds on the summit of the Jebel Akhdar, this protracted war emanated from the rugged jebel to the north at Salalah, the most important city in the southern province of Dhofar. During 1964 a growing band of wild and nomadic Dhofari tribesmen in the mountains north of Salalah mounted a rebellion against the authority of Sultan Said bin Taimur. These tribesmen with long hair and indigo-dyed faces were skilled riflemen and masters of fieldcraft. They could exist for days on a few handfuls of rice. As their ranks swelled, the Sultan's Armed Forces were compelled to deploy their forces to the remote Dhofar region with a long re-supply line back to Headquarters.

Encouraged by the discovery of oil and by early operational successes in a fearsome country of cliffs and gorges that they knew so well, the rebel strength gradually swelled considerably and became larger than the Sultan's Armed Forces. Leadership of the rebellion was seized by Arab Marxists calling themselves the Popular Front for the Liberation of Oman and the Occupied Arab Gulf (PFLOAG).

In contrast to the campaigns of the 1950s when the rebels were trained and paid by Saudi Arabia and then infiltrated covertly across the border near Buraimi, this had now become a professionally planned and confrontational rebellion of considerable ferocity. The original local threat had now escalated to one of grave regional significance.

When the British withdrew from Aden in November 1967 the first revolutionary Marxist government in the Arab world took over Aden Colony and the former Aden Protectorate. This whole area became the People's Democratic Republic of Yemen. This brought the PFLOAG threat right up to and beyond Oman's south-westerly border. The Soviet Union, as well as other Marxist countries such as China and East Germany, sensing the imminent overthrow of a British supported isolationist Oman, sent arms, advice and training teams. One more push on the already open back door to Oman would open up the heartland of Middle Eastern oil. Indeed, by the late 1960s, despite Britain reinforcing the hard pressed Sultan's Armed Forces with the Special Air Service and Royal Engineers most of the Dhofar region was in rebel hands.

Tactics were similar to Radfan operations in 1958 and 1960. These included picquetting of high ground, the building of sangar walls when in defensive positions, use of rocket-propelled projectiles, mines, bomber and fighter ground attack support. To these were added deployment and re-supply by helicopter and the use of infrared for night attacks. However, although helicopters helped to speed up deployment, the rugged terrain continued to place a premium on the skill, courage and endurance of the soldier on his feet. The Sultan's Armed Forces showed great tenacity and gallantry during this painstaking and ferocious conflict (93–96).

When Sultan Qaboos succeeded his father in June 1970 there had been six years of bloodshed in the Dhofar Region. The outlook was grim. Britain was already fully stretched and other Arab rulers were loath to join a struggle that seemed to pit Arab against Arab. Moreover Oman's money was running out because its newly discovered oil reserves were too small to finance a prolonged war.

Sultan Qaboos and his British advisors decided that it was time to adopt a new approach to the war. Gradually the Dhofari rebels were wooed with promises of amnesty, rewards, medical aid, schools and jobs. By 1972 many hundreds had joined the home guard units, called firqas, and had returned to the mountains in the pay of the new Sultan. These growing reinforcements allowed the Sultan's Army to penetrate deeper into the rebel strongholds.

Following a visit to the Sultanate by Sir Gawain Bell, the former Governor of Nigeria, Sultan Qaboos established a Civil Aid Department in Salalah that was responsible to the Wali of Dhofar. This small team of dedicated British and Omanis worked towards providing schools, clinics, shops, mosques and water supply schemes all over the jebel in Dhofar. New services also included provision of food supplies, a flying doctor service and Government vets to advise the Jebalis with their livestock.

Although this new approach was clearly succeeding, the outcome of the war still remained in the balance. The need to close the border supply routes to the rebels from South Yemen required more resources than Oman's forces could muster. Fortunately, fuelled by the Sultan's enlightened policies towards his people, a shift in international perceptions began to take place. By 1973 the main force of the Arab revolution was on the wane and this allowed Arab moderates to take the Sultan's side. Saudi Arabia offered financial aid and started to use its new, oil-based muscle to persuade South Yemen to abandon PFLOAG. King Hussein of Jordan sent military help while the Chinese abandoned the Dhofar Marxists. The huge increase in oil price that followed the Arab oil embargo helped to focus more foreign minds. It dawned that Oman and Iran shared the guardianship of the Strait of Hormuz, 'the Free World's jugular vein' for oil supply to half the globe. The Shah of Iran, initially fearing he might upset other Arab rulers by intruding on Arab territory but sensing a change in international perceptions, sent 3,000 ground troops and many helicopters to Oman.

These welcome reinforcements to the Sultan of Oman's Forces finally tipped the balance after eleven years of fighting. By 1975 the war was over and peace was imposed throughout Dhofar. This victory signalled the first occasion that a modern revolutionary guerrilla army had been defeated in the field since Malaya in 1960. The Sultan's Armed Forces' fifteen years of British military training and leadership had been put to the test and had passed with distinction. The Force had gained battle experience during a prolonged and bloody war. As

**87** Burning off oil from the first drill stem production test at Natih 1, 1963. *By kind permission of A. J. M. Lush.*

**88** Oil rig in operation at Natih in 1968. *By kind permission of C. R. Butt.*

**89** On military escort duty to explosives convoy for PDO, 1964. *By kind permission of J. R. Darbyshire.*

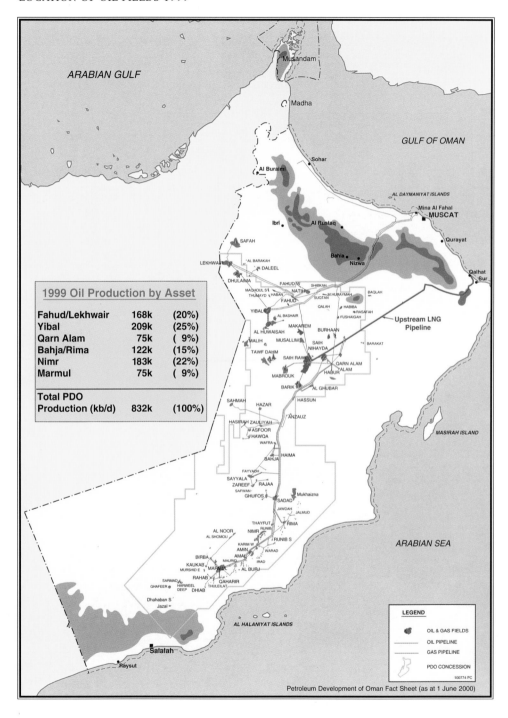

**1999 Oil Production by Asset**

| | | |
|---|---|---|
| Fahud/Lekhwair | 168k | (20%) |
| Yibal | 209k | (25%) |
| Qarn Alam | 75k | ( 9%) |
| Bahja/Rima | 122k | (15%) |
| Nimr | 183k | (22%) |
| Marmul | 75k | ( 9%) |
| | | |
| Total PDO | | |
| Production (kb/d) | 832k | (100%) |

Petroleum Development of Oman Fact Sheet (as at 1 June 2000)

LEGEND

OIL & GAS FIELDS

OIL PIPELINE

GAS PIPELINE

PDO CONCESSION

100774 PC

**91** Brigadier Colin Maxwell, Deputy Commander, Sultan's Armed Forces, 1973. *By kind permission of C. R. Butt.*

**92** Lieutenant-Colonel Naseeb bin Hamad Salim al Ruwahi in May 1978 as Commanding Officer, Royal Guard Regiment. In 1982 he was to become first local Commander, Sultan of Oman's Land Forces (CSOLF). *By kind permission of C. R. Butt.*

**93** Platoon picquet convoy as it climbs track at Aqabat Mushaila, August 1968. *By kind permission of C. R. Butt.*

**94** Ferret scout car and CO's Land Rover wait for the call forward at Wadi Narhiz, April 1969. *By kind permission of C. R. Butt.*

**95** A sentry in a sangar at Akoot, 1972. *By kind permission of Colonel N. Knocker OBE.*

**96** Alex Lamond, Operations Officer, The Desert Regiment, briefs members of the Firqat Tariq bin Zaid (FTZ) at Akoot, 1972. *By kind permission of Colonel N. Knocker OBE.*

**97** Sultan Qaboos Mosque, 2001. *By kind permission of the Ministry of Information, Sultanate of Oman.*

**98** A small herd of white oryx in the shade, 1994. *By kind permission of Gigi Crocker-Jones.*

**99** His Majesty Sultan Qaboos bin Said Al-Said. *By kind permission of Mohamed Mustafa.*

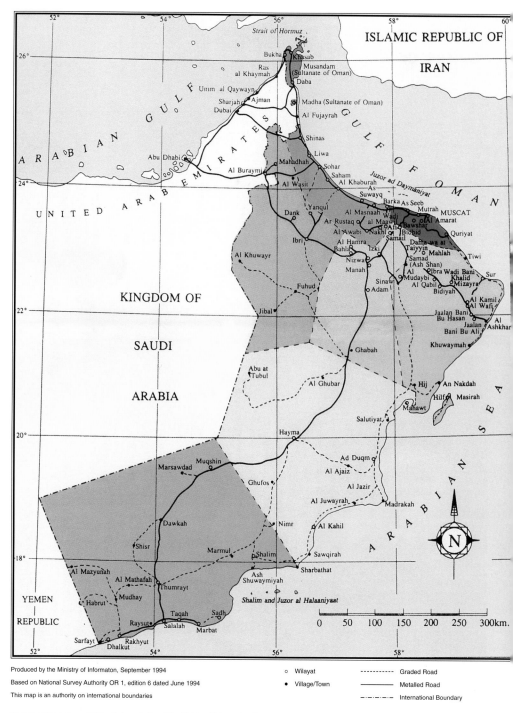

| | | |
|---|---|---|
| o | Wilayat | ---------- Graded Road |
| • | Village/Town | ——— Metalled Road |
| | | —·—·—·— International Boundary |

they gradually regained the initiative over the Marxist rebels so a growing sense of confidence and pride in achievement followed. The Sultan of Oman's Forces had come of age.

## Massive changes to infrastructure

Despite Oman's victory over Marxist rebels in 1975 this protracted conflict in Dhofar had taken its toll. Many Omani, British[35] and Iranian lives had been sacrificed or scarred during this eleven years of ferocious fighting. When in 1972 Sultan Qaboos offered an amnesty to the Dhofar rebels and an opportunity for them to join Firquat Forces, both sides were war weary. By then this campaign had imposed a considerable drain on Oman's resources. The Omani people had witnessed their country gradually emerging revenues being diverted to a costly war in remote Dhofar. An impatient thirst for peace prevailed.

As soon as the Dhofar rebels accepted the amnesty, the Omani government decided to give priority to spiritual and moral issues. It is as well to remember that in a Muslim world Church and State are one and the need for spiritual refreshment and moral rectitude comes before both physical and political considerations.

Accordingly, to encourage Omani people to seek spiritual refreshment, priority was given to improving the provision of mosques for civilian and military communities. Much emphasis was devoted towards addressing issues of justice and human rights. Land near the Christian Cemetery in Ruwi was given for Christian communities to build churches. This in itself was remarkable, bearing in mind that in 1947, Wilfred Thesiger and his companions were forced to flee from outside Ibri. His Bedu companions were told that they would die because they had brought a Christian into Oman.

This enhancement of spiritual opportunities was linked to improving the moral livelihood of Omani people. With the notable exception of the Army, education within Oman had been virtually non-existent. Ambitious young men had either joined the oil company or one of the Services or travelled abroad to attend schools. Now the government embarked on the recruitment of teachers and technical instructors. Much emphasis was devoted to establishing a sound educational basis from which to progress. Five-yearly infrastructure plans set targets for the number of schools required and specified the levels of apprentice training needed.

At the same time infrastructure plans were drawn up for the regeneration of the industrial and business sector and the promotion of employment opportunities. By then it was known that Oman's oil reserves were relatively modest so the government embarked on a programme of diversification of industry. This included expansion of fishing, mining for minerals other than oil, agricultural programmes, experimental farming, desalination plants and improving water reserves. All this created new employment opportunities that together with banking and contract tenders, helped to counterbalance those employment opportunities that depended on oil. It was also important to ensure that all Bedu tribes had their fair share of oil-related employment opportunities. Indeed, soon after the PDO struck oil in 1964, Sultan Said devised a three-month roster system designed to preserve equal opportunities between tribes. Despite these good intentions some inevitable friction arose between the Duru and the Harasis.

While health, education and employment were central to the moral regeneration of Oman, there were other supporting concerns that were essential to the need for enlightened moral progress. There were concerns for the environment and national cohesion. Accordingly, the government took specific initiatives designed to set appropriate standards for the landscaping and cleanliness of capital areas. In the interests of national pride and cohesion, the government embarked on a series of national day celebrations, military tattoos and sporting events. Finally, and most importantly, there was a proclaimed and well-funded plan to develop proper communications throughout Oman. This included not only the establishment of telephone, postal and information technology networks but also a determination to keep the Omani people well informed of progress made during the government's five-year plans.

The sheer scale of progress which flowed from these programmes between 1970 and 1990 was massive and a matter of great pride to Omanis. While oil revenues were the catalyst for sustained renaissance, it is as well to remember that Oman's oil resources in terms of reserves and annual production do not match her neighbours. Consequently, proactive and prudent development planning were essential during a time when the concept of development planning was under severe attack. Some books[36] now record Oman's transformation from an unknown underdeveloped country into a respected member of the international community within twenty years. 'Some Facts and Figures' (Appendix 4) give some indication of the huge advances made in Health, Education and Communications Services 1970–1998.

With so many physical improvements needed, Sultan Qaboos had to establish clear priorities in his post-1970 five yearly infrastructure plans. Initially, the building of a network of roads by Strabag Gmbh was followed by the development of sea ports at Muttrah and Raysut and of airports at Seeb and

Salalah. Financial resources were also allocated to projects to preserve Oman's national heritage such as museums, archaeology and history. Environmentally specific initiatives were taken to conserve flora and fauna and to combat poaching. Examples of such projects include the White Oryx and Wahiba Sands.[37]

On the political scene there was much progress made in the creation of instruments of government such as councils and ministries. There followed a programme of building of government offices and also palaces to receive heads of state. After Sultan Said's forty-eight years of isolationism, Sultan Qaboos embarked on 'catch-up' reciprocal diplomacy with Jordan, Egypt, Iran and the Gulf States.

Internally the need for a co-ordinated approach to civilian security matters throughout Oman led to Brigadier Malcolm Dennison being appointed as National Security Advisor. The Oman Police force was expanded so as to fulfil its responsibilities throughout Oman. In this process it became an integrated male and female force. The Sultan's Armed Forces (SAF), which had been too big and unwieldy to remain a single entity, was divided into three arms – The Sultan of Oman's Land Forces (SOLF), the Sultan of Oman's Air Force (SOAF) and the Sultan of Oman's Navy (SON) and, somewhat later, the Royal Guard (RG). This was accompanied by a significant expansion in manpower, armament, equipment, buildings and deployment.

## Summary reflections

When embarking on this book, I had one advantage over my contemporaries – Charmian had kept the letters which I had written to her in 1962 and 1963. They were the kernel which made it possible to extract vividness from recollection. Otherwise, just like others, I treasured memories of unusual and pioneering times. Could this combination form the basis for a book?

Somewhat inevitably doubts began to take hold, rather like a mountaineer climbing alone. By no stretch of the imagination were my experiences particularly exciting – frequently challenging perhaps but otherwise somewhat routine.

Yet what were the ingredients which made this time unusually memorable for us all? Muscat and Oman was an outstandingly beautiful country of contrasts – desert, jebel and fertile coastal plane – still virtually unscathed by westernisation. And above all else the charming, inquisitive and resilient Omanis.

Somehow I needed to capture this brief period in Oman's history just as the discovery of oil beckoned an intense period of cultural change. How could I contrast the feudal early 1960s that I had experienced, with the bold advances of the 1970s that I had not?

While this seemed an insurmountable problem at the start, happily it has not proved to be so. I have discovered in the course of my researches a nucleus of my former contemporaries who, together with selected experts, have volunteered to help me by 'roping up' so that I no longer felt that I was climbing alone. In particular, I would like to thank Colin McLean for his generous and painstaking help that has enabled me to summarise the cultural changes of the 1970s. One of the most delightful consequences of my researches has been the renewal of old friendships and the forging of new ones. A glance at the Acknowledgements shows just how lucky I have been. It is they who have helped me provide a balanced view of life before and during Oman's emerging years.

On reflection I can do no better than quote two passages which seem to epitomise the cultural challenges between the 1960s and 1970s.

David Coppin wrote in a letter dated April 20th 2000:

'We were romantics – all of us in the 60s, but I think our admiration for the Omanis stemmed from their courage under adversity and to see them finally get education, schools, hospitals and a fair share of the material benefits which we all take for granted has compensated for a loss of the glamorous isolation which we enjoyed.

'The development (since 1970) by and large has been brilliantly conceived and executed under Sultan Qaboos and the people have retained their hospitable and generous nature. You must go back on a visit!'

David Holden, Chief Correspondent of *The Sunday Times,* reported a conversation with Sultan Qaboos in 1977:

'Although the Sultan admits some shortcomings in his new order, he suggests that many were unavoidable. "After 1970, we had to keep our promises and do things at once", he told me recently. "So we pushed ahead quickly and perhaps spent more than we should. But the money has been spread all over the country. Before our people had nothing. Now, with schools, hospitals and community development projects opening up the nation, they have things they were crying out for."

Extract from *Oman's Unsung Triumph* by David Holden
for Reader's Digest, February 1978

In summary the combination of the discovery of oil (1964), the succession of Sultan Qaboos (1970) and the end of the Dhofar War (1975) triggered unprecedented changes in Oman during the 1970s. That these massive changes were so successfully achieved is of enduring credit to Sultan Qaboos, his government and not least the resilient Omani people (97, 99, 100).

# Epilogue

With few exceptions I have found that anyone who has had the privilege to serve in Oman has discovered that this beautiful country and its charming people tend to linger in the mind. Indeed many of my contemporaries were reluctant to leave at the end of their tour of duty, whether with the services, oil companies or the banks. Several fell under Oman's spell, resigned their commissions and became contract officers. Others managed to engineer second or third tours of duty. However the majority of us left with pangs of regret, to take up more conventional career postings elsewhere. Only in later life, when our recall of earlier experiences becomes surprisingly vivid, have we come to realise how special our time in Muscat and Oman was.

I hope that *Letters from Oman* will help to rekindle similar memories in the minds of others. Some readers will have enjoyed much more exciting times in Oman since the early 1960s. Most will have held more responsible positions and a few will have influenced the course of Oman's history. Yet despite my relative lack of credentials for putting pen to paper, I have done so because Charmian kept my letters. Their existence has brought Muscat and Oman of the early 1960s into focus again. Much pleasure has been derived from paying tribute to an Omani–British partnership, which like our marriage has happily endured.

How can we all help to preserve and perpetuate an Omani-British relationship fostered in the early 17th century and nurtured with care ever since? Mutual respect for each other's culture has been and will continue to be intrinsic to working together successfully during the communications revolution of the 21st century. While Oman has come of age under Sultan Qaboos during the last thirty years of the 20th century, her new found confidence and self reliance has coincided with Britain's changing role in world affairs. Although both changes have occurred within a single generation, both countries still need to rely upon each other's bedrock of friendship during the 21st century. Economic and commercial considerations, however persuasive, should not prevail to the detriment of mutual respect and affection.

# Postscript

*September 11th, 2001*

This intensely evil outrage wrought on 7,000 people from 60 nations has stunned the world. Everyone is struggling to come to terms with a world campaign against terrorism. A real concern is that intense media coverage often heightens anxiety, oversimplifies cultural differences and can encourage extremism. Yet, if we do not strive to understand what is going on, polarisation between the Western and Muslim world could become unstoppable. This is precisely what the terrorist cells are seeking to achieve.

This situation calls out for level-headed leadership, lack of prejudice and a determination to understand each others cultures. Only then can common decency prevail.

In HRH Princes Charles' speech to the Oxford Centre of Islamic Studies in 1993, he said "Extremism is no more the monopoly of Islam than it is the monopoly of other religions, including Christianity." All peace loving nations now pray that the coalition's response to this recent outrage will be porportionate to the need to isolate and neutralise those responsible.

As I write this postscript there are 25,000 British servicemen on exercise in Oman. Planned several years ago to test our logistical capability to deploy a major force to the Middle East, Oman is being used as a staging post. What this now means in the context of the "War on the Taliban" remains to be seen.

However, one thing is certain. Had there not been a history of respect and trust between Omanis and British, Sultan Qaboos would not have made Oman available at the outset. Recent intense insecurity has not deflected him from welcoming Christians to a Muslim world.

The world is witnessing an evil minority holding civilised people to ransom. In such insecure times, we need to be on our guard. However, this is also precisely the time we need to respect, understand and trust the vast majority of our fellow human beings. We can help this process by our determination to foster and improve our multi-racial communities.

13th October 2001

# Notes

1. This compares with an army strength of 100,000 in 2001.

2. Some Muslim traditions place the Garden of Eden in the green and pleasant hills of Yemen, citing the name of the port of Aden to substantiate this.

3. Hunter's *Statistical Account of the British Settlement of Aden, 1877*, p. 169.

4. The Port and Legislative Council Records. Sir Tom Hickinbotham, author of *Aden* (Constable and Company, 1958) took over as chairman of the Aden Port Trust in 1948.

5. *Farewell to Arabia* by David Holden, p. 30.

6. *Yemen: Travels in Dictionary Land* by Tim Mackintosh-Smith, p. 157.

7. The Treaty of Friendship of 1800 between Muscat and Oman and Britain "envisaged friendship between our two countries lasting until the end of time . . ." and provided that "an English Gentleman of respectability should always reside at the port of Muscat".

8. David Holden was the *Sunday Times* special correspondent on Foreign Affairs and author of *Farewell to Arabia* published by Faber and Faber Ltd in 1966.

9. Tarik bin Taimur subsequently became Director of the Municipality (Muscat and Muttrah) 1945–1957.

10. *Full Circle: the memoirs of Sir Anthony Eden*, pp 334–5.

11. When Sultan Qaboos succeeded his father in 1970 a broadcasting station was opened within one week of his accession; Sultanate of Oman Television followed in 1974.

12. Introduction to *Sultan in Oman*, by James Morris.

176

13. *Farewell to Arabia* by David Holden, p. 226.

14. Lieutenant Wellsted of the Indian Navy in 1835.

15. Ramniklal B. Kothary, PO Box 66, Cable: Kothary, Muscat (Arabia) were suppliers to the Sultan's Armed Forces.

16. Shamagh. A red and white cloth headscarf worn by soldiers on patrol. Square with tassles at the edges, it is folded into a triangle, the base of which is wrapped around the forehead while the central point of the triangle drops down the back between the shoulder blades. A black aghal, a double headcord which is adjustable, keeps the shamagh in place and displays the SAF badge. This headress protects the head, can be wrapped in across the face below the eyes and the side points tucked back into the aghal. This provides good protection from sunburn, dust and sand, particularly when riding a camel or travelling in an open vehicle or during a sandstorm.

17. UN General Assembly Report of the Special Representative of the Secretary-General on his Visit to Oman, October 8th 1963.

18. While indeed it may be cooler in wadi beds, it is important to add a note of caution before adopting this practice, particularly when there is the slightest prospect of rain. Within half an hour heavy rain can convert a dry wadi bed, particularly when fed by others, into a raging torrent capable of engulfing anything in its path. Although these are rare occurrences, it is always wise to note where the high ground lies, in case of emergency.

19. This climb would normally take seven hours with donkeys carrying heavy equipment.

20. Some years later David Pank commanded 3rd Battalion The Light Infantry and ultimately as a Major-General, became Colonel of the Regiment. On retirement from the Army he became Chief Executive of Newbury Racecourse.

21. Likely to have been Carl Seton-Brown and Sandy Gordon.

22. Subsequently succeeded by Major Colin McLean.

23. Branding was commonplace, a feudal treatment for most internal disorders. Scar tissue tended to rub sore under military equipment and become re-infected in the heat. The skin wall was often 'wafer thin'.

24 Some years later Brigadier Leask was to become Lieutenant General Sir Henry Leask, KCB, CBE, DSO. In retirement he became Chairman of the 78 Division Battleaxe Club Committee. This was the highly successful division in which my father had commanded 36 Infantry Brigade in 1944.

25. *Maverick Guide to Oman* by Peter Ochs II, Pelican, Gretna, 1998 p. 151.

26. When the British left Aden in 1967, this became the Yemen.

27. GSO 2 (Int), General Staff Office Grade 2 (Intelligence).

28. MTB 219, Motor Torpedo Boat 219 has a proud Royal Naval history. When with the 6th MTB Flotilla based on Dover, she participated in the attack on the German Battlecruisers *Scharnhorst, Gneisnau* and *Prinz Eugen* in passage through the English Channel on the 12th February 1942.

29. PDO – Petroleum Development of Oman – an oil exploration company which, at that stage, was owned 85% by Shell and 15% by Partex.

30. By an 'Exchange of Letters' dated 25th July 1958, the British Government promised financial and military assistance in exchange for a reorganisation of the Sultan's Armed Forces under British supervision. This subsidy of between £1m and £2m per annum continued until 1967. Also Sultan Said was required to establish a development council, as an agent for change, which the British Government also funded with about £250,000 per annum between 1959 and 1967.

31. Both Colin and Malcolm were promoted to the rank of Brigadier in due course.

32. In February 1970, Colonel Hugh Oldman became Defence Secretary and later Sir Hugh Oldman, KBE.

33. Lieutenant-General Sir Kenneth G. McLean KCB, KBE was military Secretary to the Secretary of State of War 1949–1951 and Chief of Staff to the Ministry of Defence 1951–1952.

34. See-through plastic on which chinagraph pencils are used.

35. The SAF Book of Remembrance in the Royal Military Chapel, Sandhurst, records the names of thirty-five British servicemen who were killed during the Dhofar War (1964–1975).

36. *Oil and the transformation of Oman 1970–1995* by Mohamed bin Musa Al-Yousef and *Oman under Qaboos* by Calvin Allen, J. R. and W. Lynn Rigsbee, II, published by Frank Cass, 2000.

37. A detailed survey of the Wahiba Sands (1985–87) by the British Royal Geographical Society with generous support by Oman. This is an area as large as Wales of longitudinal sand dunes. Rust red at their base and honey coloured higher up, these dunes rise to between 300 and 600 feet. Inhabited by Bedouin tribes, they account for a fair proportion of the Sharqiyah, Oman's easternmost province. Beneath the sand lies the largest area of acolianite rock in the world.

# Appendices

*Appendix 1*

'Guide to Officers and Junior Leaders serving in Oman' by Lieutenant-Colonel C. C. Maxwell, Commander, Sultan's Forces. Undated, but issued to the author on joining The Sultan's Armed Forces in February 1963.

*Appendix 2*

Extracts from the first training manual for the Sultan's Armed Forces, dated 21st July 1964, drafted by the author.
        Tactics – Section Level iv – Patrols
        Tactics – Section Level v  – Picquetting

*Appendix 3*

Press Release issued by HM Sultan Qaboos, 26th July 1970

*Appendix 4*

Some Facts and Figures. To show the huge advances made in the development of Health, Education and Communication Services, 1970–1998.

## APPENDIX 1

### Guide to Offrs and Jnr Leaders
### Serving in OMAN

The following hints are for the guidance of all officers
and Junior Leaders who will command Arab or Baluch troops while
serving with the Sultan's Armed Forces in Oman.

.................

1.  These hints are aimed to assist you to recognise the
essential differences between yourselves, Arabs and Asians
and the degree of flexibility required by you to teach the
standards and discipline of the British Army and at the same
time foster a close and mutual understanding.

2.  The basic difference is temperament. Nevertheless it is
possible by daily contact with the men you command to understand
their temperaments and to get to know them sufficiently well to
induce a very large degree of mutual respect between you.

In order to achieve this you must realise that whereas
you have had the advantages of education, the men you command
have had practically none. They are tribesmen with simple up-
bringing and accustomed to a far lower standard of living than
you. They are mainly sons of the soil, agriculturists, cattle
herders and camel men, and some are fishermen and sea-farers.

Bear in mind that they are unaccustomed to routine habits,
these have to be taught and explained to them. But they are
adaptable and quite soon merge into the pattern of military
life which they enjoy.

Their families mean much to them .They are apt to fret
and worry when they are separated for long periods without
news of them. So pay attention to their problems which they
will bring to you and try to help them, and ask for the help
of the Welfare officer when necessary.

They will often talk at length on matters which appear
to you trivial but to them are major problems. Try to advise
them and solicit the help of your local officer. Above all
be patient and a good listener, and let them realise you are
out to help them. There is no better way of gaining their
confidence and once you have done that they will respect you
and serve you loyally and well. As you will soon find out they
are good military material, obedient and keen to learn all you
can teach them about soldiering.

Make their training interesting and vary it as much as
possible. Avoid monotony, appeal to their eye, they have
photographic minds – keep training periods short with frequent
breaks in between; you will find they lack the power to concentrate for long periods; avoid dreary lectures.

You will find they will always rise to the occasion with
a few spirited words of encouragement before a special ceremon-
ial parade, or a long and arduous patrol; you will be surprised
and rewarded by the results.

4.  The reason you are here is not only to command and lead
the local Forces, but to teach them modern military methods,
to train NCOs and teach them to instruct, and to train them to
provide their own officers in the course of time.

..../2

181

-2-

Although this is necessarily a long term measure, what you contribute towards it will be of lasting benefit to the Forces, so please keep this in mind while you are here.

Thus you are here to improve their military efficiency: do not attempt to change their way of life but respect their religion and customs. They may seem strange to you, but accept them and remember your customs are strange to them, but they accept them. By doing so you will gain their confidence.

5. Watch your own conduct and talk at all times. What you say in the office or the mess will be repeated and discussed by the men. Being mainly illiterate they are endless talkers.

6. Your brother officers come from a variety of regiments and backgrounds. This may seem strange to you after experiencing the intimate and close-knit life of your own regiment. But always remember the closeness of relationship between the officers will automatically reflect throughout your unit and indeed the Forces. Curb any feeling you may have of destructive criticism; be loyal to your superior officers. Concentrate on your military duties; avoid politics, the Foreign Office is still quite competent. Never forget that you represent in Oman all that is best in the British Army.

Some 'POTTED' Hints

1. Go easy to begin with: assess their standards and aim to raise them gradually. They will be watching you, closely to begin with, and they form their judgements on externals. Be smart in appearance and bearing (but avoid arrogance). A smile and a friendly hand-shake breaks the ice, and try to talk to them.

2. Keep a watchful eye on the cook house, rations, preparation and standard of cooking. Then men prefer a system of family feeding in small groups round a tray and bowl of food, which they are accustomed to at home. Investigate complaints and deal with them on the spot. Northing tends to lower morale more than good rations poorly cooked or unevenly apportioned. Contented feeding is of high importance to morale and cannot be over-stressed.

3. Learn all you can about your NCOs and men, their customs, previous work and domicile. Do this by watching, listening and indirect inquiry. Be friendly but don't over do it, and don't ask questions about their domestic affairs unless it is relative to a personal problem over which they ask your help.

4. Both Arab and Baluch have a keen sense of humour and the ridiculous, if you have one too, use it. Laugh with the men but never at them. Do not use sarcasm.

5. Never lay hands on them; you degrade yourself. It may be difficult to keep quiet when everything is being done wrong, but if you control your temper, the greater your advantage. Never swear at them, and when you feel inclined to shout, be firm and severe instead and you will find you will maintain your dignity and authority over them.

-3-

-3-

6. Personal example set by you is all-revealing  They will look up to you and copy you, therefore much that you what to teach them in the way of military life can be done by setting your standards before them. Be therefore always exemplary when moving among them.

7. When you introduce a new idea, herald it with explanation and give reasons for it. They will accept it once they understand the object. Familiarise them to new conditions gradually. Strange events sprung on them tend to cause panic. Appeal to their sporting instinct which the Bedu have so strongly. In short, don't attempt unusual things until they are familiar with the idea.

8. They are willing and capable of hard work. When performing menial work, however, ensure that they realise they are doing it to benefit themselves. Lend a hand yourself. Don't keep them at it too long.

9. Try to inculcate the team spirit into your unit. Run competitions in shooting and in games and sports. Turn out with them and teach them games. They appreciate this.

10. Run a Soldiers Bank in your unit. They like to hand in their pay for safe keeping. This builds mutual confidence.

11. Ensure that your senior local rank keeps you informed of all that goes on in your unit, and insist that he brings at once to your notice any grievances he hears from the men. Unless you are confident he can deal with them, investigate and put them right yourself. Never allow grievances to build up. Be sure that you are in the know of any personal feuds the men may have between themselves. If not dealt with at once these are apt to simmer under the surface. Do not suppress them, but have them brought into the open. Always allow a man to air his grievance, and be patient and a good listener. Talking about it to a sympathetic ear prepares the ground for an easy solution. Remember this, they tend to talk round the point of issue to begin with, so again, bear with the, and they will come to the point after a little while, then offer advice and help.

12. By nature both Arab and Baluch are excitable. When two men argue they both appeal to all round them to join in, hence a difference of opinion can quickly flare up into a major row. A calming influence is necessary. Deal with the situation at once, ascertain the full facts and don't on any account leave it until 'office' the next day.

If at any time men form up to complain or protest at what they may consider an unfair order, listen to and investigate their complaint. Always be fair in your dealings with them.

The ideal to aim for is unremitting study of them, watch yourself and them all the time. Listen to all that goes on, search out what is going on beneath the surface, read their characters, discover their tastes and their weaknesses and devote mental effort to it. You will be rewarded with an efficient happy unit.

C. C. Maxwell.

Lt Colonel,
Commander Sultan's Armed Forces.
(C. C. MAXWELL).

Annx 'D' PRECIS 8
TRG/29 dtd 21 July 64.

TACTICS - SECTION LEVEL - IV

PATROLS II

1. The following is a guide to the type of info required from a normal routine patrol. Patrols covering new ground are asked to include a sketch or a marked map of the route taken.

2.   a.   Dates of patrol and weather during period.

    b.   Names of any local guides used. Details of how they can be obtained again.

    c.   Composition including number and type of vehicles.

    d.   Route taken.

    e.   Timings between each village or halting place.

    f.   Going and track surface including any particularly difficult places.

    g.   Villages with names and grid references.

    h.   Distances between villages in miles from vehicle speedometer.

    j.   Grid references of wells and water.

    k.   Names of village Shuyuk, population of villages and type and extent of cultivation. (This applies to new areas or those areas infrequently visited).

    l.   Local news, rumours and gossip.

3. It does not matter if reports are handwritten. Names when reported should if possible include three, plus tribe and village, eg. MOHAMMED bin SAIF bin KHAMIS al HINAI of ALAYA.

4. Patrols for special ops should be briefed as required by Bn/Coy Comds in the light of situation and info required.

5. It is important that all patrols are properly briefed by a British officer before leaving their base so that the patrols are quite clear as to the aim of the task and the info required. On return all patrols must be debriefed and a report submitted to a Bn HQ and HQ SAF.

6. Patrols may be given special tasks in addition to the above. For example to check the names of all men resident in a village. Details of this should then appear in the patrol report.

TACTICS SECTION LEVEL V

PIQUETTING - PROTECTION ON THE MOVE

1. INTRODUCTION AND PRINCIPLES

    a. AIM. The purpose of piquetting is to protect the column as it passes them on the route below by preventing the enemy from occupying ground from which they can bring direct fire to bear on the column.

    b. METHOD. This is done by allocating a certain number of piquetting troops to come under the direct command of the Advance Guard Commander.

        The piquetting troops, who will provide protection on the move to the main body, will move with the Advance Guard. Whilst advancing along the route the Advance Guard Commander, using his discretion, will appreciate those features which, if held by the enemy, would comprise a threat to the security of the move of the main body. On to these features, he will post Route Piquets. The number of men to each piquet will depend on the size and shape of the feature being piquetted. Not until each feature has been secured by the piquetting troops will the main body be allowed to proceed along that particular bound of the route.

    c. PRINCIPLES

            (1) Vigilance.
            (2) Speed.
            (3) Supporting Fire.
            (4) The correct use of ground.
            (5) Offensive Action.

    d. AIR SUPPORT

        SOAF can provide support for the move of the Main Body in one or more of the following ways :-

        (1) Air Strikes. Bombing, rocket and/or straffing attacks against known enemy strong points.

        (2) Harassing attacks. Bombing, rocket and/or straffing attacks against forts, villages, water supplies and crops.

        (3) Close support. Offensive air action in direct support of the troops.

        (4) Visual reconnaissance.

        (5) Psychological warfare. Leaflet dropping.

    e. DUTIES OF THE ADVANCE GUARD COMMANDER

        (1) Selecting features to be held by piquets.

        (2) Deciding the strength of each piquet.

        (3) Giving the Company Commander of the detailed piquets all orders in relation to each piquet.

        (4) For arranging fire support if required.

..... 2

APPENDIX 3

*Press Release issued by HM Sultan Qaboos, 26th July 1970*

Fellow countrymen. I speak to you as Sultan of Muscat and Oman having succeeded my father on 24th July 1970, 19 of Jamada al Uwla 1390. I have watched with growing dismay and increasing anger the inability of my father to use the new found wealth of this country for the needs of its people. That is why I have taken control. My family and my armed forces have pledged their loyalty to me. The ex-Sultan has left the Sultanate.

I promise you all that my immediate task will be to set up as quickly as possible a forceful and modern government whose first aim must be to remove unnecessary restrictions under which you, my people, now suffer, and to produce as rapidly as possible a happier and more secure future for all of you.

I ask the help of each one of you in this task. In days gone by our country was great and powerful, and with God's help, if we work together to recreate our nation we shall once again take our rightful place in the Arab world.

I am taking the necessary constitutional steps to receive recognition from foreign countries with whom we have relations, and I look forward to the early establishment of friendly cooperation with all nations, notably with our neighbours, and to an era of active consultation with them on the future of the region.

My friends, I urge you to continue with your normal lives, knowing that I will be coming to Muscat within a very short period, and that my concern will be to tell you, Oh my people, what I and my new government plan to do to achieve our common aim. My friends, my brothers, yesterday was dark, but with God's help, tomorrow will dawn bright for Muscat and Oman and all its people.

May God's blessing be upon us and on our endeavours.

Reproduced from Appendix III, page 121 of *Oil and the Transformation of Oman 1970–1995* by Mahommed bin Musa Al-Yousef.

# Some Facts and Figures

**To show the huge advances made in the development of Health, Education and Communication Services 1970–1998**

| | 1970 | 1975 | 1980 | 1985 | 1990 | 1995 | 1998 |
|---|---|---|---|---|---|---|---|
| **1. Population** | 600,000 | 1,085,757 | 1,250,831 | 1,503,936 | 1,817,739 | 2,131,000 | 2,287,000 |
| **2. Health** | (1971) | | | | | | |
| Hospital beds | 216 | 1,000 | 1,784 | 2,813 | 3,431 | 3,958 | 4,443 |
| Doctors | 46 | 147 | 289 | 638 | 994 | 1,800 | 2,099 |
| Nurses | 77 | 450 | 903 | 1,947 | 3,512 | 5,128 | 6,365 |
| Inpatients | 3,974 | 56,119 | 108,208 | 150,798 | 183,201 | 220,846 | 215,477 |
| Life expectancy at birth | under 50 | | 57.5 | 61.6 | 66.5 | 67.4 | 72.2 |
| Infant mortality per 1,000 births | 118 | | 64 | 45 | 29 | 20 | 18 |
| **3. Education** | (1972) | | | | | | |
| Schools | 16 | 214 | 388 | 606 | 800 | 965 | 970 |
| Teachers | 196 | 1,980 | 5,259 | 10,131 | 15,587 | 22,505 | 24,181 |
| Students | 6,941 | 56,104 | 108,324 | 221,694 | 360,066 | 490,482 | 528,834 |
| **Communications** | (1971) | | | | | | |
| Roads asphalted (Km) | 10 | 714 | 2.192 | 3,768 | 4,976 | 6,257 | 7,771 |
| Telephone Lines | 989 | 3,701 | 15,044 | 41,320 | 107,409 | 169,603 | 214,358 |

Source: **Oman, Statistical Year Books** and **Ministry of Information**, Sultanate of Oman

Note: In 1963 there was one hospital (the American Missionary Hospital) in Muscat and one primary school for boys in Muttrah. In 1999 there were 54 hospitals, 116 clinics and 1,135 schools.

# Sources and References

This book is intended primarily for the general reader. As explained in Chapter One, much of the book has been sourced from my letters, which I wrote home to Charmian from Aden and Muscat and Oman between November 1962 and December 1963. As also explained in the first chapter, Charmian did not retain the originals of my letters, but transposed them, suitably edited, into a hard-backed exercise book. Extracts from this compendium of letters, together with my commentary thirty-six years later are the main source for chapters 3, 5, 6, 7 and 8. Because my letters and commentary are a mix of description and opinion, and mine alone, other sources and references are few.

So as to provide the general reader with some background to both Aden and Muscat and Oman in the early 1960s, I considered it essential to provide an historical and geographical briefing to both countries. This introduces each country and helps paint the scene when I arrived and started writing letters to Charmian.

I have sourced most of Chapter 2 'Aden: A Brief History to 1962' from *Aden* by Sir Tom Hickinbotham and from *Yemen: Travels in Dictionary Land* by Tim Mackintosh-Smith. I have also included some information from *Farewell to Arabia* by David Holden. My experience on operations in the Radfan during 1958 also provided useful background.

The majority of Chapter 4 'Muscat and Oman: A Brief History to 1962', comes from *Farewell to Arabia* by David Holden, but with some reference to *Sultan in Oman* by James Morris.

Clearly my brief histories of both Aden and Muscat and Oman rely heavily on such classical sources of information. Consequently out of respect for the authors and to conform to copyright law, I have provided a full cross-reference to the relevant pages in their books.

As I have explained at the opening of Chapter 9 'Memories without Letters', our decision not to write to each other during my final six months in Ghalla, converts this chapter into a series of recollections. Some of these highlight comparisons between the early 1960s and today. I have referred heavily to *Maverick Guide to Oman* by Peter J. Ochs II as a source of information about Oman today. I would strongly recommend this guide to anyone who intends visiting or revisiting Oman.

Finally, Chapter 10 'Oil and the Quickening Beat of Change' has been sourced from the *Maverick Guide to Oman*, while in support of 'Bedu Succumb to the Twentieth Century', I have also quoted from *Seven Pillars of Wisdom* by T. E. Lawrence and from *Arabian Sands* by Wilfred Thesiger. Thereafter and for the remainder of Chapter 10, I have relied on information provided by the Reverend Father Colin McLean who witnessed at first hand the events and cultural changes which the Omani people experienced between 1964 and 1977. Where appropriate sources and references have been included.

## Chapter-by-Chapter Sources and References

*Chapter 1 My Reasons Why*
Strengths of the services from *Britain's Army in the Twentieth Century* by Field Marshal Lord Carver.

| *Reference* | *Pages* |
| --- | --- |
| Pre- and Post-National Service in 1962 | 407 |
| BAOR's contribution to NATO in 1959 | 408 |

*Chapter 2 Aden: A Brief History to 1962*
Mainly sourced from (a) *Aden* by Sir Tom Hickinbotham, (b) *Farewell to Arabia* by David Holden and (c) *Yemen: Travels in Dictionary Land* by Tim Mackintosh-Smith.

| *Reference* | *Source* | *Pages* |
| --- | --- | --- |
| Biblical reference to Eden | (a) | 7 |
| Cain worshipped fire here; site of Abel's grave | (c) | 143 |
| Natural harbour and strategic position make it a prosperous trading centre | (a) | 8 |
| Tahirids, succeeding the Mongols, recognise Aden's great potential and revive the port by introducing preferential duties | (c) | 144 |
| Cape route to India in 1500 awakens interest of Europeans | (c) | 144 |
| Portuguese try unsuccessfully to seize Aden 1513 | (a) | 8 |
| Ottomans seize Aden in 1538 and still in control when British ships arrive in 1551 | (a) | 9 |

| Reference | Source | Pages |
|---|---|---|
| President Nasser closes Suez Canal and points finger of derision at the British and also at the Indians who had come to dominate commercial and political life | (c) | 152 |
| Strike action and general subversion | (b) | 20, 25,51 |
| Britain forms Federation of South Arabia, 1959 | (b) | 47 |
| Qat addiction undermines fabric of mixed society and causes breakdown of internal security | (a) | 236, 237 |
| Colony of Aden – shape, size and harbour and how in 1850 Front Bay succeeds Holkat Bay | (a) | 8, 11 |
| Little Aden (now Bureikha), Crater, Jebel Shamsan, Tawahi and Ma'alla | (a) | 11,12 |
| Harold Ingrams's description of buildings in Aden, Building of Falaise Camp, Bir Fukum, Little Aden 1960. Contract Papers of R. Horne | (c) | 146, 147 |
| Four grades of housing in Little Aden | (c) | 153 |
| Aden Protectorate a 'cordon sanitaire' | (b) | 30 |
| Political Agents and Advisory Treaties, 1930–1950 | (b) | 37,38 |
| Federation of South Arabia, 1959 | (b) | 47 |
| Aden Protectorate in 1960 – size, people and frontiers | (a) | 54–58 |
| Aerial bombing of dissident villages | (b) | 35, 36 |
| Shipment of Soviet arms and ammunition to the Yemen in 1957 | (b) | 42 |

## Chapter 3 Learning Arabic in Aden

Sourced from extracts of my letters to Charmian. Commentaries are sourced as follows:

| Reference | Pages |
|---|---|
| Regarding the Arabic language, after letter dated November 15th 1962: from *The Maverick Guide to Oman* by Peter J. Ochs II | 166<br>167 |
| 'Bugle on the Matterhorn' by Captain D. J. G. James KSLI. *British Army Review* No 17, October 1963 | 65–73 |
| Giving 1970 as the date when Omanisation of the Sultan's Armed Forces began, following letter dated January 12th 1963: from *The Maverick Guide to Oman* by Peter J. Ochs II | 48 |

| References | Pages |
|---|---|
| Commentary within letter dated January 19th, 1963 regarding the Labour Government's decision in 1966 to leave Aden is taken from *Yemen: Travels in Dictionary Land* by Tim Mackintosh-Smith | 157 |
| Commentary at close of the chapter regarding Aden Colony becoming Aden State within South Arabian Federation in January 1963 is taken from *Farewell to Arabia* by David Holden | 61 |
| The Rev Father Colin McLean is the source of supplementary recollections regarding: | |
| Our unexpected arrival at the Officers' Mess; | |
| Use of Dunhill cigarette tins to hold word group cards; | |
| Last course on which students learnt Arabic script. | |

## Chapter 4 Muscat and Oman: A Brief History to 1962

Sourced from *Farewell to Arabia* by David Holden, 1966 except where otherwise indicated.

| References | Pages |
|---|---|
| Portuguese trading post (1550 to 1700) | 12, 215 |
| Greatest independent power in Arabian Peninsula (1700 to 1840) | 215 |
| Treaties with GB and USA | 215, 144 |
| Footnote 7 on the 1800 Treaty of Friendship is sourced from *Desert Wind and Tropic Storm* by Donald Hawley | 169 |
| Abolishment of slavery signals decline | 144 |
| Britain keeps other powers at arms' length | 13, 215 |
| Muscat hibernates (1870 to 1960) | 215–222 |
| Sultan Said bin Taimur al bu Said | 217–222 |
| Footnote 9 on Tarik bin Taimur is sourced from *Oman under Qaboos* by Calvin Allen, J. R. and W. Lynn Rigsbee II | 10 |
| Buraimi Oasis focus of protracted triangular dispute (1949 to 1963) | 201–213 |
| Enforced change in Arab thinking | 202 |
| GB and USA at odds | 204 |
| American Secretary of State John Foster Dulles claims 'British aggression in Buraimi' is sourced from *Full Circle: the Memoirs of Sir Anthony Eden*, pages 334 and 335 | 204 |

| References | Pages |
|---|---|
| British troops assist in three small campaigns 1955, 1957 and 1959 | 225, 226 |
| 'The only shot in a bloodless campaign was fired at, or more probably in the general direction of a Land Rover which had me on board' 1955 comes from *Sultan in Oman* by James Morris, 1957 | 16 |
| 'In less than a month of occasional shooting, daily air attacks and minimal bloodshed, some 500 British soldiers subdued the rebel villages and then promptly were withdrawn' 1957 | 226 |
| Natural divisions within Muscat and Oman, geography and people | 226, 227 |
| Omani rebellions; Britain drawn in | 229, 230 |
| Jebel Akhdar had been 'a green mountain of trees and fruits – pomegranates, citrons, almonds, nutmegs, walnuts with coffee bushes and vines'. Source – Lieutenant Wellsted of the Indian Navy, taken from *Explorations in Oman*, 1835 | |
| From 1957 Great Britain trained, led, armed and paid the Sultan's Armed Forces | 230 |

### Chapter 5 Joining the Sultan's Armed Forces

Sourced from extracts from my letters to Charmian and *Guide to Officers and Junior Leaders Serving in Oman* written by Colonel Colin Maxwell and issued as part of induction process. Original copied and shown as Appendix 1.

### Chapter 6 An Arab Company in the Desert

Sourced from extracts from my letters to Charmian and (a) *Farewell to Arabia* by David Holden, 1966, (b) *The Maverick Guide to Oman* by Peter J. Ochs II, 1998. Other sources are referenced in full below.

| Reference | Source | Pages |
|---|---|---|
| Commentary following letter dated February 22nd 1963 regarding Arabs greeting one another in the desert extracted from *Arabia of the Wahhabis* by H. St John Philby, 1928 | (b) | 166 |
| Commentary following my letter dated April 21st 1963, describing the Sultan's Navy, sourced from David Coppin | | |

| Reference | Source | Pages |
|---|---|---|
| Commentary following my letter dated June 1st 1963, regarding claims made by Omani Freedom fighters over Cairo Radio's 'Voice of the Arabs' | (a) | 224 |
| Commentary following my letter dated June 1st 1963, regarding the visit to Oman in 1963 by Mr Herbert de Ribbing, U Thant's Special Envoy | (a) | 225 |
| Also extract from Report of the Special Representative of the Secretary General to the UN General Assembly, October 8th, 1963 | (a) | 225 |

## Chapter 7 A Baluch Company in the Jebel Foothills

Sourced from extracts from my letters to Charmian and (a) *The Maverick Guide to Oman* by Peter J. Ochs II, 1998 and (b) *Oman 1972*.

| Reference | Source | Pages |
|---|---|---|
| Opening paragraphs to this chapter regarding Rostaq village and fort and related history | (a) | 258 |
| Commentary following my letter dated June 21st 1963, regarding falaj system | (a) | 157–159 |
| Description of how falaj system is built and operates | (b) | 15,16 |
| Extract from His Majesty Sultan Qaboos's National Address, 18th November 1991 | (a) | 128 |
| Note to my letter dated July 9th 1963, regarding the risk of camping in wadi beds | (a) | 37 |
| Commentary within my letter dated September 15th 1963, regarding the history of Hazaam Fort | (a) | 262 |
| Commentary following my letter dated September 15th 1963, regarding high temperatures during the hot season in Rostaq | (a) | 33 |
| Supplementary recollections by John Darbyshire regarding: shooting incident in which he was involved; the food we ate; cause of his heat exhaustion; Commanding Officer's visit to Rostaq after mutiny at Saiq | | |

## Chapter 8 Training Recruits on the Batinah Coast

In addition to extracts from my letters to Charmian, this chapter was sourced from the *Maverick Guide to Oman*, 1998.

| Reference | Pages |
|---|---|
| Commentary within my letter dated September 26th 1963 regarding the coup in 1970 when Sultan Qaboos succeeded his father | 125 |
| Commentary within my letter dated November 10th 1963 concerning the enormous advances made by Sultan Qaboos since his accession in 1970 in the fields of health and education | 127, 128 |

## Chapter 9 Memories without Letters

Extract from original first draft of the English version of the Sultan's Armed Forces Training Manual. Brief extract from the original by Captain D. J. G. James copied and reproduced at Appendix 2. Other sources are (a) *Arabian Sands* by Wilfred Thesiger, reprinted with a second preface 1991; (b) *Maverick Guide to Oman* by Peter J. Ochs II, 1998; (c) *Thomas Cook Travellers Egypt, 1995* by Michael Haag.

| Reference | Source | Pages |
|---|---|---|
| Limits of photography: the reasons for Omani reluctance to be photographed | (b) | 52 |
| Description of Omani men's and women's dress | (b) | 150–152 |
| Return of the white oryx – how it was saved from extinction and reintroduced twenty years later into its natural native habitat. Draft amended by Major Roddy Jones, Field Manager White Oryx Project (1989–1995); his wife Gigi Crocker Jones provided supporting photograph of a herd of white oryx in the shade | (b) | 90–92 |
| Christian soldiers in a Muslim world: | | |
| Principal beliefs of Islam | (c) | 16 |
| Five practical Pillars of Faith | (b) | 139, 140 |
| Muslims urged to practice various virtues | (b) | 140 |
| Islamic faith focal to both spiritual and temporal law | (b) | 140 |
| Prayer | (a) | 54,55 |

| Reference | Source | Pages |
|---|---|---|
| Ramadhan | (b) | 140 |
| Ibadhi faith | (b) | 142, 143 |
| Specialities of the day: | | |
| Dates, varieties and production | (b) | 128, 154 |
| Limes, second largest crop | (b) | 87, 154 |
| Fish, crustacea and shellfish on the Batinah Coast | (b) | 96 |

Western prejudice against Islam was sourced from an article entitled 'The West is still demonising Islam' written by Karen Armstrong and published in *The Times Weekend*, Saturday May 27th 2000 following the publication of her book *The Battle for God: Fundamentalism in Judaism, Christianity and Islam* (Harper Collins, 2000). Supplementary information on some topics in this Chapter was sourced as follows:

| Reference | Source |
|---|---|
| Shawl, often from Kashmir | David Coppin |
| Town and country women in the interior | David Coppin |
| Silver jewellery and anklet pods worn by children | Colin McLean |
| Description of mine incident near the Training Centre | David Coppin |

## Chapter 10 Oil and the Quickening Beat of Change

Sources for this chapter are: (a) *Seven Pillars of Wisdom* by T. E. Lawrence; (b) *Arabian Sands* by Wilfred Thesiger, 1991; (c) *Oman '99*; (d) *Maverick Guide to Oman* by Peter J. Ochs II, 1998; (e) *Oman under Qaboos* by Calvin Allen, J. R. and W. Lynn Rigsbee II; (f) *Ponder Anew: Reflections on the Twentieth Century* by John Graham.

| Reference | Source | Pages |
|---|---|---|
| Discovery of oil, 1962: discoveries at Yibal (1962), Natih (1963) and Fahud (1964) and production levels 1970 and 1998, reserves guaranteed for 50 more years, restriction on annual production levels, diversification towards non-oil sectors | (c) | 136, 88, 140, 89 |
| Ownership of Petroleum Development Oman – shares | (e) | 23 |

| *Reference* | *Source* | *Pages* |
|---|---|---|
| Could the speed of change be governed? Undertakings given in the Exchange of Letters July 25th 1958 | (e) | 18, 19 |
| Bedu succumb to the twentieth century: | | |
| Customs and habits | (d) | 147 |
| Independent and loyal | (d) | 147, 148 |
| 'Bedouin ways were hard, even for those brought up in them and for strangers: a death in life' | (a) | 31 |
| 'Yet even as I waited for my identity to be discovered, . . .' | (b) | Preface 8 |
| 'I shall always remember how often I was humbled by those illiterate herdsmen who possessed . . .' | (b) | 329 |
| 'Yet I know that for them the danger lay . . .' | (b) | 329, 330 |
| 'I realised that after all these years and under these changed conditions . . .' | (b) | Preface 9 |
| 'On this occasion I found myself reconciled to the inevitable changes . . .' | (b) | Preface 10 |
| How the resilient and opportunistic Bedu have come to terms with the twentieth century | (d) | 148 |
| Sultan Qaboos succeeds father July 23rd 1970 | (d) | 125, 126 |
| | (e) | 29 |
| | (f) | 334, 335 |

Oil revenues become catalyst for renaissance: from *Oil and the Transformation of Oman 1970–1995* by Mohamed bin Musa Al-Yousef, 1995.

Arabisation of the Sultan's Armed Forces: personal communication, the Reverend Father Colin McLean.

Lieutenant-General Sir Kenneth G McLean KCB, KBE from Kelly's Handbook, 1968.

Dhofar War 1970 to 1975 sourced from:

| | |
|---|---|
| Britain's Army in the Twentieth Century by Field Marshal Lord Carver | 445 |
| 'Oman's Unsung Triumph' by David Holden, *Readers Digest*, February 1978 | 74–78 |

The Reverend Father Colin McLean, who served during the Dhofar War, first as Second-in-Command of the Northern Frontier Regiment and then as Commander of the Dhofar Forces

*Reference*                                                                 *Pages*

Colonel Nigel Knocker OBE, Chairman SAF Association,
who commanded The Desert Regiment (1971–73) during
the Dhofar War

Visit of Sir Gawain Bell, formerly Governor of Nigeria –
the Reverend Father Colin McLean

Establishment of Civil Aid Department in Salalah – David
Coppin

Massive change to the infrastructure – the Reverend
Father Colin McLean

Threat to life of Wilfred Thesiger's bedu companions in 1947
– David Coppin

Oman's oil resources do not match neighbours and need
for proactive development planning: sourced from *Oil
and the transformation of Oman 1970–1995* by Mohamed bin
Musa Al-Yousef, 1995

Summary Reflections:

David Coppin's letter to me dated 20th April 2000

Sultan Qaboos in conversation with David Holden, as            74–78
reported in David Holden's article in the *Reader's Digest*,
February 1978

*Sources of Maps, Documents and Illustrations*

Sources, acknowledgements and, where appropriate,
copyright approvals have been obtained for all Maps,
Documents and Illustrations within this book.

These appear:

◆ on the Maps
◆ beneath Illustrations and Documents

The only exceptions are:

◆ on Maps drawn by The Five Castles Press Ltd which
are:     Middle East 1962
         Muscat and Oman 1962
◆ Illustration numbers:
         83 Bedouin boy, Wahiba Sands
         84 Bedouin succumb to Westernisation
         While sources are shown beneath each, despite
         every reasonable effort being made, copyright
         approvals have not been forthcoming
◆ Photographs taken by the author.

# Bibliography

Akehurst, John *Generally Speaking* (Michael Russell Publishing, 1999)

Allen, Calvin, Jnr. and W. Lynn Rigsbee II *Oman under Qaboos: from Coup to Constitution, 1970–1995* (Frank Cass, 2000)

*Discovering Oman: Apex Explorers' Guide I* (Apex, 1992)

Asher, Michael, *The Last of the Bedu* (Viking, 1996)

Carver, Field Marshall Lord, *Britain's Army in the Twentieth Century* (Pan Books in association with The Imperial War Museum, 1998)

Clarke, Shaun, *Soldier C: SAS* (22, 1993)

Eden, Sir Anthony, *Full Circle: the Memoirs of the Right Honourable Sir Anthony Eden* (Cassell, 1960)

Field, Michael and Tony Axon, *The Face of Arabia* (World of Information 1977)

Fiennes, Ranulph, *Living Dangerously* (Futura Publications, 1988)

Fiennes, Ranulph, *Where Soldiers Fear to Tread* (Hodder & Stoughton, 1975)

Graham, John, *Ponder Anew: Reflections on the Twentieth Century* (Spellmount, 1999)

Haag, Michael, *Thomas Cook Travellers Egypt* (AA Publishing, 1995)

Hawley, Sir Donald, *Desert Wind and Tropic Storm* (Michael Russell Publishing, 2000)

Hawley, Sir Donald, *Oman: Jubilee Edition* (Stacey International, 1995)

Hickinbotham, Sir Tom, *Aden* (Constable, 1958)

Hoe, Alan, *David Stirling SAS* (Warner Books, 1992)

Holden, David, *Farewell to Arabia* (Faber & Faber, 1966)

Holden, David, 'Oman's Unsung Triumph' (*Reader's Digest*, February 1978)

Hunter's *Statistical Account of the British Settlement of Aden*, 1877

*Kelly's Handbook*, 1968

Lawrence, T. E. *The Seven Pillars of Wisdom* (Jonathan Cape, 1936)

Mackintosh-Smith, Tim, *Yemen: Travels in Dictionary Land* (John Murray, 1998)

Mahomed bin Musa Al-Yousef, *Oil and the Transformation of Oman, 1970–1995* (Stacey International, 1995)

Morris, James, *Sultan in Oman* (Faber & Faber, 1957)

Muscat Department of Information, *Oman* (T. & A. Constable, 1972)

Ochs, Peter J. II, *Maverick Guide to Oman* (Pelican, 1998)

Oman Ministry of Information *Oman '99* (The Ministry, 2000)

Oman Ministry of Information *Oman 2000* (The Ministry, 2001)

Peyton, W. D., *Old Oman* (Stacey International, 1983)

Phillips, Wendell, *Unknown Oman* (Longmans, 1966)

Salma Samar Damluji, *The Architecture of Oman* (Garnet, 1998)

Skeet, Ian, *Muscat and Oman: the End of an Era* (Faber & Faber, 1974)

Smiley, David, *Arabian Assignment* (Leo Cooper, 1975)

Thesiger, Wilfrid, *Arabian Sands* (Penguin, 1991)

*The Arabian Peninsular* (Time Life Books, The Library of Nations, 1989)

# Index

Numbers in brackets refer to illustrations.
Army ranks are included only when normally used in the text.

201

56° · 57° · Khaburah

Wuqba · B · Qusuf · Sūr Hau · Kha

24°

W e s t · Dogal · W. Mabtah

Pass 935 · W. Umra · Ghaizain · Tharmad

Siya · Furfur · W. Hawasinah · Suddom · Hailain · Dihas

Towi · Miri · H · W. Ba · Libda

Dhahir · Lislat · Falaj al Hadith

Fida · Suwaida · Beda · W. Bani Ghafir

Dut · Yanqul · 1494 · Biya

W. Miri · i · Qanat · Miskin · W. Sahtan

W. Dhank · Dhank · 1515 · 1000 · n · H · JABAL · A · K

HAMIS · Aflaj Bani Qitab · R · J.SHAM · 3107

Mazum · Arid · Maqmyāt · J

Araqi · D'ariz · A

Ibri · Salaif · Wahrah · T

J. JIFARA · 488 · W. Ain · Mathar

Dabai · Najd al Barak

Tan'am · Y

23° · Saifam · Bahlah · Hamrah

Kubarah · Jabrin · O

ARU · H

J. HADDAH

ASIS · J. HAMRAH

W. Aswad · Bir-al-Ha

AR · W. Almairi

22°